ABOUT THE

Boris Mihailovic first began riding motorcycles more than thirty years ago and soon after became a telegram boy for Australia Post (the only other option at the time that would pay him to ride motorcycles was to become a police officer). It was a job that left him with plenty of time to write vitriolic letters to motorcycle magazines, one of which offered Boris a job as a 'cadet journalist'.

The magazine was *Ozbike* and in a few years Boris became the editor of that title, which went on to be the largest-selling motorcycle magazine in Australia. It was there Boris discovered that he had a knack for telling a good yarn. He then landed a job at *The Picture* magazine. Eventually Boris was offered an editor's position at *Picture Premium*. And apart from a stint as editor of *The Picture*, he has remained in the role of editor of *Picture Premium* and *Premium Babes*. Boris has contributed to a host of other magazines, including *Ralph*, *FHM*, *UFC*, *Zoo Weekly*, *Australasian Dirt Bike*, and *Australian Motorcycle News* and Britain's *Motor Cycle News* (MCN).

Boris continues to enjoy the entire rich smorgasbord that motorcycling offers – racing, enduro trails, commuting, drag-racing, motorcycle lobbying, shows and trade expos. He was also the president of an outlaw motorcycle club for ten years. Boris has ridden all over Australia and Europe – and plans on doing just that until it is no longer physically possible.

Boris has a wife and son and a large and joyfully angry dog.

ABOUT THE AUTHOR

MY MOTHER WARNED ME ABOUT BLOKES LIKE ME

MOTORCYCLE STORIES OF BROTHERHOOD, DEMONS, DIRT AND DANGER

BORIS MIHAILOVIC

hachette
AUSTRALIA

Special thanks to publisher Ross Wiggins for permission to include
'The Christmas Run', which first saw life in *Ozbike* magazine.

The author and publisher would like to acknowledge the following works from
which the author has quoted: *Playing by Heart* by Fred Donaldson; *A Farewell to
Arms* by Ernest Hemingway; *Dune* by Frank Herbert.

Every endeavour has been made on the part of the publisher to contact copyright
holders and the publisher will be happy to include a full acknowledgement in any
future edition.

First published in Australia and New Zealand in 2012
by Hachette Australia
(an imprint of Hachette Australia Pty Limited)
Level 17, 207 Kent Street, Sydney NSW 2000
www.hachette.com.au

This edition published in 2014

10 9 8 7 6 5

National Library of Australia Cataloguing-in-Publication data:

Mihailovic, Boris.
My mother warned me about blokes like me / Boris Mihailovic.

ISBN 978 0 7336 3267 9 (pbk.)

Mihailovic, Boris.
Motorcyclists – New South Wales – Biography.
Motorcycling – Psychological aspects.
Motorcycle gangs – New South Wales.

796.7092

Cover image by Getty Images
Cover design by Josh Durham
Text design by Shaun Jury
Author photograph by Andrew McClymont
Typeset in FF Scala by Shaun Jury
Printed and bound in Australia by McPherson's Printing Group

MIX
Paper from
responsible sources
FSC www.fsc.org FSC® C001695

For my beloved wife, Lynette, and my wonderful son, Andrew. Thanks for putting up with the anguished screaming inherent in my creative process.

CONTENTS

INTRODUCTION   1

A MAN CALLED GRONK   5

THE FIRST SUMMIT   25

TALES FROM THE PILLION   39

RIDING INTO MORDOR   47

RALLY OUTSTANDING   63

THE PRICE OF FREEDOM   77

OUTLAW DAWN   87

HOUSING CRISIS   99

THE CHRISTMAS RUN   117

JAM TO JUPITER'S   167

THE WRONG WAY DOWN   187

RON'S RIDE   231

DEMON NIGHT 243

THE LINE IN WINTER 255

THE FAST, THE FIRST & THE FEAR 265

ACKNOWLEDGEMENTS 288

INTRODUCTION

I can no more stop riding motorcycles than I can stop breathing. I am far worse than any toothless crackhead or wee-stained smack freak when it comes to servicing this addiction. Believe it. If I had to climb through your window in the middle of the night and steal your kids' fluffy toys (or your kids, for that matter) and hock them for petrol or tyres so I could go riding the next day, I would.

Of course, there have been times when the law has decreed that for my sins against the *Motor Traffic Act* I would not be permitted to ride upon a public road for a certain length of time.

Did that stop me riding? Did it shit. As soon as I could organise it, I'd be lurching wildly through the nearest scrub on some barking dirt-bike full of hate, or cartwheeling it down some scree-strewn precipice as my internal organs rearranged themselves in horror. Hell, I once decided I needed to go motorcycle racing after one particularly long and stressful period on the sidelines – a decision which promptly served me up several broken ribs, scared a steamy kilo of excrement out of me, and

1

made my dumb, middle-aged head ring like a Chinese gong for a week after I face-planted on Turn 11 at Eastern Creek Raceway. On Lap One, no less.

Certainly various injuries and illnesses have prevented me from riding for brief periods of time, but these enforced pauses have always been nothing but short commercial breaks in the ongoing motorcycling soap opera that is my life.

And that soap opera is pretty much what this book is all about. The stories on the following pages span three decades of riding, and while they are by no means all of the stories I could tell, they do provide a good indication of what happens when one sells one's soul to the Blessed Bastard Motorcycle in all of its many incarnations.

Are the stories true? Of course they are. A man couldn't make this shit up . . . um, except for the bits that could otherwise see me doing lengthy jail time. Those bits are entirely fictional. Honestly. Cross my heart, your honour.

A few of the yarns would be vaguely familiar to regular readers of my column in *Australian Motorcycle News*. But so as not to damage the almost childlike sensibilities of some of its readers, I chose to leave out or change various segments of those tales. The salty, angst-filled tears of the magazine's editors were always a good indication of what they were uncomfortable with. You might be pleased to know that those parts have now been put back in.

My mum will not share in your pleasure. I'm not even sure I want her to read this book. You see, my mum really believes that one day I shall come to my senses and stop riding these wretched, stupid and improbably perilous motorcycles. She has believed this since the first day I started riding them, more than thirty years ago. It is a constant in our relationship.

Every time she sees me she asks me if I'm still riding bikes. I tell her I am. She frowns and advises me, yet again, that they're very dangerous.

Because I love her, I refrain from telling her that that is exactly what attracts people like me to motorcycles in the first place. Instead, I lie to her and assure her that I am always careful. I know she doesn't believe me, but I tell her anyway.

The uncomfortable truth is that I actually came to my senses the day I started riding bikes. I so very much came to my senses it was simply not possible to come to them in any greater degree. All the senses there ever were for me to come to, had been arrived at on that fateful day. And the ensuing decades of riding have only served to confirm that arrival.

Of course, it is entirely possible that riding motorcycles has driven me completely insane. I have no way of knowing, since everyone I happen to be good friends with is as deeply obsessed with riding motorcycles as I am. But in this very ignorance lies my bliss.

Either way, to know about any of this is completely surplus to my mum's requirements. So please don't tell her. Thanks.

And while I am dispensing gratitude, I am very grateful to my boss, Peter Holder at ACP Magazines, whose professionalism, reassurance and tolerance has always been an inspiration.

I must also thank my friends, Nick and Klavdy, without whose cruel and searing encouragement I'd still be scratching my arse and wondering what to write about, when the answer was always staring me in the face.

'Write about what you know, stupid,' they said to me at various times. And so I did, and this is the result. I hope you get as much of a kick out of reading it as I did living it, but I somehow doubt that.

Boris

A MAN CALLED GRONK

Every serious addiction has a definable beginning. Every junkie worth his scabby track marks recalls the first time he felt the fanged kiss of a syringe. But once motorcycling gets into your veins, the need to ride makes the hankering for heroin feel like a mild craving for something with chocolate in it. The syringe full of my addiction began to fill in the early '70s when I started reading magazines like Australian Motorcycle News, Revs *and* Two Wheels. *My father worked in the printing industry and alongside copies of the* Australian Women's Weekly *and* The Bulletin *he would bring home each month, there'd be the odd motorcycle magazine. He also brought home copies of the iconic surfing magazine* Tracks, *but while I liked the bikini ads and the 'Captain Goodvibes' cartoon, the chances of a tubby, badly myopic wog kid named 'Boris' ever carving the glassy break at South Bondi were slim. I also started to read the American biker bible,* Easyriders. *Initially attracted to the tits on its pages, I stayed for the motorcycles and for the incredibly vivid fiction stories by writers like Jody Via and illustrations by the legendary*

Dave Mann. The bike magazines spoke to me in a voice promising everything a teenage male wants – adventure, rebellion, camaraderie, speed, danger and girls who would suck your dick for beer. So by the time I grew some proper pubic hair, the motorcycle syringe was full, the rubber hose was around my arm, and the pulsing vein was evident. All that remained was the prick and the plunge.

'To know what you prefer instead of humbly saying Amen to what the world tells you you ought to prefer, is to have kept your soul alive.'

ROBERT LOUIS STEVENSON

It would be fair to say I owe my entire desperate motorcycle fetish to a man called Gronk – and may the Road Gods bless him and keep him from harm – all 130 marijuana-enriched kilos of him.

But I'm getting ahead of myself.

Unlike many motorcyclists, I did not learn to ride bikes in the great outdoors. I was a city kid. I learned to ride them in the back streets of inner Sydney's Camperdown – an altogether incredible and disturbing feat when viewed through the prism of today's nanny-state fascism.

But in the '70s the world was a very different place. People gave less of a shit back then. A bunch of kids buggering about on noisy motorcycles was not all that uncommon, and it was beneath the dignity of the cops to do anything more about it than kick the juveniles in the arse and send them home.

I think most kids in those days knew someone, or knew someone who knew someone, who had a motorcycle. Most of us played in the streets all the time, and what growing boy isn't going to look with desire upon a fast, loud, enginey thing with handlebars – a motorised extension of the pushbike he was riding every day?

It all began for me the day a seventeen-year-old man called Gronk arrived at my school one glorious lunchtime astride a noisy, oil-splashed XL250 Honda, as I was struggling through Fourth Form (Year 10 in today's money) and puberty.

To be perfectly honest, it had actually started some years prior to Gronk's oily advent in the Fort Street High School car park. But motorcycling didn't really sink its greasy fangs into my soul until that day.

I had ridden a few times before. For example, I had ridden a minibike into a tree as a child at a picnic ground near the Colo River. It made my mother cry and slap me upside the head. So I didn't essay motorcycle riding again until I was about twelve, when I managed to talk a friend's heavily stoned older brother into letting me scrape his Z900 Kawasaki (and my thigh) along his neighbours' front fences for about twenty metres. He cried, and slapped me upside the head too.

But by the time Gronk turned up, the scars had healed and I was at that awkward age when everything from sniping cats with slug guns to wrestling pythons in vats of porridge seemed like a good idea. The siren song of motorcycles would find a receptive listener in me.

Gronk wasn't a student at my school, but he was mates with one of my mates who *was* a student, and Gronk had brought his bike along to show him. Our little four-man posse of teenage proto-criminals immediately surrounded him as he sat astride this proper man-sized bike in the school car park, blipping the throttle and out-cooling every cool thing I had ever imagined.

'Giz a go!' I screeched unthinkingly, convinced I'd never get one, but I was a little maddened by the smell of burning oil and exhaust fumes.

'Can you ride?' he asked. A fair question, given Gronk didn't know me very well.

'Yeah!' I lied, fully aware that a detailed rundown of how I crashed a two-stroke Rockhopper into a tree six years before was clearly not what Gronk would want to hear at this pivotal moment.

He shrugged and got off. I had a quick look around to see if there were any teachers nearby, and got on. My toes could barely touch the ground and the bike felt vast. It was hot too, and seriously heavier than I had imagined.

Suddenly I was a little scared. My mates all stood around me, honking and giggling and keeping a look out for teachers, so there was no question of a change of heart. In the eyes of my peers, a backdown would be tantamount to admitting you preferred kissing boys. It was a ride-or-die moment.

I revved it. Nothing happened.

'Put it in first!' Gronk instructed.

Easy for him to say. I had a vague notion he was talking about gears, but none at all about where they might be found.

'Hold the clutch in!' he demanded, tapping helpfully on the lever.

I duly pulled it in and held it. He kicked the bike into first for me, via a small lever near the left foot peg, and I felt the Honda lurch a bit.

'Now give it some revs and let the clutch out slowly.'

And that was pretty much that, as far as my riding lesson went.

It also pretty much sealed the deal on the sale of my soul to the infernal two-wheeler. I was doomed before I'd even pogoed madly out of the car park and onto the street, helmetless and in school uniform – an instant and irredeemable motorcycle tragic, world without end, amen.

I couldn't sleep that night. I had never got the bike out of first gear, stalled it 100 times and ripped open my leg kick-starting it 101 times. But something profound had occurred inside my head in the hour I'd spent 'riding' Gronk's bike in the streets behind my high school – and it was playing on a constant loop as I lay awake in my bed. The sheer atavistic rush of speed that only a motorcycle can provide is so addictive it makes crack cocaine look like a bitch. The incomparable coolness, rebelliousness and pure 'otherness' of being a motorcyclist (albeit one dressed in a school uniform) spoke to my puberty in a language as old as mankind itself. And I listened. Oh how I listened.

The next morning, I was sand-eyed with lack of sleep, but my mind was clear and focused. I was not the same fifteen-year-old kid who went to bed the night before, leaking blood from his kick-starter-gouged leg and smelling of burnt fossil fuel. I was now a motorcyclist.

Luckily, my schoolmates were dedicated truants and dope smokers and would visit Gronk (who had happily eschewed school altogether by having been expelled from every educational possibility in a twenty-five-kilometre radius of where he lived) at least three times a week. I had rarely gone with them – not because jigging school bothered me, but because I didn't smoke dope back then, and Gronk's house was a veritable shrine to that pastime.

So you can imagine the big fellow's surprise when I fronted there the very next day. Gronk apparently lived with his parents in a large house just off Parramatta Road in Camperdown. I say 'apparently' because I had never met his oldies. The only evidence they even existed were three stunningly pornographic photos of them Gronk had discovered in their bedroom one day and shared with us.

Such was his immense generosity and magnanimity of spirit.

And it was that very generosity and magnanimity I was counting on as I climbed over his back fence.

As usual, security was tight. The back door was wide open, and Gronk and my mates were happily lazing about his smoke-wreathed lounge room, discussing the benefits of chillums as opposed to joints, when I appeared in the doorway.

'Changed your mind about a smoke?' he grinned, proffering me a crackling seven-paper bunger.

'Um, actually I was wondering if I could have another go on your bike?'

Gronk peered at me through bloodshot Chinese eyes for a bit. He may have been demandingly stoned, but he was not stupid. He knew I couldn't ride worth a shit, and was obviously considering the implications of what would happen if I crashed and burned.

'If you wreck it, you gotta fix it,' he finally said, and handed me the key. 'You can borrow my helmet if you want.'

I grinned my thanks and bolted out to where the XL250 was parked in the garage.

There was no fear in me today. My hour of power yesterday had annealed me and flushed the trepidation from my glands. Even my kick-starter-kissed leg was ready for more action. Teenagers heal like only teenagers can. Which is handy given how batshit crazy most of them are.

One sniff of Gronk's white Bell helmet convinced me I would be much better off without it, and I clumsily wheeled the bike into the lane behind his house. My leg still ached, but not enough to prevent me kicking the XL into life rather quickly. And I'd certainly had enough practice the day before.

Being sans helmet or licence really wasn't all that big a deal, legally or emotionally, in the mid-'70s. I certainly didn't give it a second thought as I roared off up the lane in first gear, fiercely determined to work out where the other gears were and what would happen when I found them.

I was hugely motivated not to stack. Primarily because I believed Gronk would beat the bubbling shit out of me, which would then deprive my father of that privilege and cause him untold angst, thus setting into motion a ruinous cascade of events that would ultimately result in my being shipped off to some joy-forsaken religious academy full of kiddie-touching priests and weeping Jesus statues.

But that was a bridge I would cross if and when it was built.

Right then I was about as thrilled as a fifteen-year-old boy could be without bursting spontaneously into flame. All of this excitement stemmed directly from the fact that I was at the controls of a proper motorcycle for the second time in my life and I hadn't the vaguest idea what I was doing.

I understood that a horrible outcome awaited me if I crashed. I wasn't precisely sure what it would be, but I was sure it would be horrible on a scale yet unimagined by me. Interestingly, I did not even consider the physical implications of hitting the road at 80 kms per hour dressed in a school uniform. I was more concerned about how I would explain riding and crashing bikes to my father, who was delusional enough to imagine his only son was at school being taught to read and write and hate quadratic equations.

Although right then I had my own wretched delusions to deal with – and they were all centred on the erroneous belief that I could actually ride. I knew there was more to it than buzzing up and down a lane in first gear, staring fixedly at the road directly before the front wheel. Obviously the other gears would need to be found and utilised before I could return to Gronk's house and inform the stoned proto-crims in his lounge room of my riding prowess. And quite frankly, after an hour of yammering about in first gear, I felt I had explored all of that cog's potential.

But where was second gear? It certainly wasn't in the same place first was. No matter how ferociously and repeatedly I stomped on the lever, the Honda stayed stubbornly in first.

Eventually, fate intervened. A man in paint-splattered overalls walked out into the lane from his spray-painting business and waved me down. I stopped awkwardly in front of him, but only because I lacked the skill to veer around the bastard, and we stared wordlessly at each other for a moment.

He had a half-smile on his face and it widened into a full one as he beheld me – helmetless, clueless and dressed in a somewhat stained school uniform.

'What the fuck are you doing?' he asked.

'Nothing,' I muttered defiantly.

'That's right,' he nodded, his smile brightening as he raised his arm. 'Fucken nothing.'

I revved the bike and prepared to make a noisy first-gear getaway if he started belting me in the head. But instead of me, he hit the Honda's large red kill switch on the right side of the handlebars.

I shat myself. I had been turning the motor off by stalling the bike – a procedure I felt was not correct and which I fully intended to look into as soon as I had this gear-changing shit sorted out.

'Look,' he said, squatting down on his haunches beside me and pointing at the gear lever. 'This thing works both ways. You already know where first is, and if you hook your toe under it and pull up, you'll find second. Then third, fourth and fifth. Just toe the lever down if you want a lower gear.'

'Thanks,' I stammered, slightly embarrassed that this paint-splattered tradesman had seen so easily through my facade of motorcycle-riding brilliance, and utterly appalled by the number of gears yet to explore.

'Um, what was that thing you pressed to turn it off?' I ventured.

'That's the kill switch here,' he said, pointing. 'Did you steal this bike from Gronk?'

I was instantly offended, though in retrospect I could understand why any reasonable person would think that. But I was also a little concerned he knew Gronk.

'No!' I protested. 'Gronk lent it to me. Do you know him?'

The man grinned lopsidedly. 'Yeah, I know him.'

Then he fixed me with a serious look. 'Be careful,' he said. 'It really fucken hurts when you fall off.'

I nodded, kicked the bike into life and roared off. It took me thirty seconds before I successfully slotted the Honda into second gear.

My heart sang and I must have been grinning and gurning like a fat chick eating biscuits. I subsequently found third and fourth and ultimately fifth, whereupon the bike stalled violently and slammed my balls hard into the petrol tank as I slowed to make a U-turn.

Obviously, there was more to this gear-selection caper than my spray-painted mate had revealed. It took me the best part of the next hour to work out that one must be judicious in one's gear selection by picking the gear most suitable for the speed at which one is travelling. The price for failure was pulped testicles. I was also quickly discovering that motorcycling is a cruel, Darwinian mistress.

But as I worked the gears and felt the bike responding with even greater speed as I careened up and down Cardigan Lane, motorcycling held me ever tighter in its grip and bound me ever closer to its bosom.

I had yet to muster the courage to go farther afield, but I would do in the following days. Eventually I nutted out a proving ground that consisted of hammering up Cardigan Lane, turning left onto Salisbury Lane, then cutting across O'Dea Reserve and into Ross Street, which would then dog-leg into Denison Street. Then just before I hit busy Parramatta Road, I'd duck into Kilner Lane and be back on the street I started on. If I was feeling especially en-testicled, I would explore O'Dea Reserve or the bigger Camperdown Park, which was in the next block.

That day, as I was returning to Gronk's house, I was pleased I had managed 80 kms per hour in fourth and had resolved to work on my downchanges. The noise coming from the gearbox each time I slammed down through the gears was not encouraging. I had yet to learn how to give the bike a little rev as I changed down, but I was positively glowing with self-assurance and personal gratification as I wheeled the bike back into Gronk's garage.

I thanked Gronk, gave him a dollar for the petrol I had used and limped home. My hands were tingling from the bike's vibrations and my legs ached from being tensed with terror and ignorance for two hours. The left one burned from being whacked with the kick-starter again, and my arse was numb from the vinyl-covered plank Honda was pleased to offer as a seat in the '70s. I was as happy and contented as I had ever been in my entire short life as I waddled through the streets to my home in Marrickville.

My mother wasn't so pleased. In fact, she looked as profoundly unimpressed with me as a mother could look.

'Vy you smell like petrol?' she asked, wrinkling her nose at me. 'End vy you so much derty? Vere you go?'

As an Australian-born child of Serbian immigrants, I always found my mum's interpretation of the English language utterly hilarious, but now was not an appropriate time to laugh.

'I was at school,' I lied. 'Some kid brought some petrol and spilled it in the playground and I got some on me.'

Of course she didn't believe me. It was patently obvious I was up to crap that involved dirt and petrol but not education. Did I care? Not in the slightest. An entirely new and wondrous world had that day been revealed to me. A world of wind and noise and speed and personal fulfilment I had never hitherto imagined possible. Nothing in my young life would ever be the same again. I think I even stopped masturbating for a day or two.

My mother looked at me for some time in stony silence. And she must have seen something in me she didn't understand and most certainly didn't like, because that evening I noticed her on her knees in her bedroom before the icon of the Virgin Mary holding the Baby Jesus, praying up a storm.

It didn't work. I was back at Gronk's house the very next day, ready to explore the Honda's top speed.

It was Day Three of my burgeoning motorcycle career. Day One had seen me master the kick-starting process and first gear. Day Two saw me conquer gears two through to five and the mystery of the Kill Switch. The progression to 'Now how fast does it fucken go?' was obvious, natural and inevitable.

As it turned out, the top speed of Gronk's rather used XL250 Honda was a shade over 120 kms per hour – which was quite . . . um, invigorating in the narrow confines of a 600-metre-long inner-Sydney laneway. And it was to hell and gone faster than I had ever been in my life. The family car, a venerable 1963 XL Ford, boasted thirty-seven steering-wheel turns lock-to-lock and was powered by something laughably called a 'Pursuit' motor. It had never been over 80 kms per hour on any of the interminable Sunday drives I had been subjected to as a child.

So for me to be kissing the wind at 120, my school shirt flapping madly behind me as its collar savagely whipped my neck, was a singular triumph. I don't think my heart had ever beaten as hard as it was thudding as I pulled up at the end of Cardigan Lane, just short of Parramatta Road. I was literally breathless, having unintentionally held my breath during the clumsy, short-shifting embarrassment I was pleased to call my first ever top-speed run.

Panting like a beaten dog, I immediately performed a wobbly, ham-footed seven-point turn (feet-up U-turns eluded me for more than a decade), and did it again. And again.

And then my mate in the paint-daubed overalls came out of his workshop and waved me down again.

'This is not the fucken place to see how fucken fast it goes,' he observed.

'Yeah, it is,' I said and revved the bike to show him I was serious and he was interrupting important motorcycle shit.

'No, it's fucken not,' he replied and hit the kill switch so I would know *he* was serious. 'I'm too fucken busy to shovel you off the road when you fucken come a-gutser.'

'I won't, but,' I insisted.

'Too fucken right you fucken won't!' the bloke declared. 'Slow it fucken down or I'll call the fucken cops.' He glared at me pointedly then went back inside his shop.

The cops? My stomach roiled sickeningly. Yesterday I held him to be a sainted Samaritan of motorcycling wisdom and today I thought he was a cunt. And the last thing I needed was the cops turning up on the Camperdown Salt Flats during one of my top-speed passes.

Hindsight's inherent wisdom now tells me the bloke was quite within his rights not to want to rake up my juicy meat-flavoured jam if I crashed, although at the time I cursed him as only someone who speaks three languages can curse. But I did it under my breath in case he heard. Then I went back to Gronk's Buddha-stick palazzo and put the bike away.

'Hey,' Gronk wheezed, taking the keys off me and blowing out a rich cloud of THC-impregnated smoke. 'We thought you'd crashed. There was all this noise going up and down the lane a few times, then silence, and then I remembered I should have told you about the back brake being rooted.'

'There's a back brake?' I asked, genuinely astonished at this revelation.

'Yeah, but it would lock up if you used it, so I took the brake pedal off.'

'Fair enough,' I shrugged, thinking I was truly blessed to have such a mechanically savvy bloke to mentor me through the early stages of my riding career.

'So what happened?' Gronk asked, toking deeply on a bong.

'The spray-painter told me to piss off or he'd call the cops.'

Gronk pondered this development as he packed another cone, lit it up, sucked back and then expelled what looked to be ten cubic metres of incinerated marijuana mist and coughed for a bit.

'Wait until the cunt goes home at four o'clock,' he advised me sagely.

What wisdom, I remember thinking at the time. First the back brake and now this. At precisely 4.01 pm I wheeled the bike back out into the lane. Thirty short seconds later, as I was de-clutching and kicking down through the Honda's long-suffering gearbox in a bid to slow down before I speared onto Parramatta Road and ruined everyone's day, a car turned into the lane, head on to me.

I didn't have time to swear. But I remember I did have time to close my eyes and avert my head. Which was just as well, because otherwise I would have hit the exact centre of the EH Holden's all-steel grille like a mince-filled artillery round.

As it turned out, one of riding's Great Rules saved me in spite of myself. It's the rule that says you're going to go where your head's pointing. Mine must have been pointing at the gutter because that's where I ended up. But because I had (via reflex brought about by years of watching Fred Flintstone cartoons) tried to assist the front brake by dragging my feet along the ground, I'd lost both school shoes, shredded my pants and smeared some of my skin along the gutter I was now lying in.

I'd already slowed down a lot when the car turned into Cardigan Lane and probably wasn't doing any more than about 15 kms per hour when I ended up 'a-gutser' in the gutter, just as the spray-painter had predicted.

I was in a decent amount of pain, and was seeping a lit-tle of my youthful-truant blood into the convict-era gutters of Camperdown. But I managed to groan my way to my feet and hobble over to Gronk's bike, which was on its side and oozing a little petrol out of its tank. I hauled it up and looked it over. It appeared remarkably unmarked by the ignominious halt to my crucial top-speed testing.

The same could not be said for me. My school shoes, a pair of well-worn desert boots (*de rigueur* for any aspiring young hooligan in the '70s) were a torn and battered mess, as were my school pants and the limbs inside them, and there was some pain and bruising on my hands. Still, all things being equal, I'd hurt myself much worse when I fell off my skateboard a few months prior.

But as I would discover, limping home with skateboard-related injuries was different from limping home with motorcycle-related injuries. Especially when you've been jigging school to acquire them.

For his part, Gronk was entirely indifferent to the incident and only laughed hoarsely from within a thick cloud of bong smoke when I told him what had happened.

'Suck shit,' he said, utterly devoid of sympathy and peering at the scuffed XL250 through the puffy red slits that served him as eyes. 'As long as the bike is all right.'

The bike was fine. As a result of the stack, one of the levers was bent and it stank a bit more of petrol than usual, but then so did I. I remember stopping at a tap and trying to wash off the stink and to mitigate the resultant burn that goes with being splashed with fuel as I gimped my way home. My wretched shoes flapped on my feet in concert with my ribboned school trousers, which looked and felt more like some wino's party pants with each painful step.

'Aaargh!' my mother exclaimed as I shuffled into the house, and went to wake my father. My father worked night shift, and rousing him before the approved hour was only ever done in times of profound social upheaval or massive familial catastrophe, ie Not Too Bloody Often. In my mother's view, my appearance clearly fell into the latter category and thus the Kraken must be awoken.

Thankfully, I was required to deliver my explanation in his bedroom, as he sat on the edge of his bed, scratching his balls, tousled and ominous with broken sleep, ill humour and son-bastardry. The bedroom was quite dark, so my injuries were not affronting him, but the stench of petrol certainly was.

'Vy you smell like det?' he grated.

'I got petrol spilled all over me when the bike fell over,' I offered.

'Vot bike?'

'My friend's bike.'

My father stared bleakly at me and turned on his bedside light. I dry-swallowed and dropped my eyes. Now was not the time to challenge for control of the herd by staring back at him. Humility, meekness and profound regret were the only accept-able behaviours at this point.

'Dis is motorcycle det make dis?' he stated flatly, his large hand indicating the tattered wreckage arrayed before him.

I nodded.

'How much is demege?' he asked.

'I'm all right,' I shrugged.

'Not you. How much is demege to bike?'

'Nothing. The bike is fine.'

My father pondered this for a minute or so, while I contin-ued to ooze blood and pain in his bedroom.

'No more dis motorcycle,' he eventually rumbled. 'Go to school.' His tone clearly indicated this was not a subject he would entertain debating with me. 'Understend?'

I nodded. That's cool, I thought. Theoretically, all he was asking for was my comprehension – not my compliance or any meaningless no-more-motorcycles promises I might make under such duress.

Well, that's how I saw it.

My mother was a different matter. She was in the kitchen when I left my father's bedroom, and there was more praying going on than I had seen in quite some time. But there was also sympathy for my plight – sympathy that had been completely absent thus far.

Mum cleaned my injuries, took charge of my tattered clothing, and cried profoundly for some hours as I lay on my bed throbbing and stinging with bruising and gravel rash.

Gravel rash is uniquely maddening as an injury. It burns and pulses and after a day or two begins to itch with such intensity, it actually overpowers all other injuries, such as broken bones and pulped organs.

I replayed the stack over and over in my head, seeking a cause. But when that proved altogether pointless, since I really had no clear idea why I crashed, I began to brood about far more important things – specifically, the long-term continuation of this motorcycle caper.

There was no question that it would continue, despite what my father imagined. Riding motorcycles, even like a clueless arsehat, was several orders of magnitude greater than anything else I had ever done in my life and stopping now was simply inconceivable. None of my many motorcycle magazines even came close to articulating the sheer unbridled joy, the deep visceral fulfilment, and the adrenal gland orgasms that were going on as I rattled Gronk's bike through the back streets of Camperdown.

Gronk knew this. Which is why he smiled knowingly when I limped back into his house the next week, scabbed up, itchy as hell, and ready to ride.

'Wanna cone?' he asked, always the perfect host.

'Nope,' I smiled. 'I just want the keys.'

He tossed them to me and I remember locking eyes with him. My clear blue pools of innocence and his slitted crimson piss-holes of corruption exchanged a mutual acknowledgement of some higher and vastly deeper understanding.

This motorcycling business . . . it was something disturbingly special, shatteringly addictive and emotionally overwhelming. It was not just 'transport' as some seemed to think. It was transcendental.

And for me, it has remained thus for more than thirty years.

Thanks, Gronk. I owe you.

THE FIRST
SUMMIT

Catharsis. Some men seek some form of it their whole lives and never find it. Others find it in the most unlikely places, much as I did when I was hunched on my knees in the dirt, geysering ginger-flavoured-booze vomit out of my nose after setting fire to my tent and before going to throw bricks at the cops. This kind of behaviour was only ever possible during the Sack of Rome and the Easter motorcycle races at Bathurst. You may have heard of them. Well, I lived them, and this is how they began for me.

'The scene of savage joys, the school of
coarse good fellowship and noise ...'

WILLIAM COWPER

The sweet baby fucken Jesus knows I used to love the Easter motorcycle races at Bathurst. Mount Panorama is certainly not much of a mountain from a geological standpoint. But from the very beginning of my manifestation as a motorcyclist, those few dusty, beer-can-strewn hectares perched a scant 220 metres above Bathurst were the cultural and spiritual pinnacle of my universe.

For the five or so years that I went there, The Mountain was my mother, my teacher, my not-so-secret lover, my religion and my creed. The times I spent camped on The Mountain in the company of certifiable madmen desperately fending off renal failure were among the greatest and most life-affirming periods of camaraderie, public drunkenness and motorcycling insanity I had ever experienced.

There is now nothing remotely like the Bathurst Easter bike races anywhere in Australia. For motorcyclists, The Mountain has been replaced by The Island – Phillip Island in Victoria – which is by every conceivable measure a better venue for motorcycle racing. The Phillip Island track is faster, safer and more scenically splendid. It has world-class souvlaki, great accommodation and hot promo chicks in Lycra. It even has a campground of sorts, a nice, grassy, fenced-in area adjacent to the racetrack where the happy campers pre-book their sites – then fool themselves into imagining they're really letting their hair down for a couple of days because someone drank too much and heaved into their sleeping bag, or someone bogged their bike in some mud, or the regular Bass Strait ice gales had blown their tents all to buggery and they had to put them up again. All heady, memorable shit for sure.

But it is just not even in the same solar system as the screeching, revving, wheel-spinning, toilet-exploding, cop-bashing and sheer shit-fucking insanity that went on atop The Mountain. And that's probably just as well. We'd all be living in an Orwellian police state by now had that madness continued down the path it was on.

After all, the fact that we now have heavily armoured riot squads is entirely due to the fuckery that went on at Bathurst. The infamous Tactical Response Group (TRG) of the New South Wales Police Force (which blossomed from the even more infamous 21st Division) was born in the blood, bricks and baton charges of the Easter bike races. The police openly used these races to train their officers in crowd control and head-cracking. The media cheered from the sidelines and even facilitated 'incidents' (like the burning Channel 7 news car), which were then aired on the evening news to a shocked middle-class Australia amid demands that something be done about the bikie Ragnarok that threatened to envelop the universe.

Of course, the fact that the police behaved like insufferable cunts all weekend, booking riders at three kilometres over the speed limit, conducting strip-searches on the side of the road, maliciously destroying personal belongings, and generally earning the 'fucken pig' epithet was never mentioned in news reports. It was simply accepted that 'bikies' at Bathurst just went batshit apropos of nothing and started hating on the poor cops each Easter.

But be that as it may, from the first time I went in 1979, until the Mother of All Riots in 1985, The Mountain and its annual Easter denizens were what defined motorcycle culture for me.

27

And in 1979 I was the motorcycling equivalent of a blank slate. I was an empty memory stick just waiting to be filled with hot data. I had been riding motorcycles legally for a few scant weeks. I was living at home and hadn't even taken up smoking yet. I was still masturbating under my sheets to that blonde piece out of ABBA and the fat-titted biker sluts in *Easyriders* magazine. In fact, everything I knew about motorcycles I'd read in various motorcycle magazines. And I knew that motorcyclists didn't go to church at Easter – they went to Bathurst.

So a few weeks after I bought my first new bike, a gorgeous red Yamaha, I kissed my mum goodbye and told her I was going to Bathurst.

'Vy you go to Budherst?' she asked me for the seventeenth time, as I busied myself checking, for the millionth time, that the sleeping bag and small tent I had lashed to the seat with a billion ocky straps was secure.

'To watch the bike races,' I sighed, inwardly fizzing with so much excitement and anticipation I knew I would have to go pee once again before I rode off. Of course, I wasn't remotely interested in watching the bike races. I was interested in being a motorcyclist. In fact, for the first two years I went to Bathurst, I didn't see a single race. But what I did see more than made up for what I didn't. And what I learned – about myself, about others, and about vomiting Stone's Green Ginger Wine while crying like a woman – has stayed with me forever.

'You not raysink?' Mum asked yet again.

'No, Mum,' I assured her yet again. 'I am not racing.'

She hugged me as I zipped up my intensely new leather jacket, told me to be careful, and made the sign of the cross over me as I wedged my helmet onto my head. I waved fondly to her as I rode off, my cardboard L-plate poking cheekily from the rat's nest of ocky straps holding all my crap behind me. This was, apparently, a bureaucratically deemed 'failure to properly display' the papery yellow fucker, for which I was booked between Katoomba and Lithgow. I was then booked again just after Lithgow for speeding at 83 kms per hour in an eighty zone, then again just before Bathurst for being a 'Fucken bikie cunt'.

I was having more fun than I had ever thought was even possible to have. This bike-riding business was just great. I'd only started riding ten minutes ago, and already I was a two-wheeled outlaw glistening with fines, street cred and police abuse. It was the Thursday before Good Friday and I wasn't even in Bathurst yet. If I kept this up, I might well be doing ten years' jail by the end of the weekend. And all because I wanted to be a motorcyclist and motorcyclists go to Bathurst at Easter, and so I just kept on going.

I wasn't too fussed about the fines affecting my bike licence, primarily because I didn't actually have a bike licence. What I had was a learner's permit, which was at that time, and as the result of an altogether hilarious bureaucratic fuck-up, far better than a licence. You see, you couldn't lose a learner's permit like you could lose a normal licence with points on it. A learner's permit had no points, and it wasn't a licence. Oh how we used to laugh about that – almost as loudly as we cried when that loophole was eventually closed.

A few kays out of Bathurst it became obvious that there would be quite a few motorcycles at this event. They were the dominant life form on the Great Western Highway. But this was, after all, the annual Australian Motorcycle Grand Prix. It was the biggest event on the Australian motorcycling calendar. As I idled through Kelso, scant kilometres from Bathurst proper, there were bikes on the road in front of me and behind me as far as I could see. All loaded much like mine and all heading for the big hill now visible on my left. Some of the riders were even pointing to it and pumping their fists. I near wet myself with excitement and almost crashed into the back of a big Kawasaki because I wasn't watching where I was going. A little bit of wee did come out when that happened, but I forgot all about it as soon as I turned into the town's main drag. I had to stop. I was in awe. Lining both sides of William Street were bikes as far as I could see. There was a pub immediately to my left literally overflowing with bikers – of whom I was, now and forever unto the ages of ages, a part of. Even if I had just pissed my pants a little bit.

I rolled slowly up the wide main street, my mouth agape and my head swivelling from side to side exactly like those sideshow clowns you feed ping-pong balls to. Bikes gleamed on both sides of the street almost all the way past Machattie Park. Then as I looked ahead to where William Street steepened beside the big private boarding school there were no more parked bikes. Just bikes like mine, loaded and moving slowly towards the racetrack, which loomed above and before me like some vast ceremonial mound speckled with motorcycles and madness.

I came to the ticketing barrier – essentially a gantry bridging the road with people standing beneath it flogging tickets. Directly behind them was the racetrack – specifically Murray's Corner, which was the ninety-degree bend that ended the straightline speed orgasm that was the now-mythical Conrod Straight.

I bought a three-day pass, then took off my helmet like every-body else, looped it around my arm and followed the line of bikes turning right. I made my way carefully up the dirt access road that runs vaguely parallel to the racetrack from Pit Straight, left past Hell Corner, and up Mountain Straight before spitting you out at Reid Park, which was the first section of the vast three-park camping area on top of the mountain. I think I was maybe 200 metres into the climb when the first motorcycle passed me at about 90 kms per hour, the back wheel sashaying from side to side and spraying dirt. The rider was shirtless and helmetless and his two passengers (!) were each holding a carton of beer and dragging their thonged feet through the dirt as the bike hared up the mountain. About twenty other bikes passed me shortly afterwards, all going much faster than me. I pulled over, totally affronted. What the fuck were these mad pricks doing? I thought. Who the bastard fuck puts three helmetless cunts wearing thongs on a bike, then goes tearing up a steeply wind-ing dirt road heavily trafficked by other motorcycles, all drinking beer and hooting like whores when the navy comes to town?

I had my answer as I summited. Everyone on top of this bloody mountain, apparently. I actually didn't know where to look first. As I rode slowly through Reid Park, then Sulman Park and finally past a fenced compound and small brick building (which I later learned was the notorious police compound), and into McPhillamy Park, the mountain was one vast roiling mass of activity, tents, wood smoke, revving motorcycle engines and empty beer cans.

Fuck me, I remember thinking. I was so going to get me some of this meaty happiness. I idled around McPhillamy Park for a few minutes being buzzed by bikes hurtling past, their rear ends snaking as abused tyres fought for traction on the loose surface of the many one-lane dirt tracks that crisscrossed the camping areas, while drunks from the many smoky-fired camps cheered and roared and laughed. This is what Genghis Khan's Mongol hordes must have looked like – but instead of yurts, shaggy ponies and steaming horse dung, this barbaric horde slept in multi-coloured tents, rode a lot of ponies all at once, and left piles of empty beer cans in its wake. The similarities were confronting. Was there something in my genetic memory that was responding to this, like it's said all men respond to Mother Africa upon first beholding the womb of mankind? I didn't know, but I was literally carbonated with sensory overload. If I didn't stop soon, I would probably faint.

I found a cleared area approximately in the middle of every-thing, pulled up and parked the bike. A few people stared at me in benign condescension. It was obvious, even to the most booze-addled motorcyclist beholding me clumping around my shiny new bike in my shiny new gear, that I was quite shiny and new to all this. But I sure as shit knew how to put up a tent, which I busied myself doing, when a bloke walked up to me and proffered me a can of cold beer.

'Here, mate,' he said, holding it out. 'You look fucken thirsty. Where you from?'

'Sydney,' I grinned, gratefully popping the top.

'I'm from Melbourne,' he said. 'Name's Ken. This your first time?'

'Yep,' I nodded, taking a noisy sip of my beer.

'Best fucken place on earth,' Ken said, and indicated over his shoulder at a big fire with some cheery drunks standing around it. 'Come over if you want any more beer. We got tons.'

Then Ken wandered back to his fire and left me to my tent. As I fiddled with the poles and fly, I was smiling like a donut and trying to rationalise what had just happened. I was quite unused to strangers giving me their alcohol, seemingly with no hidden agenda, and while I had read much about the 'brotherhood of the bike', my first encounter with it was still surprising.

I knew immediately what I had to do. The tent was standing, so I crawled inside and dug out the little bag of marijuana I had brought with me. I had only smoked marijuana once before. It was at some party not long after I'd left school, and someone passed me a joint. I had a drag, coughed badly and felt a little light-headed for half an hour. I didn't even think about dope again until I decided to go to Bathurst. From everything I'd read, marijuana and motorcycles went together like shit and stink. The Easter races were the ground zero of all things motorcycling. It therefore followed that a supply of marijuana was simply *de rigueur* if I was to have a genuine motorcycling experience and become a proper motorcyclist. I had even brought rolling papers.

Tragically, I had no more idea about how to roll a joint than I did about breeding alligators. So it was a good twenty minutes before I had something approximating a smokeable bone in my hands. The plan was for me to light the joint, have a few manly tokes, then casually saunter over to my mate Ken's fire, offer it around and maybe have a few beers with my new motorcycling friends. What happened instead was that I took three deep drags, coughed so hard I felt something tear beside my pancreas, and had to lie down on my sleeping bag with my eyes closed for a while.

When I emerged from the tent it was early evening and I saw the Laverda Owners Club had camped itself around me. There were only six of them, with only two Laverdas between them – Jotas, in fact, which are arguably the most beautiful three-cylinder bikes ever made. The other four blokes split a Ducati 900SS and three big Suzukis between them.

Time has erased their names from my memory, but I remain ever grateful it was this lot I found as I crawled out into the fading light, and not some jolly, middle-aged, family-based touring organisation. My life might well have taken a different road. I am also grateful they didn't kill and eat me, given how I was so young and pink and fresh and they were all such hard-bitten road warriors. And I am beholden to them for all the things they taught me over the next three astonishing days.

The first lesson was joint-rolling. All else proceeded from this. It is a skill that has stood me in marvellous stead over the years, making me feel useful when some mate's bike breaks down in the middle of nowhere and the ensuing wait for salvation becomes intolerable. I have honed this talent and am now able to roll a serviceable joint in a Force Six gale, with a bad moon rising and a hard rain falling.

I was shown how to tow 200 kilograms of dead tree behind my bike without completely burning out my clutch, leaving just enough friction-grab on the plates to get me back home. Towing immense lengths of firewood from the various wood dumps, which the local council would top up from time to time, was a salutary lesson in bike control, clutch-feathering and throttle management. It also sorted the size of everyone's testicles quite ruthlessly. The men with smaller and less robust cags would idle up to the pile with a girlfriend or a mate on the back of their bike, load them up with a big armful of dead branches and idle slowly away to their campsite. But men with big, hairy, bullock-sized yams would skid to a halt with vast aplomb, skilfully lash a few metres of rope to the biggest stump in the pile, then using their feet as outriggers, lurch wildly back to their campsites, with the bike revving like mad and the slipping clutch smelling like unwashed genitals. There are no prizes for guessing which gonad size I promptly aligned myself with. Once towing was learned, the skill could be applied to humans as well as logs, and until you've dragged a shrieking drunk behind your bike till he shits his pants with fear and lets go of the rope, you haven't lived.

I learned how eye-opening it was to sit around a campfire and tell massive lies about one's riding prowess, even if you had none, then greet the sunrise beside a beer-drinking bull terrier called Gloria, who would lick you gently on the arm as you hunched forward on your hands and knees projectile vomiting Stone's Green Ginger Wine into the soil. Which Gloria then helpfully ate, to her eternal glory.

I discovered true fear by riding the track at night, the wrong way around, which meant going up Conrod Straight in the other direction – back when it was a real straight and not the effete chicane-shamed atrocity it is today. I can still taste the acerbic tang of pure dread as I hammered up that long, long straight at almost 190 kms per hour behind one of the Laverdas, then leaned my bike into the sharp, totally blind uphill right of Forrest's Elbow, followed by the even blinder and steeper uphill horror of the Dipper. This feat was made all the more memorable because people were actually riding the other way at the time. Oh, and we were drunk. So that helped.

I tried my hand at donuts – a hugely crowd-pleasing stunt that involved hopping on one leg as you held your bike in a rearwheel-spinning circle around itself. I managed one-and-a-half clumsy revolutions before dropping the bike, smashing the end off my clutch lever and breaking a blinker. None of which prevented me from enthusiastically entering countless impromptu short-course dragraces between the campsites, with nothing but lines of cheering human Armco keeping me out of the local casualty ward. Skill played no part in it whatsoever.

I understood that on Saturday evening, just as the sun set, I was to go to the police compound to throw burning rolls of toilet paper soaked in petrol at the police. I would do this until darkness fell, then I would start throwing half-bricks and cans full of dirt at them. I would do this because it seemed to be what all the cool kids were doing. After all, the cops had been totalitarian cocksmokers all weekend, clearly looking to antagonise the restless crowd into action. It was inevitable. We knew that and they knew that. I also learned that each time the cops came charging out with their batons, I would run like a yelping cur. Then I would return and throw more shit at them. It was like the tide going in and out. I quickly worked out that hiding in someone's tent during a baton charge was not smart: many occupied tents and occupants were trampled under angry police boots. Moreover, I learned that when running like a startled faun, one must look where one is running. Peering over one's shoulder, wall-eyed with terror only means you'll kneecap yourself on some bastard's hotplate full of snags, enabling the police to catch you, baton you like a hired mule, then drag you face-down through 100 metres of broken glass, dirt and beer cans, before charging you with 'Being a cunt' and fucking your Easter right the fuck up.

I also became a mewling slave to the volcanic arse-lava that came geysering out of my inflamed rectum after three days of eating sauce-smeared Pluto Pups washed down with beer. In turn, this taught me to always buy the softest toilet paper in the supermarket and to always carry a travelling roll of it wherever I wandered. Always.

And I learned incontrovertibly that all I ever wanted to do until the stars fell from the sky and the oceans swallowed the earth was ride bikes and hang out with like-minded psychotics, social misfits and beery misanthropes.

All up, I was a much more educated and developed motorcycle rider when I finally returned home on the Monday evening. My mum could see the marks of all that quality learning in the way I limped when I walked, and croaked when I attempted human speech. She told me later that my right pupil was larger than my left and that I reeked of un-Godly corruption.

She made many signs of the cross over me that evening. They all failed to take.

TALES FROM THE PILLION

Pillions are the damned of the motorcycle world. Perched behind the rider like a massive organic backpack, they totally ruin a motorcycle's handling and force an entirely unwanted responsibility on the poor rider. Most times, it's all I can do to keep myself alive. Having to bear full liability for a person whose very presence on the bike makes it handle like a drug-addled bullock is vastly surplus to my riding needs. That said, if the pillion is cute and blonde, wearing a short dress and holding a half-empty bottle of cheap wine, I am prepared to make all sorts of compromises. Personally, I make a crap pillion, despite all the various circumstances that have seen me hunched on the back of some motorcycle. Even so, being doubled relatively short distances is nothing compared to being piggybacked 600 kilometres by a frost-bitten drunk.

MY MOTHER WARNED ME ABOUT BLOKES LIKE ME

'Enjoy when you can, and
endure when you must.'

JOHANN WOLFGANG VON GOETHE

It will surprise no one to discover I am the world's worst pillion. It dawned on me that this was the case one frigid summer night about sixty kilometres north of Albury in the early '80s.

Prior to that realisation, the world's worst pillion was, without a doubt, a mad chick called Lana I was doubling around Sydney in the vain hope she'd surrender the contents of her panties to me if I managed to frighten her enough. In the end, she scared me far more than I ever scared her and we parted company after I handed some bloke on a Jaffa-coloured Kwaka Nine his arse in an impromptu dragrace one Saturday evening; a dragrace which left her best going-out heels somewhere on George Street and her feet looking like hamburger.

In my defence, I had repeatedly told her not to put her feet down when I stopped, but I may as well have been talking to an egg carton for all the mind she paid me. It was almost impossible for me to get her to adhere to pillioning basics and lean with the bike as we banked into a corner, so advanced shit like when not to put your feet down was still some way off. And the cunt on the Kwaka really did need putting in his place that night. What did he expect was going to happen when he began revving his engine and jerking his fucken head up the road in the ancient ritualistic challenge to establish whose man-piss was richer and stronger?

In the end, I won the drag, but only because he must have missed a gear laughing so hard at the sight of Lana's flailing legs disappearing up George Street as my perfect drag start tore the strappy heels right off her well-manicured feet with a violence that almost crippled her.

Anyway, fast forward a few years and here's me, sitting out the last six weeks of my very first licence suspension. My mate Terry had ridden up from Melbourne and we'd been out drowning my no-licence sorrows, when he came up with this awesomely brilliant idea.

'You're not allowed to ride in New South Wales, right?'

'Right,' I grated.

'But you're allowed to ride in other states, right?'

'That's what I understand the words "You are disqualified from riding or driving a motor vehicle in the state of New South Wales" to mean.'

'So come and ride in Victoria for the last month.'

How this hadn't occurred to me before he said it is a mystery. It was a genius idea. And absolutely legal back then (though legality was a stupendously grey area for me when I was twenty years old).

Three days later, Terry and I were happily tying my beloved Suzuki GSX1100 to the inside of a freight car at Sydney's Central Station. Our plan was for Terry to pillion me to Albury and beat the train there, unload the bike, then spend the rest of my New South Wales down-time riding around the state of Victoria. A simple plan for simple people, and even simpler times.

With the bike 'safely secured' on the *Spirit of Progress* choo-choo, Terry and I geared up and prepared to hurtle down the Hume Highway through the night. The *Spirit* was due in Albury in about 12 hours, so we figured we'd beat it easily, even two-up on Terry's GSX750.

I had been riding for some years at this stage and my gear reflected my vast experience. I had jeans over long underwear, a thick Walden Miller leather jacket, a woollen jumper, and rabbit-skin gloves and sheepskin-filled flying boots – rather like a WWII fighter pilot but at a much lower altitude.

Terry was a relative newcomer to motorcycling. He had bought his Suzuki GSX750 two days before riding it to Sydney to visit me. He only had a cheap vinyl parka, desert boots and an old visorless helmet to withstand the rigours of the road.

'But so what?' we told ourselves. We were young, strong and armed with a bottle of Stone's Green Ginger Wine. It was high summer and it was 31 degrees in Sydney when we rolled away from Central and headed for Albury.

By the time we hit Goulburn, it was 10 degrees. By Gundagai, we were into the low single digits and it was getting colder by the kilometre. I was wearing everything I had and using Terry as a windbreak. I also had a helmet visor, so while I was cold, I was not in the claws of crushing hypothermia like Terry. Even the Stone's was not helping anymore. It did at first, just the other side of Goulburn, when Terry dozed off due to the cold and drifted us across the double yellow lines and into the path of a semitrailer. He said later what jolted him awake was the truck's blazing lights, and not my screams of terror or the repeated headbutts I was hammering into the back of his helmet.

We stopped immediately afterwards so Terry could col-lect himself and we had a few fortifying belts of Stone's. This proved to be rather spiritually efficacious, raising our morale to previously unattained heights, so we stopped every thirty kilo-metres or so after that to have a few more pulls on the bottle.

Just the other side of Gundagai the bottle was empty, the tem-perature was just above zero and Terry was now suffering bouts of crazy shuddering spasms every kilometre or so. Each time this cold-based palsy would hit him, he'd cramp up and tremble like a shitting dog, and the GSX would veer wildly across the road. I would start screaming and headbutting him (I didn't dare let go of the grab rail) until he regained control of his body and the bike.

After a really lengthy spasm almost sent us arse-up in a table drain we surrendered and sought the heated sanctuary of a truck-stop at Holbrook.

Terry was effectively blind. Both his eyes had swollen enor-mously from the constant ice-fanged wind hitting them through the visorless opening of his helmet, and I had pissed myself when he'd merged into the table drain ten kilometres back. I didn't think it was possible for two humans to be any more miserable than we were that evening. Which only serves to demonstrate how little I knew at the time.

'What's that fucken smell?' Terry groaned as we stood beside a heater inside the Holbrook truck-stop at some obscene and frigid hour of the night.

'It's piss,' I hissed.

'What piss?' Terry asked, his nostrils twitching and his head swivelling from side to side due to his recently acquired blindness.

'My piss,' I said through clenched teeth. 'I thought we were dead when you ran off the road. I didn't see any point holding it in.'

That was a lie. I could no more have held in that wee than I could have turned the tide. When Terry's bike left the road and started tankslapping along the verge, my bladder unilaterally emptied, clearly of the opinion I should arrive at the Throne of Jesus with a freshly flushed urethra.

'Why's the back of my pants wet?' Terry gasped in horror as his hands patted the arse of his jeans, which were steaming as they dried in front of the heater.

'Please don't make me tell you,' I grated.

'AARRGGHH,' Terry moaned, wincing in revulsion as my fright-wee dried on his body and made his skin prickle.

It was too cold to go outside and wash our clothes in the toilet, and in any case our more immediate concern was Terry's blindness and how that would impact on the fact that we had to be in Albury to get my bike off the train in three hours.

'How blind are you?' I asked him.

'What?' he keened, his head radaring from side to side as it locked onto my voice.

'Are you too blind to ride seventy kays to Albury?'

'Yes . . . no . . . probably . . .' he stammered. 'Why can't you ride us into fucken Albury?'

I grabbed him by the front of his parka and pulled him close enough to smell the Stone's Green Ginger Wine on his breath, which was mixed with the sour tang of my evaporating urine in a way I still dread remembering.

'I cannot ride us into fucken Albury because I do not have a fucken licence,' I said slowly. 'That is why *you* were doubling *me*, remember? That is why I have pissed myself and that is why you are blind.'

Then I frogmarched my blind friend outside into the pre-dawn frost and into the toilet. I turned on the tap, waited a few seconds for the frozen water to spit its way out of the juddering fitting, then started splashing it into Terry's face. He began screaming, but there had already been so much screaming that evening both of us were kinda used to it by now.

'Is that better?' I shrieked over his howls. 'Open your fucken eyes and tell me if you can see!'

'Yes, yes!' he yelled back. 'It's better! Stop! The water's freezing!'

It was better but only a little. Terry's eyes had undergone several hundred frigid kilometres of wind-blast and needed to rest. I gave him my helmet because it had a visor which would assist him by not ruining his eyes any further and I put his horribly ancient bucket on my head.

Then we hit the road again.

There are three small towns between Holbrook and Albury – Woomargama, Mullengandra and Bowna – before the Hume Highway turns sharply west to run around Lake Hume, then south again into Albury. Terry didn't see any of them. He told me later that all he could see were lighter shadows picked out of the dark by his high beam. And he was very grateful to me for helping him lean the bike into corners that he didn't see in time to do the leaning himself, and for yelling out helpful instructions like 'Change down!' and 'Truck . . . truck . . . TRUUUUUCK!'

But we made it to Albury station with an hour to spare. The sun was coming up and I had stopped smelling of piss. Well, it is probably more accurate to say that I could no longer smell that I still smelled of piss. I didn't care. I could have a shower later and wash my clothes and then spend the next few weeks hurtling around Victoria on my beloved Suzuki. Life was looking better by the moment.

The *Spirit of Progress* pulled in, and I waited impatiently for access to the freight car where my bike was secured. Except when I was given access, the bike was no longer secured – and it appeared that it hadn't been secured since about Redfern. It lay on its left side, but it had obviously been lying on its right side at some stage. And upon closer inspection it had also spent some time with both wheels in the air. The tank was dinged all over, the handlebars were bent, the levers were broken, the instruments were smashed, the blinkers jagged ruins and my beaut CRC exhaust-can was now flat-sided years before such things became fashionable.

'I thought you knew how to do truck hitches,' I said to Terry.

'So did I,' he muttered as we wrestled the wrecked bike onto the platform, much to the giggling delight of the station staff.

But repairing a smashed motorcycle on a station platform, while reeking of piss and shaking with cold, still beats the hell out of riding pillion. Every time.

RIDING INTO MORDOR

Motorcycling, done with the correct amount of dedication, can teach you many things. Not only about yourself and the size and soundness of your testicles, but about the laws of this great land, how they vary from state to state and what happens to your shit when you disregard them – even if those laws are dumb and stupid and reek of nannying and communism. I count myself fortunate that I was able to learn some of these lessons at a relatively early stage of my motorcycling career – lessons that were administered when I was handcuffed in a suburban Melbourne gutter several hours before I wasn't arrested for breaking and entering.

'Good decisions come from experience, and
experience comes from bad decisions.'

AUTHOR UNKNOWN

It was a different time. My world was less claustrophobic, but still filled with powerful motorcycles, crazy mates and the odd police siren. I was twenty-one – or possibly younger, but still suitably immortal and quite poisonously brazen. It is the only reasonable explanation I have for riding from Sydney to my mate Terry's place in Melbourne without a helmet.

Now you have to understand that in those days, the state of New South Wales had helmet exemptions. The NSW Roads and Traffic Authority (RTA) was called something less authoritative, had yet to begin its great social engineering crusade and was still to rent the greasy behavioural scientists it would later use to justify saving us from ourselves. The Fun Nazis had not yet ripped the soul out of motorcycling, and any decent doctor would sign a piece of paper stating helmets gave you headaches, which you would present to the RTA who would then cheerily issue you with an open-ended helmet exemption. This could be shown to any police officer, and if he didn't tear it up and give you a touch-up with his baton, you'd be permitted to proceed sans helmet.

The other option was to declare oneself a Sikh, and refuse to wear a helmet on religious grounds. But every time I tried to tie a turban around my head, it ended in a farce, and I was not about to tempt fate by insulting a religion whose practitioners all carry knives and are called 'Tiger'.

So I found a doctor who agreed that my helmet gave me an insufferable headache and shortly thereafter tucked a genuine RTA-issued helmet exemption into my wallet. Happy days.

But the state of Victoria was an altogether different prison camp to Stalag NSW. Dire inbred fascists had long held sway in that part of the world, chewing over the eldritch bones of lost opportunities to rule Australia as the de facto and de jure capital city and home of the country's cultural apparatchiks. The state's noisome capital, Melbournistan, was thus viewed by those of us in the Free North as something akin to Mordor. So when I first touted the idea of riding there without helmets to my mate Badger, the notion was treated with some incredulity.

'We're never gonna make Melbourne,' he shook his head. 'The fuckers will shoot us at the border.'

'Bullshit,' I sneered. 'Don't be a poof. We have valid helmet exemptions. The law's on our side!'

Of course, I had no idea what the actual law stated, or even whose side it might have been on in this case. But such paltry details were of no concern to me. I had a legal, government-issued piece of paper that said I didn't have to wear a fucken helmet because it made my bonce hurt, and I was going to party with Terry in Melbournistan after riding there with no helmet, and that was pretty much bloody that.

Badger pondered his incipient homosexuality for a few seconds, then shrugged and said, 'Okay, I'll go'. Two days later he and I were packed and rolling down the coast road to Victoria, helmet-free and grinning our fool heads off.

I could write volumes on the sheer visceral, bestial and splendidly sordid pleasure that can be had riding a long distance without a helmet, but it would only make the old-timers weep over what we've lost, and the young blokes scoff ignorantly about what they've never known and will never have – because once you've sacrificed your freedom for safety, there's no going back. Suffice to say that riding without a helmet rocks, and rocks fucken hard. And while the tail-tuckers among us will always mewl about such bizarre concepts as 'safety' and 'responsibility', I would remind them that one doesn't take up riding motorcycles because one is wedded to the twin prisons of safety and responsibility.

Anyway, Badger and I were belting down the coast in bright spring sunshine, looking *tres* cool and feeling *tres* badarse. Which, I hasten to point out, is exactly how one *should* feel when one is riding a motorcycle. Interestingly, we were not riding Harleys – the ultimate two-wheeled incarnation of male villainy. We were still unworthy, and had yet to approach the level of personal wickedness needed for Harley ownership (required by laws unwritten yet totally understood). And we couldn't afford Harleys, anyway.

Badger was riding a GS850 Suzuki and I was astride an almost-new GSX1100. They were powerful, angry-sounding beasts and as we wended our way south through achingly beautiful New South Wales coastal regions, the traffic was light and the warm air being force-fed into our faces smelled sweeter than joy. The whoosh of the wind and the muted growl of the bikes filled our ears, and made talking impossible over 140 kms per hour, so we would communicate with thumbs-up signs, crazy grins and frantic nods.

The New South Wales cops ignored us. Helmet exemptions were not all that uncommon and you'd see helmetless blokes on big Jap fours, hair whipping in the breeze, most days of the week. Quite frankly, there weren't that many police around in days of yore. The fanatical drive to build a vast, heavily militarised police force to subjugate the citizenry had yet to seize our government. So Badger and I were managing a stately

120–140 kms per hour, which was totally acceptable on the free-fire zones that were, back then, this nation's great highways. These zones were indicated by a sign that bore a black circle with a line through it. Older riders would be familiar with it. It kinda meant 'Off ya go, mate. We'd rather you pay attention to the road than your speedo, and the state government's not yet a money-grubbing pack of arsehats ruled by the megalomaniacal fascism of the RTA. Just don't be doing anything really stupid, okay?'

Such commonsense seems completely at odds with today's nanny state-ism. And it just goes to show how much personal freedom is missing in today's world. But as Badger and I pulled over outside Timbillica, a few kays north of the state border, and treated ourselves to a zesty five-paper bunger, today's world was still light years away. The Victorian border was not. It was just down the road a ways.

'How do you reckon we'll go?' Badger gagged, lunging back a goodly cloud of bought-in-Cabramatta Buddha, before passing it to me pinched, as tradition dictated, in the circle made by his thumb and forefinger.

'Mate, we'll be sweet,' I wheezed, taking a manly toke. 'You got your helmet exemption, haven't you?'

Badger nodded.

'Piece of piss then.'

I flicked the smouldering roach onto the road with what I felt was the appropriate amount of rebellious *savoir faire*, and watched it bounce twice shedding happy orange sparks. Then we got on our bikes and headed into Mordor.

The first thing Badger and I noticed as we wended our hel-metless way deeper into Victoria was that the roads were much nicer. The Germans noticed the exact same thing about their roads a few years after Adolf stepped up to the crease, but then they got over him pretty quickly. The Victorians, by contrast, have kept right on goosestepping to a succession of crazed fascists and don't look to be coming to their senses any time soon. Still, the roads are beaut.

Anyway, the second thing we noticed was that lots of people stared at our bare heads as we made our way to Melbournistan. As there were no helmet exemptions in Victoria, the sight of two righteous road warriors hurtling down the highway with their mullets tossing rebelliously in the wind was clearly the stuff of awe and wonder for the smelly southern proles.

And didn't we just ham it right the fuck up for them. At one stage we even tried passing a joint to each other as we banged along a little west of Sale – just like Captain America and Billy would have done during their iconic, drug-funded odyssey across the American heartland of *Easy Rider*. But instead of attaining still greater heights of coolness, Badger got some wayward sparks blasted into his mouth, veered wildly into oncoming traffic and ended up sporting a burn-blister on his mouth the size of a marble for the next four days.

Of the police there was no sign, and our helmetless progress was unimpeded. And it remained unimpeded almost all the way into Mordor's CBD, when a policeman on a motorcycle pulled us over just near Kooyong.

'Where are your helmets!?' he shrieked. 'Why aren't you wearing helmets?!'

'It's all right, mate,' I grinned, opening my wallet. 'We have helmet exemptions.'

He snatched our proffered sheets of paper, looked at them in disgust, then glared at Badger and me like we were targets on the pistol range.

'These are not valid in Victoria,' he stated flatly, handing them back. 'You have to wear helmets if you want to ride down here.'

His armed and unreasonable attitude presented us with two clear options. Either we agreed with him that we needed helmets to ride here, or we didn't and he shot us down like dogs. I immediately chose the first option, since it seemed to offer a positive way forward.

'Can we go to a bike shop and buy some helmets?' I asked.

The policeman stared at me in silence for a few moments, as if wondering how dangerously brain-damaged I was. This was a long time before Tasers and capsicum spray, but it was also a long time before toy-sized and chicken-chested police officers, and I could see him wondering how many blows of his baton I could endure before he had to shoot me. Then he looked around at the truly epic traffic jam that had occurred as a result of us getting pulled over in peak hour on the main road.

'Look,' he said, suddenly using his human voice. 'Youse are gonna get pulled over all the time if you don't have helmets. I'm amazed youse got as far as you did. If youse go straight to a bike shop from here, I will not take this matter any further.'

Badger and I immediately agreed that was the best possible course of action, crossed our hearts and hoped to die that we would, on the instant, proceed to the nearest bike shop, thanked him for his consideration and watched fondly as he rode off. Then we pushed our bikes onto the footpath, lit up our very last number and considered our position.

Terry's new house was in Caulfield, which was kinda south from where we were, according to our mud map. All the bike shops I knew about were further west, in the city. It had also just gone five o'clock. So our next move was a no-brainer as far as we could work out.

We got on the bikes and made for Caulfield, which is why I was surprised to find myself in Prahran some twenty minutes later. And I was heaps more surprised when an unmarked police car started whooping and flashing us in the middle of Prahran shopping centre.

Now, in case you were wondering, it's not a good idea to run from the police if you don't know where you're going. Given that Badger and I had no idea where we were, let alone where we would run to when the high-speed pursuit commenced, we didn't run. We should have, given what happened next, but we didn't. Instead, we got off our bikes and were immediately nonplussed as buggery to be ordered onto the ground at gunpoint by two very large and hostile detectives who stated they were from the Prahran Crime Squad and called us 'Dirty fucken cunts', while kneeling on our spines and handcuffing us.

'Just what the fuck do you two dirty fucken cunts think you're fucking doing?' asked one of them when we were seated in the gutter and their guns had been holstered.

'We have helmet exemptions,' I puffed, thinking this treatment was all a bit harsh for no helmets.

'Not down here you don't, cunt,' the detective grinned.

'Yes I do,' I said, thinking perhaps he was under the impression that we had left them at home. 'Mine's in my wallet.'

'What kind of fucken drugs are you dirty cunts on?' the detective demanded.

Badger and I stared blankly into the middle distance, our arses already numb from the gutter we were sitting in, and our wrists aching from the arrest-tight handcuffs. We were not about to admit to anything, and it was clear the detective was not finished holding forth.

'You have to be on fucken drugs!' he chortled, his voice booming loudly. 'Only mad drug addicts and dirty fucken cunts would be riding around here with no helmets on!'

The other detective had already cut our luggage off the bikes with a penknife, and was happily kicking our meagre possessions all over the footpath, as the good burghers of Prahran walked insouciantly around what was clearly a major crime scene.

The luggage-kicker then came over to us, shunted us onto our sides with his foot and frisked us. He pulled our wallets out of our pockets and emptied their contents onto the ground. Then they both examined what fell out – maybe 200 dollars between us, a licence and helmet exemption each, and some bits of paper and cards with assorted phone numbers on them – the normal wallet detritus of two twenty-something motorcycle hooligans.

'Look at this, Inspector,' said the luggage-kicker, holding up two sheets of paper.

The inspector peered at the papers, then peered at us, then went and spent a few minutes on the radio in his car. He came back with a big grin on his face.

'Which one of you dirty cunts is Boris Makulavik?' He mispronounced my surname, but I felt it prudent not to correct him.

'I am,' I said.

He dropped two pieces of paper on the ground where I lay. 'This is your licence and helmet exemption?'

'Yes.'

He then hauled me to my feet, uncuffed me, and told me to go and stand near my bike.

'Then you must be Gabriel Stark,' the inspector leered at Badger, flapping his helmet exemption in front of him.

Badger nodded.

'Then who the bastard fuck is Peter Fucking Madison?!' the inspector roared, waving Badger's licence in the air. 'And why do you have his fucken licence, you dirty fucken cunt!?'

An icy claw of fear and nausea wriggled to life in my guts. I could see Badger was swallowing madly, his throat working like a chook's cloaca preparing to deliver an egg.

A few months prior, Badger had found a licence in some pub he was drinking in. Back then, there were no photo ID licences. They were just bits of paper with your details on them. Helmet exemptions were similar. Just anodyne bits of vaguely official looking paper. We used to deploy sticky tape along the creases to stop them disintegrating in our wallets. Today's amazing photocopiers could replicate them with ease and total accuracy. Anyway, upon discovering someone else's licence lying abandoned in a pub toilet, Badger felt it was incumbent upon him to put that licence to good use. As it turned out, Prahran was this licence's debut appearance, and as the inspector discovered when he was on the radio, Peter Fucking Madison was a man wanted by the NSW Police for crimes ranging from armed robbery to not paying child support.

'Roll up his sleeve,' the inspector instructed the luggage-kicker. Badger's sleeve was brusquely rolled up to reveal a small, badly inked tattoo of a Grim Reaper on his upper arm. Apparently, Peter Fucking Madison was similarly tattooed and this made the inspector even happier than he had previously been.

'Put the dumb bastard in the car,' he smiled, then turned his attention to me. 'You must be the stupidest cunt I've ever laid eyes on. Or maybe the second stupidest, given how dumb your fucken mate is. How far did you think you'd get with no helmets in Victoria?'

I was going to point out that we'd actually got rather a long way, but decided to keep my stupid mouth shut for the moment.

'We're gonna take that dumb cunt to the station to see who he really is. You need to pick up this shit that's all over the foot-path. And you need to get a helmet, otherwise this is as far as you'll be riding in Victoria.'

Then he got back in the car and drove off with the luggage-kicker and Badger, and left me standing on the footpath in Prahran, considering my somewhat diminished options for that evening. I picked up the gear that had been strewn across three shopfronts, retied the cut ocky straps and secured all the luggage back onto the bikes. Then I sat back down in the gutter, a little lost and confused.

At some stage, I would need to call Terry. He would come and get me. He would bring a spare helmet and things would be . . . um, better than they were at this second. We'd go back to his joint, I could grab a hot shower, we could have a few beers and then have a think about getting Badger out of the chokingly deep ka-ka he seemed to be in. It appeared the right and proper way forward out of the debacle this ride had become. Now if only I had Terry's phone number. I knew Badger had it, but he'd just been carted off to jail for being two people at once.

Fuck, I thought to myself. I needed a plan. I was alone on the mean streets of Prahran with two motorcycles, a badly drawn map to my mate Terry's place in Caulfield and the searing contempt of the nearby shopkeepers, all of whom had just witnessed Badger and me being cuffed and kicked by the cops. It was getting on to 8.30, so there weren't that many shops open, but the milk bar, hair salon and pharmacy I entered looking for change to make a phone call all responded negatively and threatened to call the police if I didn't vacate their shops forthwith. The bloke in the all-night chemist was downright hostile and showed me his under-the-counter cricket bat before threatening to call the cops.

My plan was to call the Prahran police station and see if the cops wouldn't mind asking Badger for Terry's phone number in between beating him with a coathanger. A big ask, I know, but I was really at a bit of a loss. My fabulous helmetless odyssey into Mordor had ceased to delight and amuse me some hours before. I would not leave Badger's bike unattended and the prospect of a cheerless evening asleep in some piss-splashed shopfront was looking very likely. I would probably go buy some hot chips, find the least-smelly shop to sleep in front of, and seek oblivion.

I was halfway through unstrapping my sleeping bag from the back of the bike when the unmarked police car returned and ejected a wild-eyed Badger, before screeching off into the night.

'You okay?' I asked, as Badger glared at the disappearing detectives. 'What happened?'

'They pushed me around, screamed at me, threatened to shoot me in the face, then charged me with producing a false licence and brought me back here,' he rasped.

'We should go,' I urged.

'They also said if they saw us riding off with no helmets they would run us down like dogs.'

I absorbed that information with some alarm. For all I knew, the bastards were parked in a nearby side street just waiting for us to ride past.

There was only one thing to do. I pocketed my bike key, kicked up the sidestand and started pushing. Badger was right behind me. I think we must have pushed those bikes for almost two kilometres before my strength departed and took my fear of being car-murdered by the cops with it.

'Piss on this,' I puffed, sticking my key back into the ignition and firing up the bike. Badger followed suit and after checking our mud map, we were back on our way to what I hoped was Terry's place in Caulfield. It was getting late, so we didn't bother ringing Terry, who was probably asleep.

As you no doubt know, most of Melbournistan is nothing but a vast grid of streets, so no one stays lost for long. It's relatively easy to navigate your way around, especially if you're not drunk or stoned, and almost by accident Badger and I found ourselves in Terry's street about half an hour after we'd set off. Shortly thereafter, we also found Terry's house. It was dark and devoid of life.

'Why is he not home?' Badger wanted to know.

'Maybe he's asleep,' I shrugged and continued hammering on the door.

Nothing. The house remained dark, locked and empty.

Badger and I looked at each other. I saw despair in his eyes and I'm sure he must have seen something similar in mine. Our trip had gone from being a glorious helmet-free declaration of I-don't-give-a-shit to a rather pathetic shower of criminal charges, bike-pushing and imminent homelessness. We certainly felt like a pair of really stupid cunts.

But necessity has always been the mother of invention, and in a wordless exchange of intent, Badger and I grabbed a screwdriver from my tool roll, moved to a side window, and started levering it open. We even failed at that, but Badger did manage to put his hand through the glass when it slipped off the screwdriver, so it was not all doom and gloom. There was a fair bit of blood, but at least we could now get into the house via the window. We crawled awkwardly through the opening, flicked on the lights in the living room, and took our bearings.

Badger was bleeding quite heavily and clutching his hand, so the first thing we had to do was have a beer to calm our nerves, and then consider staunching the blood. I found the kitchen, opened the fridge and marvelled at how well stocked it was. Terry obviously ate right and looked after himself, judging by the fresh vegetables I could see. But I could also see beer. I grabbed two cans, snagged some nice fluffy towels from the adjoining bathroom and went back to the living room where Badger was sitting on the couch, dripping blood onto Terry's well-polished parquet floor.

'Good fucken thing he hasn't got carpet,' I grinned, handing Badger a cold can, and tossing him a towel. I used the other towel to mop up some of the blood under the broken window. There was more of it than I thought, but the towel was thick and it wasn't hard to get it off the wooden floor once I moved all the broken glass away. Getting it off the rest of the window sill and jamb was a little problematical. Each attempt to wipe up Badger's claret just smeared it across a wider area.

It was clearly a problem for tomorrow. Right now we had shelter, a heater, two big leather couches to sleep on and a nice bathroom with lots of hot water. Badger's bleeding had slowed down some after his shower, and I made him promise he would clean the blood up first thing in the morning. The bathroom looked a bit like an abattoir when he came out in a cloud of steam, and I found it vaguely unsettling that Terry had so many pretty-smelling bath salts and lotions. But girlfriends and their jars of potpourri, jasmine and patchouli drippings were girly-ing up bathrooms all over the world, and I looked forward to meeting whoever Terry was currently cohabiting with.

I had a long shower myself, and padded back into the living room with fresh beer for Badger and me. Badger was clumsily going through Terry's sideboard and desk, his right hand swathed in a fresh and slightly less bloody towel.

'Where do you reckon he keeps his stash?' he muttered, rifling through the drawers. 'I've been right through his bedroom. He must be living with some chick – there's so much of her crap everywhere. I even smelled some of her undies. Fucken sweet.'

'The prick must be out with her now,' I said, looking at my watch. It was almost midnight. 'What's on TV?'

Badger tossed me the remote control, slammed some of the drawers shut and plonked down on the other couch, yawning like a bear. We fell asleep in our underpants in front of the big gas heater, the TV blaring and beer cans strewn everywhere.

We woke about an hour later, confronted by a concerned Terry and the very upset couple whose house we had broken into.

'I live in the flat out the back,' Terry explained to me in hushed tones, as he helped us pick up our crap. 'Just keep saying sorry. Tomorrow we'll go buy them some new towels and fix the window.'

I nodded. 'Right after we buy some fucken helmets, okay?'

RALLY
OUTSTANDING

It is never wise or clever to involve yourself in someone else's domestic issues. I have no idea why women do it, but most of the men I've known develop a kind of selective blindness and deafness when they're suddenly confronted by some melodramatic tear-stained parting of the ways between a mate and his girlfriend. And there must always be a suitable cooling-off period before you can hit on her. It's in the rules. But rules were only ever made to be broken. That's in the rules too.

'The only antidote to mental
suffering is physical pain.'

KARL MARX

I'm not exactly sure why I quite suddenly stopped going to motorcycle rallies. I tend to think it may have been due to my emerging and rather intense desire to immerse myself in the fascinating world of outlaw motorcycle clubs. After all, hot sex, hard drugs, red violence and a romantic notion of brotherhood will always trump campfires, muddy tracks, cheap port and a romantic notion of brotherhood in my life's card game.

Still, I did have some altogether magical moments at various bike rallies. There was always a great sense of achievement if the road into the rally site was especially challenging (as so many of them were), and evenings swaying drunkenly by a campfire with like-minded mates really helped cement the sale of my soul to the Road Gods.

What else really helped was the fact that I was born with a terrifyingly low threshold of boredom and a zero sense of social responsibility. So apart from distressing my parents, this combination of elements has invariably contrived to keep me supplied with vastly entertaining mates – a situation that has always ensured I never dozed off from ennui and fell face-first into the campfire.

As it turns out, my recollections of some of these rallies have been blurred by the passage of time and substance abuse. But some are seared into my mind like cattle brands for all eternity.

My first rally, for example. I can remember most of that fucker. It was held in some woebegone swamp not far out of Dungog in New South Wales and it introduced me to the horror of the Come-To-Jesus handlebars attached to Shades's Honda 550-Four.

'What the fuck are those?' I asked Shades when he arrived on his mud-splattered and altogether ancient motorcycle.

'Those are Come-To-Jesus bars,' he grinned, opening the first of the seven million cans of beer he would consume in the next 24 hours. But since I had already consumed my first million I brashly demanded he immediately cede me his keys so that I might essay these intriguingly named handlebars. Which he did.

I quickly discovered why the bars were named 'Come-To-Jesus' as the bike and I ploughed into a large campfire, scattering the embers and the people standing around it, and setting fire to one of their tents. The bars offered no leverage for steering the motorcycle – they were narrow and rose straight up from the triple tree atop the forks, before curving back like a pair of stumpy goat horns. I understand they take their name from the prayer-like position of the rider's hands when gripping them. Though the horrifying fist-fight I was forced to have when the people whose tent I had set ablaze took umbrage and attacked me led me to believe that, thanks to those handlebars, I was soon to actually find myself come before the aforementioned Son of God.

Then there was the rally at Darkes Forest, where so many people smoked so much good dope and drank so much bad homemade rum, it all got violent and hilarious before the sun had even gone down. If you've ever seen tragically stoned drunks in beanies punching on in a paddock full of fresh cow shit, you'll understand the comedic aspects.

I also vividly remember the infamous and legendary Rough Road Rally, which scarred my soul for all time and taught me that I could indeed ride a Laverda-handlebarred, Pirelli Phantomed and Yoshimura-kitted GSX1000EX two-up over the fucken Kokoda Track if I just wanted to bad enough.

And I totally remember the very last rally I attended – which was one of the weirdest, funniest and most viscerally brutal weekends of my life. I still shudder like a dog trying to shit out a pineapple when I think about it. It was the Australia Day Rally, and while the year escapes me, the events do not.

My riding buddies and I really dug the Australia Day Rally, but not for patriotic reasons, since our patriotism was an unspoken given. We dug it because it was a three-day long-weekend affair and could thus be taken most seriously because it required a little more preparation than the usual two-night soiree.

And we sure as shit knew 'serious' back then. Most of our balls had well and truly dropped, and while ignorant observers saw us as wankers, we knew we were seasoned bike riders – hard-bitten, long-distance-riding fools on stupidly powerful motorcycles, valve-bouncing on testosterone and immortality. Which is why young Susie's immaculate tits drove us all mad, and why her new boyfriend, Chokka, brought her along that evil-filled long weekend. It was certainly why Max pulped Chokka's nose with his fist – an act of sublime goodwill that ultimately caused Chokka to fall off his Suzuki GS850 in a complex visual display of beer, blood and pale blue panties. This, in turn, caused Susie to have smelly beast-sex with Max, and for me to almost bring Chokka a leaky dead wombat to enjoy while he lay in Cooma Base Hospital lamenting the loss of the front of his knee.

This cascade of cause-and-effect began when we all stopped at the pub in Gunning to get treacherously drunk for 14 hours before continuing to the rally site with cannibalistic hangovers the following morning. As you do.

That evening, we discovered that Susie liked to play pool and that the straps of her top would slip off her shoulders whenever she did so. Actually, each time she so much as breathed the fucken things would fall off, so she was constantly re-dressing herself and giggling. And drinking rum.

For reasons which are obvious, Max, who was also drinking rum, held this to be the sexiest thing he'd ever seen and played pool with her like twenty bastards. No one else could even get close to having a game unless they partnered her or Max. Then at about 2 am, Max punched Chokka in the face and broke his nose in a dispute over the Two-Shot Rule. Well, that's what Chokka said, but Max reckons he snotted him because he felt that someone really should. And since Max was available, and out of his mind with Susie-lust and sidecar ownership, he figured: 'What the fuck!' and popped him.

For her part, Susie thought this was very cool. After all, she loved guys on bikes who fought over her like only a seventeen-year-old blonde from a broken home could, and she was certainly entitled to her opinions. And besides her opinions and centrefold rack, she also had a perfect bum, lotsa leg, and a wardrobe full of sheer tank-tops and skin-tight jeans. Blokes would invariably give her their undivided attention for as long as she cared to lisp and giggle at them. Certainly, critics have pointed out that her nose was perpetually running, her mouth was sullen and full of braces, and she smelled a bit crook and meat-like up close, but she was nevertheless something to behold. And she made blokes mental – much like rum makes blokes mental.

The combination that evening . . . well, is it any wonder that friendships were severed, blood was spilled and things just got weirder and weirder and weirder?

The next morning six motorcycles turned off the highway and onto a dirt road just south of Gunning. The riders were all seedier than a freshly planted field, and one of them had a nose that resembled an exotic tropical orchid. Max's Yamaha XS1100 with a sidecar immediately roared off into the distance, demonstrating that three wheels are always better than two when the surface is loose and uncertain. Not to be outdone, Chokka and his hideously overloaded Suzuki, with Susie decorating the pillion seat, set off in hot pursuit. The rest of us followed at a more sedate pace.

Max was an experienced rally-goer. He was carrying eight cases of beer, eight bags of ice, a groundsheet and a sleeping bag – all that he needed for three days of camping. The smell of Chokka's girlfriend was strong upon him that morning, and he was clearly riding his monster outfit like a man possessed. Chokka, from what I could see as I struggled to keep up, was right behind him, his bike dangerously unstable thanks to his broken nose, his pillion, an esky containing two cases of beer strapped to his rack, two saddlebags bulging with girl-clothes, and a tankbag full of tools, make-up and hair-care products.

None of this was slowing Chokka down, and in short order both he and Max were lost to our sight. But two short, quick and very dusty kilometres later, we were all suddenly treated to the end of the pissing contest that had started the evening before when Max first signalled the kick-off.

I didn't see the actual incident, but as we crested the top of a long hill, we saw Chokka's Suzuki wheels up and off the road. Susie was seated on a log, her boobs completely unmarked, surrounded by every bit of crap that was once strapped to Chokka's bike. There were panties hanging off bushes, toiletries, clothes and chunks of esky strewn through the scrub, along with headlight and blinker bits, and many busted beer cans fizzing themselves empty all over the dirt road. Chokka was on his back, clutching his leg and keening like an IRA widow. Max was nowhere in sight.

'What the fuck!' I yelped unnecessarily, because I had a fair idea of what had happened, and slid to a stop. I could see Chokka's tyre tracks and it was obvious what had gone down. The road we were on was a timber trail used by logging trucks to ferry their cargo out of the state forest we were in. It had a big ridge of very coarse gravel in the centre that ran between the grooves worn by their tyres, and on a bike it was good for about 80 kms per hour if you stayed in one of the grooves. But it was not so good if you foolishly decided the rut you were in was not the rut you wished to be in.

'You changed fucken ruts, didn't you?' I asked Chokka.

'No!' he hissed. 'I never . . .'

'You fucken did too!' Susie suddenly shrieked.

'I fucken did not!' Chokka yelled back, then grimaced and began whimpering in pain.

He obviously *had* changed ruts, but this was not the time for me to be siding with his soon-to-be ex-girlfriend. It was the time to see what he had done to himself, so I took off my jacket and knelt beside him. It was pretty nasty, but amazingly localised to his left knee, the top fleshy bit of which was missing. A lot of rocks and sand had been embedded in the now-exposed knee-jelly, and it looked downright medieval. Clearly, immediate medical treatment was called for.

Of course, none of us possessed anything resembling a first-aid kit. After all, what need did immortal road warriors have for such wimpy rubbish? Mobile phones were still some years away, so we couldn't even call for an ambulance. But what we did have was lots of booze, which we immediately began pouring into Chokka (and ourselves) while my girlfriend helped Susie collect her crap. Then in a roar of exhaust and a cloud of dust, Max returned and we had a solution to our problem.

'I'll take him to Cooma hospital,' he declared, quickly assessing the situation. 'He can sit in the sidecar and Susie can ride pillion. I'll drop him off and bring Susie back to the rally site so her weekend won't be totally shit.'

Out of the corner of my eye, I could see Susie already stowing her gear into the sidecar and climbing on, taking care that her top was half off, and that her tits were especially enticing.

'Let me clean his knee up first,' I burped into the awkward silence that followed Max's proposal. In one hand I held a pair of Susie's lovely little blue panties and in the other a near-empty bottle of Bundaberg rum. 'His leg might get infected otherwise.'

It was the sensible thing to do, I told myself. I'd seen similar things done in the movies, so I was not at all averse to pouring overproof rum into Chokka's wound and brushing off what crud I could get at with Susie's undies. And it was also a great way to get Chokka's mind off the fact that his new girlfriend was about to spend the rest of the weekend with the bloke who had broken his nose the night before, and was now selflessly preparing to take him eighty kilometres to the nearest doctor.

In retrospect, I was amazed Chokka didn't cry longer and louder than he actually did. His ride into Cooma must have been a deeply psychotic episode in his life – insane with pain, heavily pissed and still weeping blood and that crazy clear liquid that lubricates the human knee, with his freshly minted soon-to-be ex-girlfriend sitting less than a foot from his head, her fabulous thighs wrapped tightly around the bloke who was making her giggle a lot.

I wondered how I would feel in his place as we watched the now heavily laden sidecar roar off into the distance, and decided it would be pretty bloody shithouse. Still, it's entirely counter-productive to get involved when two blokes go at it over a girl. Unless you have a money bet on the outcome, it's best to keep your mouth shut and your opinions to yourself. Telling other people how to behave is what the government is all about. Besides, I still had a rally to go to.

As soon as Max, Chokka and Susie were out of sight, the cloying mix of tension, lust and conflict dissipated faster than the dust cloud their departure had left above the road. And all the rum we had drunk ministering to Chokka had kicked in, so we were all a bit giggly. Luckily, the rally site was not very far, so we gathered our collective shit into some sort of order and wobbled our way there to set up our respective sleeping facilities.

Much later that afternoon, Max and Susie returned and set about erecting Chokka's magnificent tent. Chokka had obviously intended for him and Susie to sexually despoil themselves in grand comfort – and this was now clearly Max's intention too.

71

The vast structure loomed over our scabby hoochies, ground-sheets and swags like a Mongol warlord's pavilion, and as I sat under a tree and watched them build it, I did some maths.

It was about a 160 kilometre round trip from the rally site to Cooma and back. A comfortable speed with the outfit on that road was about 100 kms per hour. Max had left with his passengers at about eight in the morning. It was now 6 pm. Now Max may well have ridden the entire distance at 16 kms per hour so that Susie could enjoy the scenery, but I had my doubts. Susie was wearing a different top and jeans to what she had been wearing that morning and Max's face was glazed like a donut and he was greasy about the jowls and ponged of hog-sex and girl-goop. An idiot, even one as resoundingly drunk as me, could see that they had been at it like frill-necked lizards.

'So how's Chokka?' I asked Max as Susie busied herself in the tent with sleeping bags and probably lingerie and motorised rubber penises.

'The doctor reckons he'll be there for a while,' Max puffed, banging in a tent peg. 'There's a surgeon coming in to look at his knee on Tuesday.'

'How's the rest of him?'

Max sighed. 'He's not fucken happy.'

I nodded. 'Well, that'd be normal, considering the circumstances.'

'For sure,' Max agreed.

The subject really couldn't bear any more exploration, so I opened the nearest esky and asked Max if he wanted a beer.

'Very badly,' he said and smiled. 'Do you wanna ride my outfit while I drink it in the sidecar?'

'More than life itself,' I answered, smiling back. It's not like he was fucking my girlfriend after busting my nose.

Max fixed me with a stare. 'Don't hit any really large trees, okay?'

'No worries,' I vowed, climbing aboard his massive three-wheeled contraption. 'What about people?'

'Fuck them,' Max grunted climbing into the sidecar. 'It's got airhorns. Unless the cunts are deaf, you'll be fine.'

An hour later I turned off the ignition. My heart was pounding, my arms were aching and my legs were quivering like freshly set jelly.

'You've got no fucking idea, have you?' Max asked quietly as people all around the rally site stared at us in abject horror.

'Nope.'

'You've never ridden a sidecar before, have you?'

I shook my head. 'Not on the handlebar side, no.'

Max considered this very briefly. 'Goes all right, doesn't it?'

'Pulls a bit to the left,' I advised him.

'That was the tent you ran over.'

'I just need more practice. And beer.'

Max nodded solemnly. 'I'll get you that beer.'

We all went to bed really late that evening and I resolved to never again camp within earshot of a couple exploring their rum-fuelled sexuality.

The next morning, I was still too drunk to ride on two wheels, so Max and I climbed aboard his outfit and set off for Cooma Base Hospital to visit Chokka. On the way we found a dead wombat reclining on the dirt road. Max slid to a halt, dismounted and hauled the corpse onto my lap, grinning like a fiend.

'She must have done some crazy sick shit to you last night,' I yelled, cradling the coldly stiff marsupial in my arms as we roared off up the track.

'You heard?' Max yelled back.

'Not words, as such. Just noises.'

'Sorry.'

'Don't sweat it,' I shrugged, the wombat heavy in my lap. 'I'm just curious about this dead animal here.'

Max flashed me a resonantly evil grin. 'It's a message. From her to him.'

I pondered that for a while as the scenery flew past and rocks rattled under the outfit.

'When did she have time to sneak out, kill it, and leave it there for us to find this morning?' I finally asked as we lurched and slid along the track.

'No, no,' Max shook his head. 'She told me Chokka had taken to calling her girl-bits her "wombat". She says it made her crazy.'

I nodded. That much was certainly evident.

'So when I saw this dead one on the road, I thought she might appreciate it if I gave it to Chokka. As a message.'

'That's deeply symbolic,' I told him. 'But I don't really have a dog in this fight of yours, and I ain't gonna be there when this goes down.'

'Of course not,' Max agreed. 'I just need you to hold the fucken thing until we get there, otherwise it'll roll around inside the tub and smash something. They're really heavy, you know.'

'I do,' I said. 'I have had some dealings with them.'

Fortunately for Chokka and the staff of Cooma Base Hospital the dead wombat never made it into Cooma. Just as we were approaching the town, it made a strange popping noise and drenched me in rotten dead-wombat juice. I had no choice but to eject it from the sidecar, much to Max's disappointment. He sulked outside the hospital while I visited Chokka.

He looked pretty grim, but told me the pain-killers were working a treat. I told him his bike was at the Gunning petrol station. One of the other blokes had ridden back to Gunning and organised a ute. As it turned out, the bike was only lightly damaged and rideable, and would be waiting for Chokka when he got out of hospital.

Chokka told me how horrible it was getting his knee scrubbed out with a wire brush and thanked me for getting him pissed before it happened. We never discussed Susie and Max, and he eventually got back together with her when Max lost interest a few weeks later.

I still drank rum for a few years after that long weekend, but I never went to another rally. It was better that way.

THE PRICE OF FREEDOM

The severing of familial bindings came relatively late for me. I was a wog kid, and we tended to stay at home longer than the Skippy kids because the food was better and the laundry services simply top-notch. But there comes a day in every young motorcyclist's life when his bike and the lifestyle that goes with it no longer really fit within the family paradigm. Mine came hot on the heels of an amputation, which thankfully wasn't mine, but which opened the door for my moving out of home forever. Just don't tell my mum. She still thinks I'll come to my senses and return one day.

'Freedom is not worth having if it
does not connote freedom to err.'

MOHANDAS GANDHI

I moved out of home shortly after, and totally because, Grub lost his leg in a fabulously shitty and very drunken motorcycle accident one night.

Grub was my friend, and much like him, I was mortified when they lopped his leg off. My motorcycle career was only in its nascent stages and to be suddenly confronted with a mate's vast maiming was deeply unsettling. But on a positive note, it did cause me to cut the umbilical cord tethering me to my totally wonderful and utterly dysfunctional family – a severance that was well overdue.

It's a damn shame my gaining independence was a direct result of Grub's losing a limb, but such is kismet, and if my tree of freedom needed watering, Grub's claret was every bit as worthy as that of any patriot or tyrant. And I am not a man to question kismet.

Grub had enjoyed several million beers with Shades that fateful Saturday evening, then both of them climbed aboard Grub's red-and-white Honda Bol d'Or for the always-fast trip home. Grub could ride well and most blokes who ride well, also ride fast. The one has invariably informed the other.

Shades was between bikes, but he was Grub's oldest mate, so there was no question this good-hearted and amiable bloke would even hesitate in getting on the back. And in all honesty, what they were doing was nothing I and most other riders and drivers were not doing on a regular basis. Random breath testing was still at least a year or more away, so no one really thought too much about having a few beers and riding home. Or to the next pub.

Anyway, for reasons that remain vague to this day but were probably entirely due to massive amounts of piss, they decided they would make a detour through the city, check out some of the hookers up at Kings Cross, then carve through the mean-hearted bends of New South Head Road as it wends its spiteful way along the Sydney Harbour foreshore, from Rushcutters Bay to Watsons Bay.

New South Head Road enjoyed a certain reputation among Sydney motorcyclists in the '70s and '80s. It had certainly crippled and killed enough of us over the years, but it was such a gut-lurching thrill to ride at speed and so conveniently located, we continued to be drawn to it like teenage boys to stick books.

At one end is Kings Cross, a regular Saturday evening gronk-fest of seedy whores, seedier stripclubs, and rancid takeaway shops and an atmosphere positively electric with danger, despair and corruption. As a drawcard for aspiring motorcycle hooligans in the late '70s, it had no equal and catered to every food group and appetite, so my mates and I were frequent visitors.

At the other end of New South Head Road is Watsons Bay, a jewel in the glorious crown of Sydney's fabulously wealthy eastern suburbs, gateway to the legendary Lady Jane nudist beach and home to the pub with the best view in Sydney, the Watsons Bay Hotel.

In between these two social extremes is about eleven kilo-metres of snaking bitumen and uneven concrete, dramatic elevation changes and a longish 200 kms per hour straight that runs from the expensively reclusive peace of Vaucluse (where New South Head Road actually ends and becomes Old South Head Road), along the cliff-top past Christison Park, the light-house and the suicide-friendly Gap Reserve, before dipping hard to the left for a series of frightful downhill bends that spit you out near the pub like so much quivering phlegm.

There's no room for error anywhere along its length, and were you to part company with your bike, they'd be using a shovel and hose on what was left rather than oxygen, kind words and a nice soft gurney.

I've ridden New South Head Road thousands of times, and while it's hard to get a good head of steam going in today's dense traffic and Highway Patrol–rich environment, it's still possible to have a little sip from the two-wheeled trench of life on its blind and hateful corners.

But back when Grub and Shades essayed its thrill-rich bounty, that same trench was literally running over and you could slurp from it like a hog with its snout in a bottomless trough. Traffic was invariably light, and the cops thin on the ground, or at the Cross augmenting their pay packets with bribes. As a result of having the best police force money could buy, many parts of Sydney were turned into impromptu racetracks and dragstrips on weekend evenings – and the affluent eastern suburbs were just as likely to host a conga line of fast-moving motorcycles as they were to host a dinner party of corrupt politicians and motley teenage hookers.

According to Grub, their run up William Street to where the road dips under the famous Coca-Cola sign and into the Kings Cross tunnel was a bit wobbly. Shades was having a few balancing issues on the back, and was struggling to find a happy medium between leaning backwards onto the luggage rack (which unweighted the front of the bike and caused Grub to shriek as he lost the ability to steer), and leaning forward onto Grub, which caused their helmets to smash together each time Grub braked, accelerated or changed gear. Which was quite often, given that prostitutes had to be leered at and meandering cars had to be avoided. Eventually, Shades found his happy balancing space just as they exited the tunnel; the bike winding down, burbling and backfiring after the mandatory third-gear howl through the tunnel's echoing interior.

This is really somewhat of a dreary transport stage for the dash to Watsons Bay. There are a lot of traffic lights preventing rapid progress as the road descends through Rushcutters Bay. It then starts to climb past where Edgecliff station now stands, before cresting at the Ocean Street T-intersection and winding down again into Double Bay. So Grub and Shades amused themselves by pulling little wheelies off the lights and howling with beery laughter each time the bike's front wheel came crashing back to earth.

Shit only starts to get fast and real as you leave Double Bay and power up the hill past Redleaf Pool and into the magnificent superfast right-hander that runs past the Point Piper police station. If you're on your game, and the Road Gods are smiling, you'll be snicking out of third and into fourth coming out of that corner. Then you'd bang the throttle wide open, lean forward against the wind blast and howl down the hill into Rose Bay like a hot round from a long cannon.

Apparently, things were going swimmingly until they got to Lyne Park at Rose Bay, where New South Head Road kinks ever so slightly between the harbourside park on the left and the Royal Sydney Golf Club on the right.

Grub reckons he was minging along at about 190 kms per hour and setting up for what he thought was a tight left-hander by going down a gear. But what he imagined was a hard left was really the entrance into the Lyne Park car park – which Grub enthusiastically entered at about 160 kms per hour. What happened next is all guesswork, but what Grub and I were able to piece together when I visited him in hospital a few days later and stared at the emptiness where his left leg used to be, was the following.

Upon arcing into the narrowed car park entrance at Warp Factor 10, Grub drunkenly realised something was somewhat amiss because the road disappeared and his bike hit a massive bump. There was no time to hit the brakes, and nowhere to go. He remembers nothing after that except some big air-time, and a brief moment of awareness as he was slotted into an ambulance the following morning.

The bump he'd felt was the Honda seeking to escape the Earth's gravitational pull. It had launched itself off the gutter directly in its path, smashed through a Koppers log barrier that divided the U-shaped car park in half, before cartwheeling through the air and levering another log barrier out of the ground on the other side of the car park. Grub and the bike parted company somewhere between the first log and the second log, so the appalling injuries to his leg must have happened when the big Honda tore through the first wooden barrier.

Shades had departed the Honda immediately after it hit the gutter, flying through the air on an alternate flight path to the bike, and demolishing another Koppers log barrier with his fat-encased pelvis, before also cartwheeling for half the length of an Olympic pool and finally coming to rest upon the park's soft green bits, some forty metres from the initial point of impact.

A jogger found them early the next morning. They had been lying there for about six hours, oozing their alcohol-enriched body fluids into the soil, and were, quite understandably, in a pretty bad way.

The surgeons took Grub's leg off that same day. And apart from some deep bruising pretty much everywhere on his body, that was the extent of his injuries. Shades, on the other hand, had broken his pelvis, both his arms, and a leg – and literally torn more muscles than he ever imagined he possessed, bruised all the others and turned his spleen into an IED. He would walk with a pronounced limp for the rest of his life, live in various forms of crushing pain, and I was told he never rode or got on the back of a bike again. Grub was riding six months later with a new prosthesis affixed to his stump.

But while he was coming to physical and mental terms with his new life as an amputee, he needed someone to help pay the rent in his two-bedroom townhouse in the Sydney suburb of Arncliffe. And I needed to live somewhere where I wouldn't be shot by my dad.

My father and I had commenced hostilities over my motorcycling lifestyle choices a few months previously, and we both knew that his implacable will to insist that I do as I was bid would eventually collide catastrophically with my equally implacable determination to do as I damn well pleased. We were both fully aware that I was very much my father's son and the resultant impact would be like dividing by zero.

So I waited until he was out before I approached my saintly and long-suffering mother. Mum was always far more malleable than my father, which is why both of us took shameless advantage of her.

'My friend has lost his leg,' I said to her as she was simmering soup on the stove.

'Det is terrible,' she tutted. 'You vont take him some soupa, yes?'

'Sure. But the thing is, he's going to be in hospital for a couple of weeks, and he can't work. So he will lose his house if he can't pay the rent. So I was going to go and live there while he's recovering.'

My mother looked nonplussed. There were a few too many alien concepts here for her to easily assimilate in one go. I spent the next half hour patiently explaining how, as a true and righteous friend, it behoved me to render whatever assistance I could to Grub in his hour of need. And if that meant I was to sacrifice the comforts of my family home to live in un-catered-to-by-my-mum squalor, then so be it. It was the least I could do. We lived in Marrickville, and Grub's townhouse was only up the road in Arncliffe, so it wasn't like I was going to Perth, I explained. The clincher to my argument was that it was really only a temporary measure. As soon as Grub was able to pay his rent, I would be home. Of course, this was a massive con, but it was not the first one I had pulled on my mum. And it was not the first one she had seen straight through, either. Her gentle grey eyes filled with tears and she shook her head as if to deny what she knew was inevitable.

'You . . . leavink me?' she said, her voice redolent with emotion.

'Nooo,' I lied soothingly, trying not to see her tears. 'It's just until he's better.'

But both of us knew I was full of shit.

Still, full of shit and free had to be better than being shit-free and living at home, I stupidly reasoned to myself as I rode off up the road, a garbage bag full of clothes strapped to my bike.

A mate's leg and my mother's bitter tears the price of my freedom.

OUTLAW DAWN

It's kind of sad that men today are buying Harleys as a way of appeasing their midlife crisis. The proper time to buy them is when you're in your twenties and have a hot girlfriend. When you're in your fifties and your wife looks like a couch, the whole vibe is different. And today's Harleys are also several orders of magnitude improved from the offerings in the '70s. Back then, owning a Harley implied a deeper commitment to the brand and the lifestyle than a monthly sausage sizzle with fellow retirees.

'People are more violently opposed to fur than leather because it's safer to harass rich women than motorcycle gangs.'

ANON

It was obviously the right time. No other time was ever going to be as right. I felt it in my deranged, mid-twenties waters. I tasted it in the back of my throat like cheap speed, and I felt it lurching in the pit of my stomach each time I heard the booming, machine-gun staccato of an unmuffled Harley hammer up the road.

I had yet to realise I was just another brick in the tax wall. My girlfriend was actually a centrefold. I walked tall, I stood proud and I was as mad, bad and dangerous to know as any bloke could ever hope to be and not die in a shoot-out with the cops.

I had been riding for about a decade on vastly powerful and relatively ill-handling Japanese bikes, had ridden them all over Australia, attended rallies, races, protest meetings, done high-speed night runs between capital cities, engaged in illegal street racing, crashed, recovered and seen mates maimed and dead on the side of the road. I had been locked up, beaten up, done some beating up myself, tried all the drugs there were to try, could drink my body weight in rum, and still bench-press 100 kilograms the next day. I had, in my brief time on Earth, felt I had done pretty much everything there was to do on a motorcycle, imagined I was immortal, my poo pleasantly scented, and that the sun blazed gloriously from my arse. I was hovering on the fringes of an outlaw motorcycle club, and felt its dangerously thrilling siren call deep in my crazy bones. That I was going to join up was a no-brainer. It was only a question of time. And a motorcycle.

And therein lay the problem. I had the wrong kind of motorcycle. Attitudinally, I was fine. I was luminously antisocial. My resentment of authority resolutely forged in iron. My sense of honour, loyalty and sacrifice naively unshakeable. But my motorcycle was all wrong. One cannot join an outlaw club astride a Japanese motorcycle. It's in the rules.

I was having a brief and engaging fling with a 1979 Triumph Tiger I had bought (well, was paying off) from my girlfriend's stepfather at the time, but if I was going down the one-percenter route, I wanted a Harley. And when I say 'wanted' I mean craved, lusted, coveted, pined, yearned and hankered for like a dog needing to climb aboard the bitch-on-heat next door. It was like a genetic imperative, and I was just utterly insane with the whole damn thing.

Many evenings would find me smeared like inchoate jam on the big glass windows of Burling & Simmons in Lidcombe (Burlo's, as it was known, was Sydney's only Harley dealer in those days), while my girlfriend sat on the Trumpy, looking fabulous and bored.

There was no Harley Owners Group (HOG) in Australia back then and Harley itself had not long emerged from the clammy, death-like grip of American Machine and Foundry, its parent company whose intriguing operational practices saw Harley-Davidson building some of the vilest and most unreliable motorcycles ever made, and slowly going broke in the process.

Things would get much, much better for Harley in the years to come, but in those days the marque was pretty much the exclusive province of a few crotchety collectors and about the same number of dangerous outlaws. It was the '80s, and it was a great time to be in your twenties. Maniacs still dragraced their cars and bikes at Brickies (an isolated stretch of road near where the Sydney Olympic complex now stands), and cops still had .38s and augmented their shitty wages with paper bags full of bribe money.

Shovelheads (so named because the shape of the rocker boxes atop the cylinder heads vaguely resembled the leading edge of a shovel) were the Harley *du jour* and there was none of this super-reliable Evo-engined bullshit the moneyed executives dressed as gay pirates run around on today. In fact, if Shovelheads were still around, HOG would have a membership of twenty-seven, and each one of them would know how to adjust the bike's hydraulic lifters and tickle the S&S carby no matter how drunk and stoned and lost on the other side of Thargomindah they happened to be.

And I had found My Shovelhead. I saw it one evening at the back of Burlo's showroom, just as the girlfriend finished off a five-paper bunger and informed me she wasn't wearing any panties in the vain hope I would take her home and stop peering into Burlo's showroom. But this was My Shovelhead. And my girlfriend could have been swinging greasy-naked from the No Standing sign and I would have had eyes for nothing but My Shovelhead.

'That,' I moaned and coughed a bit after dragging too deeply on the joint. 'That's the one. That one.'

How did I know this?

Simple.

Nothing, but nothing on this great galloping Earth says: 'I party with strippers, play with guns, kick arse, take names and dance like no one's watching' better than a metal-flake purple Shovelhead with a leaky chrome primary cover and ape hangers.

And I had found it, and it was to be mine, and that was that. Amen.

Except, when it comes to Shovelheads, nothing is ever 'that'. And nothing is ever easy, and nothing is ever straightforward.

Viewed via the crystalline clarity of hindsight, Shovelheads were irredeemable piles of unreliable crap. But they were the only game in town, unless you counted the few British offerings, which were equally as worthless from a reliability standpoint, but didn't sound anywhere near as 'outlaw' when their mufflers were changed.

Problematically, it was about 11 pm on a Wednesday night when I found My Shovelhead, and Burlo's wasn't open, so I had to wait until the next day before I could rush in and make hot scissors action with it. So I took my girlfriend home and verified the fact that she did indeed have no panties on.

But as Burlo's doors swung open the following day, I was on the metal-flake purple bastard like a spider monkey on a coconut.

'Can I help you?' Greg the salesman asked after watching me fondle and squeak at the 1980 FLH for twenty minutes.

'I want to buy this bike,' I said.

'You sure have an eye for a good bike,' he grinned like a shark.

'Crap,' I said. 'I have no idea what's good and what's not when it comes to Harleys. I just want this bike.'

'I can see that.'

'What do you want for it?'

He quoted me a price.

I tried not to look horrified.

The bike was only a few years old and I could have bought two-and-a-half new Jap bikes for the price. Did I care? Not in the least. Greg could've added another five grand to the price and I still would have paid it.

I puffed myself up, gave him a look that eagles give rodents before they eat them and pulled fifty dollars out of my pocket.

'Here,' I said evenly. 'This is a holding deposit. Put a sold sign on it. I'll be back.'

Greg, smiling like a venomous daffodil, scrawled me out a receipt and I was out the door, my arsehole puckering with what I'd just done. I certainly wanted to buy the bloody thing . . . but until I'd actually pulled out the fifty dollars and given it to Greg, I didn't realise how much I wanted to buy it.

I also had no idea where I'd come up with the many thousands of dollars I had just committed to spending. I certainly didn't have any savings. I had a job, but the money it paid was going on my rum addiction, my rent, my girlfriend and paying off a whole bunch of crap that I couldn't remember buying on Bankcard.

What to do?

It came to me a week later, when Greg called to remind me that I still owed him thousands of dollars for My Shovelhead, which he regretted to inform me was taking up precious floor space in his shop.

'I will have the rest of the money for you in a fortnight,' I said, and hung up.

Then I quit my job and went on the dole – which you could do in those days without the government having you chemically neutered and placed in a display cage at a major shopping centre.

Freshly unemployed, I called up my superannuation fund and gave them the bad news. I would need, as a matter of urgency, to access my funds now, I told the nice lady. It was for food and shelter.

She sent me some forms to fill out, which I did, stressing my extreme hardship and providing them demand letters from Bankcard, and my landlord. Within ten days, I had a cheque from my super fund with enough left over after buying the bike to get me a bottle of rum, and my girlfriend a new bikini I could tear off her after consuming the rum.

I couldn't have been happier if the heads of my enemies were drying in my garage.

The next day I was back at Burlo's and after signing some papers, I wheeled the divinely purple FLH out onto the footpath and pressed the starter.

It burst into cacophonous life, thundering via two bowel-loosening shotgun pipes and I was grinning so hard my ears were starting to cramp.

'You know what you're doing?' Greg asked over the raw crash of exhaust explosions.

'Yep!' I yelled.

I had no fucken idea. I had never even ridden a Harley before. But how hard could it be? It was just a bloody motor-cycle, and as I orientated myself, I could see that it was indeed, just like any other bike . . . except it wasn't. It was about twice as heavy as the Triumph. Which I imagined wasn't a problem 'cos the engine was twice as big to make up for it. Then there were the footboards and the heel-toe gearshifter, which were also entirely new to me.

First had to be down, I hoped, and toed the back of the heel-toe shifter down, which put the bike into second gear. And then I let the clutch out gently and eased onto Parramatta Road feeling like the meanest gunslinger to ever ride out of the badlands. Which, in case you're a bit slow and still trying to figure out why people buy them, is precisely how one is meant to feel astride a Harley-Davidson.

I chugged on down Parramatta Road sneering like the tattooed beast I was yet to become at every car I passed. I was completely overwhelmed and involved with my sudden ascent into glorious thuggery.

How bloody good was this!?

And then I applied the brakes, shot straight through the lights at Granville and stalled in the middle of the intersection.

Shit, I thought. That is so not in the script.

So there we all were – me, My (Stalled) Shovelhead and all the traffic that was watching me and My (Stalled) Shovelhead, all sitting motionless together in the middle of a Granville intersection.

There was no beeping. There were no angry drivers yelling. My hate-filled demeanour certainly precluded that.

There was nothing but the grim whirring of the starter motor as I tried to restart the bike. Then there wasn't even that because the battery gave out and each time I pressed the starter button I was rewarded with a contemptuous click. The traffic, which had initially been shocked into stationary silence by my awe-inspiring ability to ride through a red light and then stall my shit in the middle of the intersection, began to creep around me like I was some angry purple roundabout.

I got off and made to push My (Stalled) Shovelhead off the road, and failed miserably. It was in gear, but I wasn't sure which one. Stomping on the heel-toe lever revealed nothing but more gears and nothing remotely resembling neutral.

I heaved the clutch in (and I do mean 'heaved', as owners of Shovelheads everywhere will attest) and put my weight on the handlebars, which moved about four inches on their rubber mounts and then nothing. The bike would not budge. It was still in the middle of the intersection and the traffic had come to terms with that and was simply moving slowly around us.

'Need a push?' a bloke on the footpath asked me.

'Sure,' I panted and gave the gear lever a few more futile stomps.

The bloke pushed on the guard and I leaned as hard as I could on the bars and the bike, now clearly dragging on its clutch, was inched onto the footpath, trailing behind it a long smear of oil.

'Looks like you've got a bit of a leak,' the bloke observed.

I sat down on the ground, lit a durrie, offered my new mate one and considered my options.

They were few.

I rang a friend, loaded My (Stalled and Oil-Leaking) Shovelhead into his ute and went home.

And so began my four-year purgatory with the metal-flaked son-of-a-bitch.

There were no mega-dollar Harley showrooms with spit-polished workshops full of gel-haired 'technicians' in those days. There was only Burlo's and a handful of non-Jap bike shops, all invariably owned and/or staffed by outlaw motorcycle club members and their mates. They were serious places doing serious business with serious people.

If you'd have told me that in ten years' time, shops like that and people like me would go the way of the dinosaurs and be replaced by gleaming motorcycle emporiums of floor-to-ceiling glass, complete with espresso machines, staff with collared shirts and a computerised parts inventory, I would have asked you for an ounce of what you were smoking. Radiant dealerships full of embossed leather duds, piratical bandannas and faux Nazi helmets were still some way off as I began doing time with My Shovelhead.

And what a time it was! We were nothing if not busy, that's for sure. I spent more time with that bike than with any other bike I have had before or since. And a lot of that time was spent on the side of the road in places as diverse as inner-city Melbourne and the table drain on the Hay Plain eighty-five kilometres from Balranald. I've sheltered beside it in pouring rain outside of Murray Bridge and cursed it from the shade of a solitary tree near Coonamble. I would have put in, and observed the departure of, at least 10,000 litres of 20W-50 Pennzoil, smeared a billion metres of Silastic around its ever-leaking primary and wondered how, by all that is holy, anyone could build a bike using self-tapping wood screws to hold the headlight in its nacelle. A nacelle, I might add, I had obsessively rubbed some sixty kilograms of Autosol alloy polish into over the time I owned the bike.

My Shovelhead never stopped leaking oil – though it did vary the amounts from a few drops to 'How the fuck am I gonna get home now?' And it never failed to excite me when it barked its unmuffled hatred at the world. Except that one time when I ran into the back of a stationary car while admiring my tattooed he-glory in a shop window. Then it kinda pissed me off.

And it taught me many things. It taught me the value of Loctite. It taught me how to set hydraulic lifters, gap points and 'fix' clutch-plates by rubbing them on concrete. It taught me to ride clutchless. It taught me to ride with flat tyres and what riding in the rain with no front guard is all about. I even made it into a suspension-free 'rigid' once, entirely by mistake, and that taught me all about spinal compression.

Though I cursed it and reviled it and hated it for brief, incandescent periods, I normally loved My Shovelhead with a passion that was quite breathtaking.

Do you know why?

Because it was my first Harley – My Goddamn Shovelhead, in fact – and I couldn't help myself.

Now, to complete myself as a man, all I had to do was find an outlaw motorcycle club to join.

Given my qualifications, how hard could that possibly be?

HOUSING CRISIS

I lived a relatively nomadic lifestyle up until the point where my girlfriend demanded I marry her, and even then I managed to stave off putting down mortgage-impregnated roots for several years. But when I was getting my badarse on, moving house was as regular an event as getting a new rear tyre for my bike. And of all the many places I have lived since I left home, the house in the western Sydney suburb of Merrylands was far and away the most magical, for reasons you'll shortly understand. You might not condone them, but you'll certainly understand them.

'It takes courage to play in a
world that does not play.'

FRED DONALDSON

'It's fucken green,' I said, glancing at Mark.

He nodded. The house was about as green as a house could be without being a golf course.

'And there's no glass in the fucken windows.'

Mark smiled. 'There is in some of the ones at the back.'

I laughed and clapped him on the back. 'It's perfect.'

And it was, as far as I was concerned. Mark and I were at the very end of our housing options and things were looking pretty grim. The Matthew Talbot Hostel for homeless men loomed large before us. The house we were parked in front of that morning could have been made from sundried horse dung and fenced with goat heads, and I would have deemed it beaut. I had no desire to spend another night sleeping with Mark in the cab of our rented truck, wrapped in the miasma of our unwashed stench, sipping cheap rum and pondering the lifestyle choices we had made that had led to our current housing issues.

Grub's townhouse at Arncliffe, which I had moved into when I first left home worked just fine while Grub was still at the hospital battling infection and oozing into wound drains. But then Grub came home and things got a touch disagreeable between us. Ever lived with a freshly minted amputee? They are not a lot of fun. It's as if losing a limb suddenly entitles the loser to behave like a monstrous shitcock. Which, in a way, it kinda does. But it's still very hard to live with and pay rent for the privilege of doing so. So not long after Grub came home with his horrid stump and shitty attitude, I decided to move out with my mate, Mark.

We found a rundown joint in Putney; essentially a six-roomed fibro box on brick pylons, with a killer view down to Kissing Point Bay. But we weren't there long. The tequila parties we held every weekend and the wheelie practice that happened like clockwork each pay day ensured a short leasing period. The police were frequent visitors – especially after I started breeding fighting dogs under the house and Zorro came over and showed Mark how much pants-shitting fun acetylene bombs could be. The poor neighbours were in a constant state of curtain-twitching anxiety. Our landlord, an angst-ridden young Italian guy who got the house as a wedding present from his wealthy parents, would cry whenever he came to collect the rent. We were never late with the money, but when our three-month lease expired, Roberto did not offer to renew it.

This pattern of three-month residences continued, and when Mark and I and our collection of mates grew far too horrid to behold as we added lurid tattoos, barbaric piercings, cruel jewellery, assorted weaponry and ever-louder motorcycles to our repertoire, we would send our nicely dressed girlfriends along to real estate agencies to make the rental applications. But as time went on our housing options continued to dwindle, almost as though the real estate agents were growing wise to our cute-girlfriend racket. Then there was the fact that we could only afford to live in certain parts of Sydney. While I always thought it would be utterly hilarious to take my ghastly biker mates and move into a Castlecrag mansion or a Vaucluse bungalow for shits and giggles, the cost of such a stunt was prohibitive.

And then we were told about Abdul – landlord to the scum and villainy of Sydney and one of the biggest private property owners in Australia. His family owned more than 400 houses and flats throughout the Sydney basin and Abdul and his brother Mahmud ran an impossibly shonky real estate agency near Rockdale. A true and primal capitalist, Abdul had no issue with our appearance, and even came outside to admire our bikes when we turned up at his office one warm spring afternoon.

'Sure I got a house for you,' he grinned, holding his hands out in a gesture of largesse and goodwill, as the sun sparkled off the kilo of gold he had chained around his neck. 'I have plenty of houses.'

'We don't have any bond money at the moment,' Mark explained. This was normal. We always struggled with bond money (normally four weeks' rent) because the bond on every property we had ever rented was never returned to us when we moved out. The one time we did ask for it back, the police were promptly called and we were told in no uncertain terms to 'Fuck the fuck off'.

Abdul bobbed his head up and down. 'That is not a problem. I very much trust you.'

'Fuck, you'd be the first,' I said and laughed.

Abdul looked perplexed. 'Why would I not trust you? You think because you have tattoos and big bikes I think you run away and not pay rent? Or I think you are bad men, yes? I am from Lebanon. I know what real bad men are. Everybody must live somewhere. And you must live somewhere, yes?'

We nodded.

'Of course you must!' He smiled and clapped his hands together as if the matter was settled. 'I have a house in Merrylands that is perfect for you. It is not a fancy place, but I think you do not want a fancy place, yes?'

'It needs to have a lock-up garage,' Mark explained. We got all of our houses based on the quality and lockability of the garage first and all other considerations second. Men who have slept in reeking roadside drains, speckled with their own filth, are perfectly all right about sleeping in a house with fourteen different types of rotten linoleum on the floor and armies of cockroaches patrolling the walls. As long as there was somewhere secure and sheltered for our motorcycles, we really didn't much care about anything else. It was a question of priorities. I've bought tyres instead of food lots of times. Our bikes were easily our most expensive possessions. So we always made sure they were well looked after, both in terms of maintenance and security.

We spent most of our time in the garage anyway. In Bikerland, the garage is the epicentre of all things at all times – especially at parties. And that's perfectly understandable when you consider that customised motorcycles are a joy to behold. Riders can stand around them for hours, totally absorbed in their myriad details, telling war stories and lies, drunk, stoned or dead sober. Customised motorcycles are the modern equivalent of the beautifully bred horse, just as the car is the direct descendant of the pot-and-pan-filled Conestoga wagon. From what I know of history, not many men ever gathered around their wagons, drays and wains in admiration.

Our garage was where our totems were built and stored and maintained, so it was normal that visitors would come to see and admire them. At parties, we gathered in our garage just as normal people gathered in their kitchens. Our kitchens were only used for spotting hash off the stove, cutting lines of speed on the benchtop, and maybe whipping up the odd cauldron of bolognaise sauce if someone fagged out and could no longer stomach takeaway.

Our bedrooms were similarly non-crucial. They were essentially storage areas for expensive bike parts not yet fitted to the bike, with three distinct piles of clothing (dirty, clean and the girlfriend's), and a sex platform of some type, which also doubled as a bed for sleeping in if one of the several house couches was unavailable.

'It has a great garage,' Abdul assured us. 'And four bedrooms, or six if you move some cupboards around, yes?'

Abdul was true to his word. He did let us have the place with no bond, the garage could house ten motorcycles, a fridge and a couch, and when we moved some of the cupboards around inside the house, we did indeed have six bedrooms.

The rent was very reasonable because the place was pretty rundown and half the windows sported rusty steel reo bars instead of glass. But it was a pretty big joint with a large backyard and the sense of space it offered was very welcome after the relatively cramped confines of the townhouse and the little place in Putney. Mark and I immediately decided to sublet, further defraying the cost of our rent and inadvertently creating a never-ending party, simultaneously bringing the thunderous musical goodness of George Thorogood and the Delaware Destroyers to our neighbours and plunging surrounding property values deep into the toilet.

And it's not like we couldn't fill the spare bedrooms. We had a sizeable circle of like-minded, bike-riding mates who were always passing out on the couches and floors of wherever Mark and I happened to be living, and they weren't fussy bastards. They didn't give a hot brown shit about stained bathroom fixtures, mouldy carpets and peeling wood-veneer panelling – they just needed a cheap place to live, and jumped at what we had on offer.

What we had on offer was certainly not the almost-flashy front two bedrooms, which Mark and I took for ourselves, but four other quite passable little man-caves, a viable kitchen, a big room out the back, a smaller room in the middle, and that killer garage. We had tenants by the end of our first day.

Salvo Dan got the windowless bedroom in the middle of the house. Its walls were painted red and the torn linoleum was a disturbing fleshy colour that made you feel like you were inside some bizarre flat-sided pancreas. Salvo Dan only kept his clothes in there and usually slept on the couch in the big day room at the rear of the house that overlooked the backyard. Big Dima the Russian got the bedroom we'd made out of cupboards. And because of the zero sound-proofing the cupboards offered when compared to floor-to-ceiling walls, we would hear him snorting speed and feeding his cock to his impossibly cute and compliant beautician girlfriend Svetlana every day, for hours at a time. It was like living with our own private sex show, and it made the whole place smell a bit like an excited girl's panties.

Zorro got the room at the back of the house, which adjoined the day room, but he was hardly ever in residence. He spent at least five out of seven nights living at home with his mum and dad, eating proper meals and getting his clothes washed, ironed and folded. We shit-stirred him relentlessly about his inability to sever the umbilical cord tying him to his Italian parents. But we were always quietly pleased he would bring over the odd homemade lasagna or veal to defray the awfulness of endless takeaway.

Badger got the final room. The small green-painted one wedged between the kitchen, the big day room at the back, and the Room With The Table Where We Would Snort Speed. The Table was a tacky six-seater dining table we had nailed an old

wardrobe mirror to, thus providing a vast and very handy mirrored surface upon which we would rack long lines of speed
to snort on weekends, parties and high holy days. It came into
being the day Big Dima tore the mirrored door off one of his
wardrobes in a fit of methamphetamine-induced sex-lust. He'd
tied Svetlana up with ocky straps, pushed her face-first into the
cupboard with her arse sticking out and commanded her to
remain in that position until he'd explored every erotic possibility their new Sex Cupboard offered. We were in the adjoining
room playing cards and listening to Svetlana yelling something about cockroaches and old underpants, when Big Dima
emerged from behind his cupboard wall with the mirrored
door held above his head and no pants on. He banged the door
down on top of our card game, said: 'How fucken good's this?'
and returned to fuck Svetlana in his Sex Cupboard some more.

Badger's little green room opened directly onto the Room
With The Table Where We Would Snort Speed, and that was
very convenient, because Badger was the bloke with everything.
Fate had seen fit to give him a job at a massive warehouse, and
it was like putting Ronnie Biggs in charge of Ali Baba's cave
of Seriously Awesome Shit. Not a day would go by that Badger
wouldn't arrive home with huge wheels of Jarlsberg cheese
and cases of good Penfolds Merlot strapped to his bike. But he
wasn't just into cheese and wine. Boxes of lollies, bullets and
Bic lighters, cases of thongs, gumboots and ski poles, packages
of bikinis, tank-tops and aftershave, and vast boxes of handbags
and wallets were just a portion of the stuff he'd lug home and
store in his green room. He also did a line of fake helmet exemptions utilising an official RTA stamp he'd flogged off the counter

while some dozy RTA drone scratched his arse and stared into space. And it was not uncommon for him to emerge from his green room while we played cards, plonk down his rent in cash, and follow it with five grams of speed, two bottles of tequila, a bag of fresh lemons and a box of SAXA iodised cooking salt for us to be getting on with.

From the standpoint of communal living, it was a pretty sweet deal for everyone involved. Even dole-bludgers like Big Dima could afford to live there. Everyone kicked in 100 dollars a week. Rent for the whole house was about 200 dollars. That meant we, as a collective, had 400 dollars a week to spend on communal food, booze and drugs. The end result was a form of hardcore Marxist socialism crossed with a pirate ship. It was the perfect storm.

And that was the core of the household. Naturally, our numbers were invariably augmented by girlfriends and mates, and girlfriends of mates, and mates of mates, and assorted blow-ins and wannabes and try-hards, and all sorts of utterly fascinating and deeply disgusting versions of humanity. The green house in Merrylands was never closed and never silent. There was always something going on and all of our dozens of neighbours were usually privy to most of it, since their dwellings overlooked our house.

Unlike most people, who might only have a single neighbour or family living either side of their house, with maybe one behind them, our house was ringed on three sides by four-storeyed blocks of flats whose balconies and windows all looked down upon our meth-fuelled kibbutz of outlaws, villains, thieves, sluts and gunslingers. It was a show that ran 24/7. And what a show it was.

At any given time, there were at least fifty people who could open their blinds and watch our coconut-butter-covered girlfriends sunbaking topless in the backyard or spraying each other with the hose.

On some evenings they would see us issue forth upon our Harleys, exhausts barking as we revved our motors and revelled in the sheer awesome atavism of ourselves and the noise we made being us. We had big knives strapped to our legs, and pickaxe handles wedged on our bikes. Our pillions were hot, haughty, bra-less and brazen. We yelled and roared and smoked drugs openly and frequently. When we went away on big runs we had guns strapped to our bikes and partied all night before we left in the morning. We were predictable, horrible, hostile and utterly hilarious – and we were happening right outside their windows.

Each weekday morning they could share Badger's motorcycle-starting ritual. This involved swearing of a frequency and volume hitherto unattained in western Sydney, and was accompanied by repeated mechanical explosions as his Sportster backfired each time he kicked it, spitting flames of non-starting hate at the world.

On hot summer afternoons, the flat-dwellers could behold me smashing recalcitrant bike parts with a sledgehammer or throwing tools against the fence. Or they could be lucky enough to watch Salvo Dan vomiting his lungs up because he'd had one too many West Coast Coolers after Badger had brought a case home and told him it needed to be necked before it went off.

At night, our neighbours were treated to Viking-sized bonfires, quite often made with the wood from their own paling fences and trees. And it was not unusual for their balconies and rapidly slammed windows to be suffused in carcinogenic clouds of tyre smoke from a brutal four-gear burnout when one of us felt a rear tyre needed replacing.

No doubt they had all witnessed what happened the day we bound Badger to the Hills Hoist with gaffer tape, piled crumpled newspaper around his legs, set it all alight and tried to burn him as a witch. I know for a fact they saw the Great Shopping Trolley Race because none of us was physically capable of calling the two much-needed ambulances that turned up to sew and staple the competitors back together. They may have enjoyed Big Dima leading Svetlana around the yard on a dog leash, but they probably wouldn't have enjoyed the savage beating dished out to some bloke who came to one of our parties and failed to understand that no matter how sluttily our girlfriends were dressed, they remained off limits to everyone but their respective boyfriends. But I think the incident that caused the most For Sale and For Lease signs to go up in their windows was the night my dog crawled into a stolen shopping trolley and face-fucked Johnny Squirm, a thalidomide-afflicted regular at our soirees, and one of the most courageous human beings I have ever met.

Johnny was born with misshapen flippers instead of arms and legs – a direct consequence of his mother taking the drug thalidomide to deal with her morning sickness during pregnancy. Johnny was nicknamed 'Squirm' before he came into our lives, but it was obvious why he was called that. He couldn't walk and moved by squirming along on his arse. We did organise a skateboard for him to trundle himself along on, but it was usually easier just to pick him up and carry him to wherever he wanted to be. Amazingly, he drove a heavily modified car and enjoyed more success with girls than one would have thought possible. He used to tell us girls wanted to fuck him out of curiosity or pity or a combination of both, and that he really couldn't give a rat's fuck about their motivation as long as they put out.

But the only thing my dog Curse was interested in was if Johnny Squirm put out. And in a funny sort of way, my dog's sexual fixation spelled the beginning of the end of our time in the big green house.

It began the first time the two of them beheld each other, which was at the massive four-day housewarming party we decided to hold to celebrate our arrival in Merrylands. Johnny had been a regular at most of our prior parties, and would spend many happy evenings perched on the seat of a bike out in the garage, drinking beer, snorting lines of speed and lunging back fat crackling joints, just like everybody else. The difference was that because he was so small, essentially a head and torso unencumbered by arms and legs, he'd get very shitfaced on very little. So when he was ready to fight ogres or fuck chorus lines of strippers, the rest of us were barely hitting our straps.

Curse was a purebred bull terrier I had acquired as a puppy, and was my genial, sweet-natured and adorable companion for the next sixteen years. But when Curse met Johnny Squirm, he was just out of puppyhood, and while he was always sweet-natured, the years had yet to take the edge off his insatiable curiosity and pig-headed determination. To give you an idea of just how implacable this determination was, I need to also dispel the myth that these dogs have the ability to lock their jaws. What actually accounts for the merciless and relentless way these dogs 'hang on' is their unassailable stubbornness to not let go, and not some actual physical jaw-locking ability. Once a bull terrier clamps its jaws onto something, it has been known to hang on even after death claims it. They are more stubborn than wives in that regard and on par with lawyers.

This was clear to me from the first time Curse set his slitted little eyes on Johnny's crippled body. It was still daylight when Johnny came over and was squirming and shimmying his way down our hallway on his leathery little arse. He was making his way, as custom dictated, to where we were all writing our names in methamphetamine on the mirrored table in the Room With The Table Where We Would Snort Speed. We didn't even know he was in the house until we heard him screaming 'No! Fuck off! Get off me, ya cunt! No! Fuck! Arrgghhhhh!' but Curse clearly did.

I had just finished snarfing back the letter S in my first name, and the burn of the speed had made me a little blind and teary in my left eye. Nonetheless, I leapt into action and crashed into the hallway, stumbling over chairs, empty bottles and pizza boxes, ready to help my brave dog rend the house-invaders. But instead of confronting intruders, I was confronted by something I have not seen ever again, even in these heady days of internet atrocity porn. I doubt there's an ISP anywhere on Earth that would carry footage of a dog trying to fuck a badly deformed thalidomide victim.

'Getchyafuckendogoff!' Johnny howled as I stared at the tangle of fur and flesh in the hall. He was pinned face-down on the floor by Curse, who had straddled him, clamped his jaws (quite tenderly in retrospect) on the back of Johnny's head, and was eagerly trying to wedge his pink doggy cock into where he believed Johnny's vagina simply had to be. I don't know if you have ever seen dogs mate, but it's not a loving and caring exercise like it is with people. Dogs fuck like strippers on coke – hard, fast, brutal and dirty. Big Dima often tried to emulate this with Svetlana, but always admitted failure because she wasn't really a professional stripper, he told us.

I still don't know why Curse suddenly took it upon himself to mate with Johnny. The dog had never even so much as humped anyone's leg and spent most of his time sleeping. But when Johnny Squirm came into his life, he became a sex-pest of epic proportions. It got so bad Johnny could no longer sit on the bikes in the garage because Curse would stand up on his hind legs and start to lick him endlessly in some kind of damp and vaguely spooky doggy foreplay. If we sat Johnny on the kitchen table, Curse would not rest until he had expended every bullet in his chair-scaling arsenal trying to climb up beside him and skewer him with his cock. Eventually, we had to prop Johnny on top of the fridge in the kitchen or garage to keep Curse off him, but Curse would invariably sit and wait with sphinx-like patience at the foot of the fridges.

The beginning of the end of our time in the green house was the night the police turned up and demanded to know where we had hidden the child that had been killed in a cage by a savage dog. It was also the night Johnny declared he wanted to be outside by the fire because the girls were taking off their tops and he wanted to look at their tits in the firelight. I duly carried him outside, with Curse dogging my heels and panting with lust.

'Make sure you keep that fucken dog off me, mate,' Johnny pleaded as I wondered how I was going to make this work. If I put him on the ground, Curse would rape him right there in the dirt. I certainly couldn't hold him in my arms – the little fucker might not have had arms and legs, but he still packed a bit of weight into his head and torso, and it was like carrying a smelly tattooed five-year-old around.

Luckily, one of the many shopping trolleys we had acquired was very close to hand. It was packed with fresh fence-palings to be burned on the fire that evening, so I asked one of the blokes to tip them out and wheel the empty trolley over to me. I plonked Johnny into it with a sigh.

'There ya go, mate,' I said. 'Safe as. Wanna beer?'

'You're a fucken genius!' Johnny crowed and started yelling at Curse, who was watching him like I watch girls dancing on poles.

'Fuck you!' he shrieked at the dog. 'Whatcha gonna do now, ya fucken mad cunt?! Let's see you get me here, ya stupid prick!'

Curse was nonplussed. Johnny was now quite within reach, but sealed off from his love by the trolley's thin steel bars. I'm sure he must have thought it to be some kind of kinky doggy bondage scenario. He first stuck an exploratory paw on the trolley's grate, then tried licking Johnny through the bars and was rewarded for his efforts by Johnny spitting beer at him and laughing. So he did what any sexually aroused male always does when the object of his desire is in a sex-cage he hasn't got the key to. He sat down beside the cage and started to whimper piteously.

Meanwhile, I had been distracted by naked breasts and marijuana and had wandered away from the fire in pursuit of both. The music had been turned right up, it was getting dark and the party was entering that lift-off mode where everyone has had just enough booze and just enough drugs to be carrying on like nothing in the world mattered but having a good time.

I think that's why no one noticed Salvo Dan lifting Curse up and putting him into the shopping trolley with Johnny Squirm. But we all noticed the terrible sexual thuggery that began the second Curse got up close and personal with his malformed jism-spittoon. Yes, I now know it's not funny putting a sex-crazed fighting dog into a shopping trolley containing a drunken thalidomide victim, especially when they're in a very dysfunctional relationship – but it really was funny at the time.

In the brief minute or so while we were helpless with laughter and could not effect a rescue, Curse had managed to smear his cock all over Johnny's face and neck as he frantically tried to find some hole for his staccato thrusting. His nails had gouged angry weals into Johnny's back and chest, and he had one of Johnny's hind flippers clenched firmly in his teeth as the trolley rocked madly and finally tipped over, allowing us to quickly pull the couple apart.

Salvo Dan was laughing so hard he fell into the bonfire, burning his arm so badly he would need three skin grafts in the coming months. It was probably the Road Gods' way of punishing him for being a cunt and giving poor Johnny the doggy sex-scars he would carry until he passed away a few years later from a heroin overdose.

Two of the girls who witnessed the wild trolley sex left so fast their bras and vodkas lay unclaimed by the fire for several hours. The rest of us all felt suitably ashamed and quite sorry, which is probably why the police only arrested Big Dima when they arrived shortly afterwards. They had come to investigate reports of a dog savaging a child in a cage, but saw nothing other than a big fire, some shopping trolleys, a bunch of giggling bikers standing around the yard, and two topless girls wiping thick yellow fluid off a hard-cursing, limbless gimp with a panther tattooed on his chest. They were not prepared for that. Nor were they prepared for Big Dima, who came shambling out of the house, ripped off his shirt and insisted they immediately wrestle him for their handguns. It was Big Dima's way of distracting the police from whatever it was they were doing. And it kind of worked. They promptly arrested him for being an idiot, warned us all to stop being cunts and left.

The only truly happy and guilt-free creature in the immediate aftermath was Curse, who had finally, after months of anticipation, managed to get a load off, and had succeeded in pumping what looked like half a litre of rancid dog-sperm all over Johnny's head, neck and face. Big time happy was written all over his hairy snout.

But there was some writing on the wall of our fate after that evening too. Even Abdul came over to complain to me about the complaints he was getting from our neighbours and the cops.

'Fuck them forever!' he raved, waving his hairy arms around his head. 'You pay your rent, I tell them. But they do not care, yes? They are animals, they say to me. They have many sluts in their house, and mad dogs and they are making explosions and music all the time, day and night, yes?'

'Yes,' I said. I could hardly deny it.

'Fuck them in their face!' Abdul declared. 'They want to report me to the government!'

While I wasn't entirely sure what branch of the government would be hugely interested in Abdul's noisy, slut-friendly rental clients, I did understand that the current party house paradigm could not continue. It was starting to feel more and more like the *Titanic* looking for an iceberg to headbutt. A change could be a good thing, I thought to myself. Our parties were getting wilder and wilder, and we had gotten away with so much shit in the last eighteen months, it was unlikely our luck would last. I was thinking of heading overseas in the near future and didn't need a drug charge or something worse getting in the way. There was some deeply crazy shit starting to go on in that house. It was only a matter of time before someone lost an eye.

I looked pointedly at our Pantagruelian landlord. 'What do you want to do, Abdul?' I asked.

Abdul smiled and spread his arms wide. 'I want to help you, yes?'

I shrugged. I had no idea if that was true or not, or even what it meant. It could mean that while he wanted to help, his hands were tied and we were doomed shortly to be homeless.

I sighed and resigned myself to whatever was going to happen.

Abdul peered at me from under his heavy Lebo slumlord brow. 'I have another house for you,' he declared. 'It is a very nice house, yes? Not so big like this one, but very nice. No bond is needed. I trust you, yes?'

THE
CHRISTMAS RUN

This run was a run like no other I had been on before or have been on since. It remains a testament to one man's indefatigable determination to persist and endure against all odds, especially odds that are actively conspiring to fuck his shit up. To this day I remain amazed and awed by Jabba's iron resolve to keep on keeping on, just as I remain amazed that a motorcycle could exude such hatred.

'My centre is giving way; my
right is retreating; situation
excellent, I am attacking.'

FERDINAND FOCH

'You do know it's never gonna make it, don't you?' I said to Jabba, a month before our Christmas Run. It was only right and proper I pointed the obvious out to the poor sod. It's not like the silly cunt was ever going to grasp it for himself.

Our annual Christmas Run was a big thing for me and my friends. We looked forward to it like fat German sex tourists look forward to Thailand.

Jabba glared at me in defiance. He reminded me of that poster where the little mouse is giving a swooping eagle the finger. In Jabba's case, the eagle was blind Fate, and in all the time I knew him, Fate did seem to have a bead on him despite her alleged blindness.

'It *will* make it,' he stated with utter conviction, his eyes flicking across to 'it' then back to me.

'It' was an utterly vile two-wheeled contraption that started life as a 1968 Triumph Trophy. And that afternoon, it sat in our garage, exuding all sorts of impalpable nastiness. In retrospect, its year of manufacture was somewhat prophetic – 1968 was quite the year for exuding nastiness. The My Lai massacre took place that year, the Pope banned the use of contraceptives for the faithful, and Pierre Trudeau became Prime Minister of Canada.

Twenty years later the mechanical nastiness that was built in 1968 was no less nasty. I think Jabba must have known about this on some primal level, because he had spent the last four weeks sequestered in the garage like a diseased animal, feverishly putting the bike back together after first taking it apart and apparently 'improving' it. And the Road Gods knew it certainly needed improving.

When Jabba acquired it and brought it home, I saw the Triumph had retained some of its frame and most of its motor. But the previous owner had succumbed to some kind of dire mental illness and had shitcanned the swingarm and subframe, replacing it with a nightmarish add-on known (and feared) in bike customising circles as a 'plunger' rear end. So rather than having two normal shock absorbers linking the swingarm to the subframe with bouncy goodness, a plunger system worked (and I use the term loosely) directly on the rear axle, which was suspended between two short springs. It looked really trick and worked not at all. The previous owner had also tossed away a lot of the original gear, like the forks, tank, wheels and seat, and ended up with a religiously ugly, dirt-red shitheap with a Harley Fat Bob rear guard mounted atop the plunger rear end, a Sportster peanut tank, a two-into-one exhaust system of indeterminate origin, an extended front end sporting two rectangular headlights mounted one atop the other and the dark, twisted and deeply sick soul of a true son-of-a-bitch – though this last quality wasn't immediately apparent to me when I first saw it parked in front of a bike shop on Parramatta Road.

As a matter of interest I asked the price. I was impressed with the answer and that night, over a few beers, I told Jabba about it. He was currently bikeless, but on the lookout, and felt he could scrape up the necessary dollars.

The next day Jabba brought it home. He was beaming with pride and sitting astride his new Triumph, which was clearly already bathing him in waves of mechanical loathing. It was running painfully on one-and-a-bit cylinders and missing the lens from one of the headlights that had fallen out along the way.

When he turned it off so we could all admire it without having to squint and cough through the oily smoke roiling from its engine, it promptly emptied the contents of its crankcase onto the driveway. To this day I will swear on holy books the infernal bastard housed a miniaturised oil refinery somewhere in its hate-rich gizzards. It vented oil like the *Exxon Valdez* – even when there should not have been any oil left to vent.

'Needs a bit of work,' was all Jabba said as Ankles, Mark and I wiped our oil-stained boots on the grass beside the driveway. He then wheeled it into the garage and hooked into it that very night. And pretty much every night after that as well. It was a phenomenon you sometimes read about, when men begin to obsess about something well past the point of rationality and into the realm of black madness. And it was happening to Jabba. As far as he was concerned, he was going to build a masterpiece; a showbike to stun the masses – an unassailable monument to English engineering and Aussie customising.

Two things stopped him. Money, because he didn't have enough to buy a new motor, frame, gearbox, running gear, electrical items and cosmetics; and the bike itself, which had no intention whatsoever of allowing its new owner any chance of succeeding in his intentions.

Over the next two months, as our annual Christmas Run approached, Jabba and the Triumph developed an altogether unique relationship. It was like Battered Wife Syndrome, with Jabba as the brutalised but optimistic spouse. A sane man would have put a match to the bike after a month, but not Jabba. He would spend many hundreds of his hard-earned dollars and endless nights sorting out the bike's panoply of problems, only to have something else go wrong the next day. Or hour. Yet he never gave up. He was constantly covered in grease and sweat, his pockets perpetually torn and bulging with tools, while determination and despair leached from him in equal amounts. He developed that hunted look Triumph riders get from never knowing if they're going to get to where they're going. He never had any money, since every spare cent was claimed by Zener diodes, tappet covers and the millions of Nylok nuts he kept buying to replace the millions that kept falling off.

After one particularly long breakdown-free period of four days, Jabba felt the Times of Trouble had passed and he could now start customising. All the bike's problems had been sorted, he declared, and since our Christmas Run was drawing near, he wanted to impress the hippy chicks in Mullumbimby. As far as he was concerned, the rest of us would be soiling our sleeping bags with jealousy while the local girls showered him with sex, drugs and booze. All it would take, he told us, was one look at his Triumph.

High on his list was chrome-plating. 'It's gotta have lots of chrome,' he told me as he loaded half the bike into boxes. 'It drives hippy chicks crazy – all that shiny stuff.'

'So what colour are you gonna paint it after the chrome's done?' I asked.

A far-away look came into his eyes as they glazed over with divine vision. 'White,' he breathed. 'Pure white. White as the driven snow. White as a virgin bride's wedding dress. White as . . .'

'White as the fucking space between your ears,' I muttered to myself as he wandered ever farther into vivid comparisons.

I left the garage and went to bed, half wondering if he was actually going to mate with the parts he was putting into boxes and was just chatting them up first.

Early the next morning I could hear Jabba on the phone to Zorro. Zorro was our spray-painter. He mainly sprayed cars in his father's workshop, but could be prevailed upon to throw a coat of paint onto our bikes from time to time. He was a large, good-natured Italian and an absolute genius with a spray gun.

The following weekend, I drove Jabba and his bits to the chromers, then to Zorro's spray-painting shop and marvelled at the big fellow's patience as Jabba intoned his 'white as the foam of a storm-driven wave' shit at him.

'Yeah, I know what you want,' Zorro said and took the parts off to be prepared.

'Should we wait here?' Jabba asked me. 'You know, the parts . . . I mean, I don't think they should be without me . . .'

'No, I think it'll be okay,' I said evenly. 'I'm sure they'll be fine with Zorro.'

As we left, Jabba cast forlorn looks over his shoulder. I think he wanted to be held, but our friendship did not extend to such things.

Several days later, the newly chromed bits were ready. Jabba feverishly stripped the linen and blankets from his bed, took the pillows from each of our rooms and threw them all into the ute. Ankles drove him to the chromers and returned an hour later with Jabba perched in the tray like a grease-stained chicken nesting on its eggs.

Ankles joined me on the verandah as we watched Jabba carefully transferring the wrapped parts from the ute to the couch in the garage.

'There is something fucken wrong with him,' Ankles said, his eyes never leaving Jabba.

'What makes you say that?' I asked.

'He spent fifteen minutes arranging pillows and blankets in the back, then he screamed at the chrome bloke for not washing his hands before handling the parts, then he threatened to kill me and my family if I went over fifteen kays.'

The phone rang. It was Zorro. Jabba's tank, guards and frame were also ready to be picked up. When we arrived, Zorro led us to the baking booth where the bits were hanging like some massive biker mobile. Jabba entered the booth and froze, staring at the parts in glazed adoration. I've seen pictures of primitive villagers with the same rapturous, idiot look on their faces as they stare at a rock and imagine it to be the Virgin Mary.

'I don't know what to say,' he mumbled hoarsely, clearly overwhelmed by what was unquestionably an incredible paint job. Zorro carefully took the parts down and rubbed them softly with a piece of flannel. 'It's basically Alpine White,' he explained. 'But I whacked a coat or two of Candy Apple Electric Blue down as a base. It really makes the white "white", eh?'

Jabba, Ankles and I nodded in agreement. There was no doubt we were looking at the whitest, brightest parts in existence. The washing powder people would have been jealous. We transported the parts home, humouring Jabba by driving at 15 kms per hour. All the way back to the house he stared at the parts like a wall-eyed zombie, transfixed by the impossibly white paint. Ankles and I stared out the windscreen. We found that looking at the paint made something behind our eyes ache.

The reassembly commenced that very night. The other blokes came over, not to help, since Jabba would not let anyone else touch his bike, but to behold one of the few true fanatics of our time at his labours. We all knew the Triumph's reputation. We'd become used to it taking six hours for us to ride 100 kilometres on our runs. We had made peace with drawing straws to see who'd go back for the ute. But that was all during winter and on relatively short rides. During Christmas, we'd planned an epic journey of several thousand kilometres. The laws of physics, chance and probability all pointed to a major catastrophe occurring somewhere in country New South Wales. But Jabba was our mate. He had his heart set on coming and we could not deny him. Besides, maybe he really *had* fixed everything. When I stated this, Ankles told me to go fuck myself.

Out in the garage, I quietly repeated my statement of faith to the hunched figure patiently stripping bolt after bolt on the primary case as he tried to reattach it to the motor.

'It will make it,' Jabba declared, looking around for more bolts to destroy. 'I'll make sure of it.'

We all exchanged looks, wondering if this was the point when we acknowledged that one of us had become irredeemably feeble-minded. Of course, our jibes, ridicule and knowing looks were not entirely wasted on Jabba. He understood this run was a matter of honour for him. And his bike. And he was fervently determined to make the run. No matter what it took or what price had to be paid.

———

In the final weeks preceding our journey, Jabba steadily assembled, disassembled and reassembled every conceivable part on the Triumph. Gallons of Loctite and Silastic were shoplifted and applied, torque settings were meticulously exceeded by two or three grunts, clutch and throttle cables were purchased by the metre and spark plugs were bought in bulk. Entire days were spent collecting and assembling enough tools to strip a nuclear reactor. Jabba's attempts to improve upon his Coventry-designed nightmare were occurring on a pauper's budget. As a result, he had to resort to using a mixture of metric, AF, and the original Whitworth nuts and bolts. Consequently, he had a corresponding array of various spanners, sockets, ratchets, extension bars and adaptors, all lined up with military precision on the garage floor. He was determined to be prepared for any eventuality or mechanical emergency, so he also stacked a large assortment of spare parts in one corner. Cables, cable ties, gaskets, Zener diodes, levers, bolts, nuts . . . all formed a massive mare's nest of potential saviours in one large and menacing pile.

And finally, the bike was complete. We stood in the garage and looked on in awe as Jabba wiped nonexistent bits of dirt from the chrome and paint. At first glance, the bike was indeed a very shiny piece of work. The old pipes had been replaced by an expensive, custom-made, stainless-steel set, which we were told were never going to turn blue under any circumstances. We'd convinced him the two rectangular headlights were dreadfully unsuited to a modern custom bike and he had replaced them with a single round Bates unit. The Cobra seat was gone and in its place was a strange-looking sprung affair like a squashed pushbike seat and an even stranger pillion pad that dimensionally resembled a James A. Michener novel formed in foam and vinyl. Flat drag bars had replaced the baby ape hangers and a secondhand Morris magneto hung jauntily from the right-hand side of the engine. And as a result of Zorro's incredible white paint, the bike literally seared itself into your brain. When you closed your eyes, you could still see an after-image of it on your retinas. We all stared at it a little self-consciously, like people do at tragically deformed animals.

'Nice, mate,' I ventured. 'Very nice.'

'Yeah,' Ankles said. 'Okay. Yeah. Nice.'

'The chrome's good,' Mark offered.

'I think the paint makes it,' Zorro grinned.

Actually, it didn't really matter what we thought of the Triumph. Jabba clearly thought it was great and he was going to ride it on the run and that was that.

'You gonna start it?' Ankles asked.

'Yeah,' Mark nodded. 'I'd like to hear that exhaust.'

A fleeting look of uncertainty passed over Jabba's face like a cloud whisking across the sun. It was quickly replaced by the cocky, complacent grin of the master craftsman.

'No worries!' he chirped, turned on the ignition and prepared to kick-start it into life. Twenty minutes later we were pushing the fucken thing down the street, much to the amusement of our neighbours, who probably thought we were on really good drugs to be doing that in thirty-two-degree heat.

Jabba had kicked and kicked and kicked the kick-starter, before he tore a hole in his shin and had to stop. Then Ankles had kicked and kicked and kicked it until something exploded in his knee, then he kicked Jabba and went home in disgust.

The rest of us weren't keen to destroy our legs so I suggested we try and push-start it. After some four kilometres of that shit, Jabba, who was quite prepared to push the bike to Melbourne if need be, realised his moment of truth had come.

'I'm going to set fire to the cunt,' I puffed. Jabba must have seen the resolve in my glowing red bike-pushing face. He swallowed and whipped out a screwdriver.

'It's probably just the magneto,' he declared. Mark's red-rimmed and sweat-filled eyes glared malice at him. Zorro flicked his lighter on and off. It was clearly High Noon. Jabba knelt on the hot bitumen and started tinkering with the magneto, all the while muttering unintelligibly to himself and the bike. It sounded like praying from where I stood with my sweaty head baking in the blazing sun. A minute later Jabba bounced on the kick-starter and the bike roared into life. Well, maybe 'roared' is a bit too strong a word. The stainless-steel exhaust and muffler certainly produced a unique sound, but it wasn't really a roar. If you rattled a giant beer can full of water and gravel near your ear, you'd be getting close to the sound coming from Jabba's Triumph.

But Jabba was grinning so hard he couldn't blink. Even I stopped scowling; it was hard to be mad at him when he was so clearly overjoyed. He said something none of us could hear – the bike seemed to be idling at 5000 rpm – clunked it into gear and tore off into the distance.

Later that afternoon, after we had walked home, we heard Jabba coming down the driveway. He'd been out test-riding the Triumph and judging by his grin, he was completely satisfied. Or at least he was until I asked him what was wrong with his exhaust pipes.

'They used to be really shiny,' I remarked. 'They're a beaut chocolate-brown colour now. It doesn't really go with the rest of the bike.'

Jabba crabbed off the bike and stared at his pipes. His face collapsed in on itself. The shiny monument to pipe-bending that had cost him an ugly amount of money had indeed turned the most displeasing brown colour.

'Hey, you were right, mate,' Mark said. 'They won't fucken turn blue.'

Zorro offered to respray the bike green. 'That way, the pipes will match the paint,' he stated. Being Italian, Zorro's colour coordination was often quite at odds with the civilised world's. And while Jabba did his best to look insulted, there really wasn't much he could say. The bloke who'd sold him the pipes had guaranteed him they wouldn't turn blue, but had neglected to mention what colour they would turn.

Jabba kicked his bike into life, his face a mask of dire and imminent retribution, and tore back out the driveway. We all naturally assumed he was going to get his money back and maybe smack the exhaust bloke around with a spanner. We couldn't have been more wrong. He was back within the hour. The pipes had progressed along the colour wheel and were now an even more intense shade of brown. But we only managed a glimpse as he rode straight past us and into the garage.

'This could be serious,' Mark said, and we all hurried into the garage after Jabba.

'Well?' I demanded. 'What happened?'

'I got it all sorted,' Jabba grinned, pulling two small plastic bottles from his jacket. One bottle contained grey muck and one bottle contained white muck. He placed them on the ground near his bike and went in search of rags.

'What's in the bottles, mate?' Mark wanted to know.

Jabba dumped an armful of his good T-shirts next to his bike and started tearing them into polishing rags. It seemed that everything he owned would ultimately be sacrificed on the altar of his obsession.

'Well,' he began, wrenching a classic Ramones T-shirt apart, 'I showed the bloke what had happened and he told me it was a chemical reaction. Perfectly normal.'

Mark snorted. 'What bloody chemical reaction? They're a set of pipes, not a chemistry set.'

Jabba paused in his rag-tearing to look condescendingly at Mark. 'You just don't fucken understand,' he said.

'You haven't said what's in the bottles,' I reminded Jabba as he opened the bottle of grey muck and poured a small amount onto a piece of T-shirt.

'This stuff,' he said, holding up the gooey rag, 'will remove that stuff.' He pointed at the pipes. 'Then that stuff,' he said, indicating the bottle of white muck, 'is rubbed on to polish it all up. The bloke reckons they'll come up like new.'

So saying, he smeared the grey goo along the length of one exhaust pipe, where it promptly became black goo. We all stared at this intriguing new development.

'Maybe you should have waited for the bike to cool down,' I suggested.

Jabba ignored me and continued to stare with frightening intensity at the dark horror on his exhaust system.

'We're . . . um, going to go now, okay?' I said. There wasn't much else to say. Jabba seemed to be in some form of catatonic state. Maybe his mind's finally snapped, I thought.

The next morning it was obvious some momentous things had occurred during the night. When Mark and I opened the roller door, we saw Jabba lying on the couch, his lips pulled back from his gritted teeth in a spooky rictus. His right hand was clutching a polishing rag, his left was cramped into a grubby claw. On the floor were the two plastic bottles, now empty. We looked at the white Triumph, which was surrounded by grey-and-white-stained rags. Then we saw the pipes. Last night they had looked like ancient wooden broom handles. This morning they looked like gleaming copper water pipes.

Mark and I exchanged looks. 'At least it looked like a mistake before,' he said. 'Now it looks like it's been done on purpose and proudly polished up.'

I nodded dumbly. To a casual onlooker, it would appear that Jabba had specifically ordered copper-coloured pipes for his bike and then polished them to the point of illness.

'They come up good, eh?' came a hoarse voice from the couch. 'It took a bit of work, but it was worth it,' he declared, rising stiffly from the couch and trying to straighten his cramp-twisted hand by smacking it into his leg. Mark and I were speechless. Jabba's departure from reality seemed to be complete. Commenting on it would be counter-productive. So we left Jabba to his madness and went back to the house to pack our stuff.

We were scheduled to depart the following morning. And since packing was a relatively easy procedure for everyone except Jabba, we were soon done. So we dragged out some maps, cracked open some beer and wallowed in that glorious pre-run anticipation that besets all bikers.

Jabba spent the rest of the day stacking everything he planned to take in the doorway of the garage. We could see him from our vantage point on the back verandah. Every now and then he'd pick up a spanner and tighten something on the Triumph, as if it was falling to bits just sitting there.

'We're fucked with that thing along,' Mark sighed. 'It will explode and kill us all.'

We all laughed when he said that. But it was a bit forced.

Evening found us all in the garage. Mark, Ankles, Zorro and I were smoking a joint and watching Jabba replacing the dozen or so stripped bolts he'd ruthlessly 'checked' during the day. He had also found a small scratch at the bottom of the frame and cursed at it for twenty minutes. Finally, he stood back from the bike, wiped his hands on his jeans and gazed at his handiwork.

'Time to load her up,' he quipped as an unearthly silence descended. Each of us had simultaneously realised there was one glaring obstacle to Jabba loading stuff. The bike had no provision for carrying anything more than a sleeping bag strapped to the handlebars. How he was going to attach sixty kilograms of tools, spare parts, a tent, clothing, five litres of spare oil and all the other items he might think of before departure was beyond us all.

Jabba abruptly comprehended the dilemma. 'Fuck,' he said, his eyes darting around the garage like a spooked animal. But the bloke was nothing if not adaptable. He ran into the house and emerged shortly thereafter with about 20 ocky straps which he dumped in a tangle next to the bike.

'Anybody got any spare ocky straps?' he asked his audience.

We shook our heads, admiring the pile he had already assembled. We were all kinda stoned and his capering looked very much like some goofy street theatre to us.

'Do you think you might not have enough of them?' I asked. Jabba's eyes went from me to the pile of gear near the garage door and then to the pile of ocky straps.

'I don't know,' he breathed, his brows furrowing. 'I hope so.' Then he began.

You probably need to know that Jabba, like some riders, had never really grasped the Tao of ocky straps – those incredible and ubiquitous-to-motorcycles lengths of nylon-sheathed rubber cordage with the evil coiled metal hooks at either end. He could just not grasp the necessity of strapping things down uniformly – with equal tension on both sides of the item. Or conversely, he would strap something down so tightly the strap would break and smack him in the ear. Four ocky straps and one snazzy red weal on the side of his head later, the sleeping bag was affixed to the handlebars, and Jabba was already sweating with the exertion required to achieve the 400 foot-pounds of tension he put on each strap. Next came the four-man tent. Jabba planned on parking his bike in the tent with him to keep the dew off it, so his tent was four times the size and ten times the weight of our crappy little one-man jiggers. He wedged it between the pillion pad and the sprung solo seat, where he held it in place with one hand and used the other to administer a massive abundance of ocky straps, securing them to various points along the bottom of the frame, the seat springs and the number plate, which promptly bent under their massive pull. A large brown flight bag containing several changes of clothing and spare parts was then strapped to the top of the tent. But the moment of truth was fast approaching. He had four ocky straps left and sixty kilograms of tools and spares to go.

'This is gonna get really fucken interesting,' Ankles grinned, opening another beer. I lit another joint and settled back on the couch to watch Act II.

Jabba strained with the effort of getting his large canvas tool bag up to seat level. It weighed more than any girl he'd ever tried to pillion. He lowered it quickly onto the pillion pad, which promptly squashed itself into a flat vinyl rectangle. The massive bag drooped across the bike like the corpse of some ratty green-skinned sheep.

'If you ride slowly enough you won't have to strap it down,' Zorro smirked, as I hacked with laughter and exhaled dope smoke.

Jabba ignored us. He was utterly fixated on the task at hand. He hooked his remaining ocky straps onto the section of frame that surrounds the plunger and made weird grunting noises as he heaved hard to secure them.

Now apart from being a wondrous piece of equipment, an ocky strap is also a vicious and spiteful cunt – especially when it comes whistling through the air at 3000 kms per hour and rips into your face like a tiger claw.

Jabba still sports the scar to this day. He tells people he got it in a pub brawl with Maoris, but all of us who were in that garage at the time know it happened on the very last tug. And for those of us watching, it happened in slow motion.

Jabba had closed his eyes with exertion and his sweat-sheened brow was creased with effort. Then just as he gave the strap one last hard tug to secure the steel hook, the secured steel hook on the other end straightened under the pressure, unsecured itself, and came streaking through the air like the wrath of God. Jabba became instantly aware that there was no more resistance and reflexively cringed in horror at the impending pain. The steel ocky strap hook brutally sheared into the side of his nose and I'm sure his scream could be heard in space.

Unfortunately, as he flung his hands upwards to cover the wound, he also fell backwards and kicked over his bike in the process.

Then shit got really fucked up. As we watched Jabba writhing painfully on the floor with blood gouting from his face and the Triumph leaking petrol as it lay on its side, as if by magic the ocky straps began unravelling themselves, savagely lashing Jabba about the lower body. An Egyptian slaver couldn't have beaten him better, or faster. A few straps even managed to clank into the bike, adjusting the paint job a little. Eventually, the sound of metal on metal and metal on flesh stopped and the silence was total. Even the seeds in the joint had stopped crackling.

'I think we should go now,' I whispered.

We left quickly. I looked over my shoulder and saw Jabba lying motionless, but conscious, on the blood- and petrol-spattered floor. He was either sobbing silently or breathing deeply. I could not tell. There was more blood than I thought there should have been, but I was so stoned I put it down to paranoia and decided to go to bed like it never happened. Our bikes were packed and departure was mere hours away. None of us wanted to think about what had just happened in the garage. Bad omens are best not pondered at any length before a big run.

The next morning I was up first and busied myself making coffee as the other blokes ambled into the kitchen,

'Do you think he's awake yet?' Mark asked, looking through the dusty venetian blinds. Zorro and I joined him at the window and peered at the ominously quiet garage. Although it was only 8 am, the sun was already beating down and it promised to be another uncomfortably hot day.

'There's only one way to find out,' I said and stepped outside.

'Ah . . . um, Jabba?' I said to the garage door.

Silence.

'Jabba? You coming, mate?'

More silence.

I reached down and pulled the roller door up. It made its normal screeching sound and it took a second or so for my eyes to adjust to the dimness inside. I made out an upright Triumph with a battered-looking Jabba sitting astride it. They were both staring at me. I stared back. I couldn't see Jabba's eyes through his black wrap-around sunnies, but his entire aspect was different. This was somehow not the same man who'd been writhing on the floor during last night's ocky-strap apocalypse. This was clearly a new and improved Jabba. He had been annealed in the fires of despair, and had emerged meaner, harder, leaner and somewhat cleaner. I say 'somewhat' because he was still amply covered in bike grime and his face bore the wounds of the previous night's savage lashing. But he looked very determined and set. Like insane concrete.

His bike had been repacked and I noticed quite a bit had been left off. The sleeping bag was still being strangled on the handlebars, but the tent now lay on the floor and the large flight bag was beside it. There was just Jabba's gigantic tool bag squatting on the back of the bike like a huge, venomous toad adorned with innumerable ocky straps.

'Well?' he asked, his voice a hoarse croak. 'We off?'

I nodded dumbly as the others filed into the garage, looked dubiously at Jabba, then wheeled their bikes out into the sun. As we zipped up our jackets and pulled on our gloves, Jabba kick-started his Triumph and rolled out of the garage, revving the motor impatiently. The bike seemed to be running all right and the scratches it had sustained the night before weren't readily visible – the paint glared viciously, reflecting the sun and making closer inspection impossible.

Our five Harleys fired up and their thunder drowned out the Triumph's droning rattle. We all exchanged nods and grins, and hit the road.

———

Our pack eased steadily through the traffic on our way north out of Sydney, feeling very much the badarse, freedom-loving outlaws among the car-loads of holidaying families peering at us through their air-conditioning. I wasn't really a superstitious bloke, but the previous night's brutal *pas de deux* as well as the previous month's catastrophes gnawed at me like a vaguely cranky ferret. The Triumph certainly appeared to be cursed. I made a mental note to ask Jabba if he had killed any Chinamen recently. But as the traffic thinned on the outskirts of Sydney, I pushed my premonitions of impending doom to the back of my mind and concentrated on looking suitably nasty for the car drivers.

As the pack stretched out on the expressway north, Zorro and I took turns riding up front, followed by Ankles (aka Mick), Ben, and the continuously bouncing Jabba. The Triumph's plunger rear end, six-inch overstock front end and sprung seat caused the rider to adopt a very entertaining up-and-down motion. Mark had designated himself tail-ender, saying his Sportster was more manoeuvrable and therefore less likely to collide with any parts that fell off the Triumph. In days gone by we had all developed the habit of pulling over at the end of any expressway to wait for Jabba. After a while, we would pull over pretty much at the end of any twenty kilometre stretch of road. His Triumph never seemed to have the top-end he assured us was there. Consequently, speeds in excess of 100 kms per hour annoyed it tremendously. Unfortunately, our Harleys seemed to like it around the 130 kms per hour mark and so inevitably started to put some distance between us.

The expressway had not been extended to Newcastle in those days and ended just south of Gosford at Mount White. We pulled into a small petrol station for a drink while we waited for Jabba and Mark to catch up. To our surprise, they were both right behind us. Although Mark and his bike had undergone an incredible transformation along the expressway. They had been completely sprayed with a fine mist of oil and looked as if they'd been dipped in treacle. I almost dropped my bike while braying like a donkey as they rolled into the servo. Mark, however, was struggling to see the hilarity. He shut off his bike, shook his head, pointed at Jabba and wiped his face with a paper towel Ankles handed him. 'He has got to be fucking kidding,' he said and walked off to buy a drink.

Jabba was deeply engrossed with his bike. He was kneeling beside it and burning his fingers on the hot motor trying to adjust something indeterminate. Everything behind the blindingly white petrol tank was glazed with oil, including Jabba. Those first 100 kilometres out of Sydney had seen the destruction of the Triumph's left-hand gearbox oil seal, the disappearance of three of its four rocker-cover inspection caps, and it was now operating a 'total-loss' oil system. Jabba's trip seemed to be over before it had started.

'What are you gonna do?' Ben asked him, handing over a bunch of paper towels.

'I'm gonna fix it,' Jabba replied, looking at Ben like he'd just asked him for a root. 'It's just a bit of oil.'

So saying, he pulled a roll of duct tape from his pocket and started taping over the inspection holes. I watched in fascination as piece after piece curled up and died on the hot motor. Jabba stared at the uncooperative duct tape for a moment then decided to leave that repair until the engine cooled down.

'What are you going to do about that?' I asked, pointing at his oil-soaked rear tyre.

'That's easy,' Jabba replied as he started rummaging through the petrol station's various garbage bins. He found a cardboard box which he then carefully tore into mudflap-sized pieces. One was taped to the front of the rear guard just behind the motor, the other went into his pocket.

'See?' he grinned. 'No worries!'

He then checked his oil, deemed it full enough and started taping over the now-cool inspection holes. There was nothing he could do about the gearbox seal, so he started wiping oil from the bike and himself while the rest of us sat in the shade and smoked a joint. With our grins back on, we mounted up and headed north again.

Mark had always wanted to see Caves Beach (as a Canadian, beaches tended to excite him more than they should), so we made a quick detour to gaze for several minutes upon this most ordinary stretch of sand and ocean.

'I didn't see many fucken caves,' Mick observed, pulling up beside me as I waited for a break in the traffic before rejoining the highway north.

I didn't have time to reply because Mick was abruptly shunted violently forward onto the highway by Jabba's suddenly clutchless Triumph. Luckily, there was no traffic and no damage to anything except Jabba's ego. However, we did have to wait for twenty minutes while Jabba performed surgery on the snapped clutch cable and Mick swore and threw rocks at him from across the road.

We then threaded our way into Newcastle, itching to be through the stop–start traffic lights and back on the open road. We weren't in any particular hurry as we didn't have a schedule, but a fair bit of time had already been lost. I suddenly saw a whole lot more being lost as Jabba, with his feet dragging on the ground, casually rolled through the red light we were stopped at, narrowly avoiding death at the hands of one very frightened mother-of-six who was proceeding through the green signal. We all stared dumbfounded as he continued rolling into a petrol station on the other side of the intersection. The light turned green and we joined him to see what had happened now.

'The clutch has gone,' he informed us breathlessly.

'Good thing you're in fucken Newcastle then,' Mick growled. 'You can whack the bike on a train this afternoon.'

Jabba ignored Mick's remark and set about dismantling the primary cover and clutch in the middle of the service station. The rest of us retired to a cool spot under a big LPG tank to smoke a joint. It served to calm us and made the waiting bearable.

After some twenty-five minutes, Jabba had managed to spread his Triumph's primary and clutch internals all over the driveway of the servo and put the fear of imminent violence into the hapless servo owner. The bloke had come out to ask if Jabba would mind moving his bike so that customers could get to the petrol bowsers. Jabba got stiffly to his feet, fifteen-inch shifter in hand, and glared at the owner like a she-bear protecting its young. The owner quickly retreated inside, not at all sure how to deal with a grease-stained maniac wielding a blunt instrument, or his five mates who were smoking dope in the shade of his LPG tank and laughing like hyenas eating a zebra. And the show went on.

'What's he doing now?' Mark mumbled from beneath a wet bandanna he'd placed on his face against the heat.

'I'm not sure,' Zorro shrugged. 'It looks like he's lost something.'

Jabba was walking around the servo in ever-increasing circles with his head down. Every now and then, he'd stop, pick something up, examine it, discard it, then resume walking in circles.

'What are you after, mate?' I called out.

'A rock,' he called back.

We all exchanged what had now become our Jabba look. Mark peered out from under his bandanna and regarded Jabba's foraging with a steely gaze.

'I'll get a fucken rock for you,' he called out, clearly running out of happy thoughts. 'And then I'll give it to you.'

Suddenly Jabba seemed to find what he'd been looking for. His excitement was tangible from ten metres away. He hurried back to his bike and started tinkering with its insides again. I figured this had to be worth a look, so I levered myself up and went over. What I saw was amazing. The Triumph's clutch pushrod had somehow flattened itself at both ends so that the adjuster, adjusted all the way, still couldn't compensate and get the clutch to engage. To get it working again, Jabba had manoeuvred a small rock between the end of the pushrod and the adjuster.

'No fucken way,' I said, kneeling beside him. 'No fucken way will that ever work.'

'Yeah, it will,' Jabba assured me. The conviction in his voice was iron-clad. He hurriedly reassembled everything, replaced the oil-soaked cardboard with a fresh piece, cast a critical eye over the last remaining rocker-cover cap and checked the oil. To our mutual amazement, the oil tank still had oil despite the steady streams escaping from the motor and inspection holes (the duct tape had long since given up the ghost). He started up the bike and rode off to test his workmanship. He returned in minutes, beaming wildly.

'It's all fixed,' he declared proudly, shutting off the bike and kicking out the sidestand, which promptly detached itself from the bike and clanked to the ground.

It was probably very wrong of us to laugh as hard as we did. Mick was almost sick with stomach cramps, Mark felt his spleen had exploded and the rest of us still had tears streaming down our faces as we rolled out of Newcastle.

By the time the suburban wasteland of Raymond Terrace had slipped behind us, I began to experience an unnatural craving for prawns. I'd heard that Tea Gardens, a picturesque assortment of fibro houses and old racists, had large cheap ones for sale in the fishing co-op. It also had a bottle shop. I figured a few kilos of prawns washed down with a million cold beers wouldn't be a bad way to end this first day. Besides, Jabba could probably use the break.

I took the turn-off, and we found a place to camp behind the caravan park. It was a great shady area right on the beach with a sign that said: 'No Camping'. We parked our bikes and started to deploy our tents, tarps and hoochies. Jabba located a melaleuca tree to lean his bike against – and set to work to see if he could fix the broken sidestand. The bolt holding this crucial piece of metal to the bracket at the bottom of the frame had fallen off and the return spring was broken. Jabba had managed to scrounge a spare bolt from his bag of spares, but no spring. Sidestand springs can be unique bits of kit, and it was unlikely there was another like the one he needed for 1000 kilometres in any direction. There was nothing to be done. Jabba strapped his sidestand to the frame with one of his many spare ocky straps, and that's where it stayed for the rest of the trip. When he had to park the bike, he'd just lean it against a telegraph pole or a fence. He then started an operation that was to become familiar whenever we stopped for any length of time: tightening, checking, swearing and glaring at various bits of his bike. It was like some greasy alien sex ritual. I wandered over to have a look, clutching twenty centimetres of prawn in one hand and a cold beer in the other.

'Look at this,' he said when I was within earshot.

I chewed noncommittally.

'Look,' he insisted, indicating the two head steadies at the back of the motor.

'What about them?' I asked around a mouthful of prawn. The two head steadies were covered in oil but looked okay to me.

'There's supposed to be four of them,' Jabba hissed between clenched teeth. I looked closer and sure enough there were two corresponding holes at the front of the motor.

'What's wrong?' Mark asked, carrying a beer over for Jabba.

'His fucken motor is going to fall out onto the road tomorrow,' I told him and went off to eat more prawns.

———

As we headed further up the coast the next morning, I found myself riding behind Jabba. It was both oily and hilarious. Sitting just behind him coming into Taree, I noticed that every few kays his bike's exhaust note would change. Apparently, one of its plug leads kept falling off. Not wishing to annoy us any further by stopping to fix it, Jabba would simply reach down and plug it back in. This would send massive spasms of pain shooting through his already road-battered body, as 35,000 volts coursed through him, causing him to swerve wildly across the road as he fought to regain control of the Triumph and his twitching limbs. I was laughing, but I also wondered just how much more of this abuse he could take.

We stopped in Taree for breakfast, which gave Jabba a chance to forage through some nearby rubbish bins for more cardboard. He also asked each of us in turn if we had any spare foam handlebar grips. When I giggled at him, he held up two very dirty and badly swollen hands. The bike's inherent vibration, amplified by the fact the motor was missing two head steadies, was causing the solidly mounted handlebars to buzz with crippling intensity. The swelling of his hands got worse the further up the coast we got. By Port Macquarie, Jabba was no longer gripping the handlebars. He was operating the throttle by pushing the heel of his right hand against it and moaning. His left hand would only go to the bars when he was forced to reach down and reconnect the plug lead with his right.

We carried on to Macksville, and I kept thinking he was going to pass out at any moment. And the omens were not improving. It had started raining gently, and that, plus the state of his hands, prompted us to pull over at the town's Star Hotel. Jabba radiated heartfelt gratitude as he shut off his bike. I've seen that same look in the eyes of wounded kangaroos just before they're shot in the head as a mercy. He leaned his bike against a telegraph pole, dismounted and stared woefully at it.

It was not a pretty sight. The battery overflow hose had parted company with the battery and battery acid had sprayed all over the once-pristine paint of the rear guard. The acid had also eaten away the cardboard and all the oil escaping from the motor had found its way onto the back tyre. A closer inspection revealed that except for the magneto, all the bike's electrics had ceased working. The cause was easily traced back to the little metal box Jabba had made to house his electrics. With typical expertise, he had made it watertight. It worked like a charm – on contact with the box, water would enter it and stay there forever. The rear brake lever arm had also parted company with the bike near Kundabung and narrowly missed skewering Zorro's knee.

Jabba managed to retrieve the lever, but could not find the connecting arm. So half the braking capacity of his bike was lost. He consoled himself by telling everyone how good his ancient front drum brake was. It was a pity his bloated hands couldn't operate the lever to activate them, but I had a few anti-inflammatories in my bag, so there was still hope.

The Star Hotel sits on the banks of the Nambucca River, and is a beaut old verandah-ed thing, with a view straight out of Mississippi. We sat out the front, sipping beer and watching the river roll past and the afternoon sun coax steam out of the road. The rain had stopped and we could see Jabba squatting by his bike vainly trying to grasp assorted tools with his swollen hands.

Mark shook his head in disbelief. 'He's not gonna to make it.'

The rest of us couldn't help but agree. The evidence was irrefutable.

'So what are we gonna do with him?' Mick asked.

I had a suggestion. 'Nambucca Heads is only twenty kays away. How about we go there, kick on for a day or so and see how he pulls up?'

Ben instantly became a human leer. 'I've heard there's heaps of blonde, suntanned surfie chicks there who can't wait to stick something salt-free into their mouths.'

It was a clincher of an argument.

'I'll go tell Jabba the good news,' Zorro grinned.

Jabba was overjoyed. He was so overjoyed he immediately tore the baffles out of his coffee-coloured pipes, and declared his undying love for surfie girls based on the immutable fact that surfie girls were much cleaner than other girls because their pelvic regions were continually submerged in salt water.

'So how come you took the baffles out of your pipes?' I asked him as he limped over to the verandah.

'Surfie chicks get off on noise,' he winked knowingly. 'They dig the roar of the surf, the howl of the wind, the thunder of the thunder, the . . .'

'The death rattle of a Triumph?' Mark grinned.

Jabba waved one of his swollen paws at him. 'You've got no fucken idea!' he said, and stomped off to buy some beer.

He came back a few minutes later with a big blond bloke named Curl. Curl was clearly a surfie and Jabba had befriended him the moment Curl had asked who owned the white Triumph propped against the pole across the road. Jabba automatically assumed any reference to his bike was a compliment. Consequently, Curl found himself dragged across the road and subjected to a detailed lecture about the joy and wonder of owning one of England's finest motorcycles. I could see Curl nodding his head dumbly as Jabba wiped oil from various bits of his bike so that Curl could see the paint and gain an understanding of the skill required to ride such an uncompromising custom machine.

As payment for this courtesy, Curl invited Jabba and the rest of us to a party in Nambucca Heads that evening. He avowed there'd be heaps of 'lowies, ganja and music'. These food groups appealed greatly, so we quickly accepted and Curl gave us the address. Then he went on ahead to let the women know we were coming.

Some hours later, with the sun setting quickly, we decided it would be a good time to go to Nambucca Heads. Jabba had no lights and it was going to be dark very soon. And after several hours of drinking we all felt sexy enough for every surfie chick south of Coolangatta. With fantasies of long brown legs shimmering with coconut-scented suntan oil and tight little bottoms barely hidden by tiny bikinis firmly lodged in our minds, we set off for Curl's party.

Nambucca Heads is not very far from Macksville. It takes about three minutes to get there when you're hectically drunk and giving it heaps up the highway. Unfortunately, one of those drunks was riding a Triumph that had another agenda. Jabba was searching for the brake lever he'd lost earlier by the side of the road as the rest of us disappeared into the distance. How he found what he was looking for in the fast-fading daylight remains a mystery, but he did find it.

In the meantime, we had arrived at the Nambucca Heads turn-off and discovered we had lost Jabba. It was now dark and we knew he had no lights and no idea where he was going. For some reason, this struck us as immensely funny. We were all still helplessly cackling when Jabba emerged from the darkness behind us, one foot outstretched to feel for the edge of the road, wrap-around sunnies firmly attached to his face, and lips pulled back in a feral snarl against all the cars that had narrowly avoided wiping him out as he blindly slid and slipped along the highway. We actually heard him before we saw him. Without baffles the Triumph now sounded like an enormous bandsaw ripping through frightened scrap aluminium. We looked at him in utter amazement as he slid to a stop beside us, his misbegotten hands resting atop his handlebars, a sneer of pain-racked determination on his face. The Triumph's grating idle seemed to come from the oily mist that cloaked them both – and the headlights of cars whizzing past on the highway swam across the whole greasy chrome, paint and leather assemblage like some kind of strobing madness.

'Let's fucken go!' he yelled.

When we got to the party, it was obvious Jabba's mate Curl had set us up. Nobody at the house knew we were coming and no one had seen Curl since Davo, the owner of the party, had punched his lights out the week before.

Quite frankly, we probably would have left peacefully if asked. As a party, the whole affair was pretty dismal. There were only four girls there and three of them appeared to have more chromosomes than they needed. But Jabba didn't care about any of this. He dragged three of the four girls out to look at his bike minutes after we'd arrived. It was propped against the telegraph pole across the street, quietly leaking oil. The three girls had no choice but to listen to a lengthy diatribe on how badly screwed up the Australian roads were and how they had taken their toll on his magnificent showbike. The rest of us made ourselves comfortable near the ice-and-beer-filled bathtub and relaxed a little.

Off to the side of the backyard, I could see Jabba deeply engrossed in conversation with one of the girls.

'Looks like he might crack it,' I said, nodding my head in his direction. Mark gave Jabba and the girl a quick glance and went back to rolling a number.

'That's been cracked a few times before, I reckon,' he laughed, licking the joint closed and lighting it in one practised, fluid motion.

As he passed it to me, we saw Jabba put his arm around his

tubby, pimply and meaningfully drunk companion and steer her towards us.

'This is Bambi, blokes,' he announced. 'She wants to come back to Sydney with me.'

'What time you catching the train?' Mick asked.

'Not gown train,' Bambi slurred through her furry yellow teeth. 'Gown on th' Truf wiv Japper!'

'Who's Japper?' Ben wanted to know.

'It's "Jabba", babe,' Jabba hissed, nudging her softly and making her head wobble from side to side. 'She told me there's a disco in town. We're going to go and have a look.'

A few minutes later, we heard the Triumph's rattling belch as it accelerated towards the nearby shopping centre. As the noise faded, three florally attired blokes came up to where we were all sitting on the grass. Mildly befuddled with beer and dope, I remember thinking how very colourful they all were. There was a pink one, an orange one and a fluorescent yellow one.

'Have youse seen me sister?' the orange one asked.

A strange feeling began gnawing at the pit of my stomach.

'I don't think so, mate,' I said.

'She's only fourteen,' sniffed the pink one. 'And she's had too much to drink.'

'That's nice, but this is a party,' Mark slurred.

'Yeah, well,' said the orange one. 'I'm 'er bruvver and she's me sister, and . . .'

'And I'm fucken sure your mother wouldn't have it any other way,' Zorro smirked, standing up.

'Don't fucken talk about me muvver, right?' the orange one boomed. 'If you blokes know where Bambi is, you better . . .'

'Look,' I said, interrupting him. 'Why don't we go and see if we can help you find her?'

More people had gathered around this exchange, and the mood was no longer indifferently friendly. It was pretty obvious there was a lot of speed being snorted inside the house – the amount of sniffling and snorting was meaningful and familiar. There was no reasoning with people like this. They just needed a bit of time to work up the courage to get really unreasonable and I didn't want to give them that time.

'Let's go find fucken Jabba,' I said quietly to the others and we all headed out to our bikes.

'This is gonna get fucked real quick,' Mark said, looking over his shoulder.

I turned and saw the entire male contingent of the party gathering into one large group in front of the house.

'I've always wanted to do time as an accessory to child molestation!' Mick yelled angrily over the roar of the bikes as we thundered towards the Nambucca Heads shopping centre. Behind us, a small herd of amphetamine-fuelled surfies were doubtlessly girding their loins and preparing to pursue us. So it was probably wise to get to Jabba and Bambi before they did.

Luckily, Nambucca Heads is a small place and we didn't have to look very hard. As we pulled up in the centre of town, we saw Jabba arguing loudly with a couple of bouncers outside a large wooden doorway illuminated by flashing lights. Bambi was snoring noisily at his feet.

We parked across the road, and the bouncers took one look at us, stepped back inside the disco, and quickly shut the door in Jabba's face.

Jabba stared at the closed door for a second, shrugged, and stepping casually over Bambi, walked across the road towards us.

'What the fuck are you doing?' Mick demanded.

'I wanted my twenty dollars entry back,' Jabba shrugged. 'We were only in there for a few minutes and Bambi was sick all over herself, and . . .'

'She's fourteen fucking years old, mate!' I said. 'Her brother and a whole heap of his mates are very worried about her.'

'She'll be okay where she is,' Zorro offered, looking about with concern. 'They'll find her. Get on your bike and . . .'

He stopped mid-sentence as two Holden station wagons pulled up. It wasn't hard to guess who was in them.

We got off our bikes and met them in the middle of the street. It was like a cheap western movie, only with no cowboys.

'Your sister is over there,' I said, nodding at the loudly snoring, vomit-flecked body lying on its back outside the disco.

'You've raped her!' one of them screamed.

'No,' I tried to explain. 'She just threw up on herself and passed out in the disco. My mate just brought her outside for some fresh air.'

The assembly shifted its attention to Jabba.

'Look,' he said, holding up his hands in a peaceful gesture, 'we were just . . . Hey! Get the fuck away from my bike!'

Jabba had left his Triumph leaning against a pole outside the disco. And while we were talking, one of the blokes from the party took it upon himself to teach us rapists a lesson by kicking it over.

Jabba's warning howl came too late; the bike crashed to the ground and started leaking petrol.

The silence following the crash was total and ominous and similar to the silence that swallowed the world when the ocky straps finished beating Jabba in our garage back in Sydney. All eyes were now, once again, on Jabba. The colour had drained from his face and his fists were clenched so tightly they were trembling. The bloke who'd knocked over Jabba's beloved bike wasn't moving. He was frozen like a statue and Jabba's gaze was fixed on his throat. Unfortunately, some fifteen blokes stood between Jabba and the bike-knocker-overer.

As if by magic a motorcycle rear axle appeared in Jabba's hand, and a strange gleam lit his eyes. He took one step forward, showed the axle to the nearest surfie, who looked at it intently, and then Jabba put his lights out with it.

It was truly amazing what an effect that thirty-centimetre-long bar of tempered steel had on those salty boys. They ran around mindlessly, bumping into parked cars, gutters and each other, as Jabba strode after them, swinging the axle at anything colourful and dressed in board shorts.

It was over in less than two minutes and we were all left staring at each other in a silence punctuated only by puffing and the odd moan. It was now about 2 am and, truth be told, we were all rather woefully wasted. We had been drinking and smoking dope for most of the day and were close to becoming unconscious ourselves.

But not Jabba. He still stalked up and down the street looking for more idiots to axle upside the head. He found none so he went and axled one of the bonnets on the station wagons. Then he picked up his Triumph and leaned it gently back against the pole. The disco had not opened its door during the scuffle, but I had no doubt the people inside had called the cops. Bambi still snored peacefully on the footpath.

'I think we should fuck off,' Mark observed.

'None of us filled up,' Mick grunted matter-of-factly. 'We have enough petrol for maybe twenty kays.'

He was right. There were only two of us with big Fat Bob tanks. The rest of the bikes sported much smaller petrol tanks and they would be nearly empty.

'Well, we've got to go anyway,' I said. 'Listen.'

Sure enough, the wail of sirens sounded in the near distance. We fired up the bikes and, sandwiching a lightless Jabba between us, headed for the highway.

I will remember the next twenty kays if I live to be 200. Picture half a dozen drunks, one of them bloodstained and besotted with the thrill of recent battle, hurtling down the Pacific Highway at 50 kms per hour (we couldn't go any faster and still keep Jabba wedged between us) in the wee small hours of Christmas Day during a much-publicised police holiday-drinking blitz. We didn't know where we were going, but we knew we had to get off the road, at least until the booze wore off. The problem was where to hide six motorcycles on the busiest highway in Australia during the busiest time of the year.

'Where are we fucken going?' Mark yelled at me over the noise of the bikes.

I turned my head, but before I could answer, I saw Jabba's petrol tank lift off from his bike's frame and clout him in the face. In retrospect, I realised that serious injury eluded him simply because the tank wasn't full of petrol and only about ten kilograms of sheet metal and bog collided with his head.

Our speed immediately dropped as Jabba slowly rolled to a halt.

'Jesus!' Ben was off his bike in a flash. 'Are you okay, mate?'

Jabba's head dangled lifelessly from his shoulders, but we could hear the slow rattle of his breath. He was still sitting on his bike, swollen hands lamely grasping the bars, peanut tank on his lap and feet firmly on the road. Both his eyes were closed in what I assumed was some truly immense inner suffering.

'I think he's hurt,' Ben said, gently removing the tank from Jabba's lap.

'Are you hurt, Jabba?' Mark asked, prodding him.

'Gllrrgllrr,' Jabba gargled in reply.

'He sounds fine to me,' Mark declared. 'But he's not going any further tonight.'

'Besides,' Zorro said, shaking the peanut tank next to his ear, 'he's got no more petrol.'

'Hey!' Mick yelled from some bushes by the side of the road. 'Come look at this!'

Mark and I walked towards his voice and found Mick standing on a fire trail a few metres off the highway and almost parallel to it.

'A perfect fucken camping spot,' Mark declared with a grin. 'Let's get off the road.'

We rolled our bikes down the fire trail for a hundred or so metres. Jabba couldn't be persuaded to get off his bike, so Ben ended up pushing him, then going back for his own bike. Jabba was finally persuaded to dismount when Zorro picked him up and deposited his whimpering body on the ground. The rest of us lay down beside our bikes, exhausted. We were soon lulled to sleep by the ticking of the engines as they cooled and the mournful whimpers issuing from Jabba.

———

None of us heard the four-wheel-drive pull up the following morning, but we all came instantly awake when its door slammed.

'Merry Christmas,' said a deep voice. Even with my sleep-fuddled senses, I could detect a note of humour in it.

'Merry Christmas,' we echoed automatically.

I got slowly to my feet, feeling amazingly bad. The rest of the blokes, except for Jabba, followed suit and we all looked at our wake-up caller.

It wasn't the police. It was a middle-aged man dressed in work boots, jeans and King Gee workshirt. He was smiling.

'Had a bit of trouble?' he asked, looking at Jabba's bloody and comatose body.

'A bit,' I agreed. 'His petrol tank hit him in the face.'

'Is he all right?'

'He's okay,' I replied. 'Are you . . . um, after something?'

The man's smile broadened. 'I was going to feed my cows but I didn't want to drive over any of you blokes.'

We followed his gaze and saw a gate a short distance away. Beyond the gate was a field full of black-and-white dairy cattle. The tray of his four-wheel-drive was full of feed. It seems we'd stopped on the farmer's access road.

'Jeez, mate,' Mark sighed. 'We're sorry. We thought it was a fire trail. We only pulled off the road to get some sleep.'

'No worries,' the farmer grinned. 'You all look a bit second-hand. Would you like some coffee?'

We nodded gratefully and he produced a big thermos and two tin mugs. While the others were drinking and talking, I walked over to Jabba.

'Wake up, mate,' I said, shaking him gently. 'It's time to go.'

He moaned and pulled back his cracked and swollen lips.

'Come on. Get up.' I shook him a little harder. He looked really terrible and I didn't want to damage him any more than necessary. Granted, most of the blood wasn't his, but he still looked admirably repulsive.

He stared blankly at me, but eventually got up and started searching for a nut and bolt to reattach his tank. The rest of us imposed on the farmer's Christmas spirit and bought a jerry can of petrol off him before he left to feed his cows.

We then got out a map and figured our best chance of avoiding capture was to turn inland at the first opportunity, riding over the Great Dividing Range to Armidale via Bellingen and Dorrigo, a distance of just under 200 kilometres. As Mark explained, the University of New England was in Armidale, so there was no reason why we couldn't bathe in the intellectual sexuality of dozens of nubile girl-students hungry for a bit of road warrior excitement. It was now 8 am. All things being equal, we'd be having them for lunch.

At the mention of girls, Jabba immediately perked up.

'What are we waiting for?' he chirped and happily kicked his Triumph into life. It suddenly seemed as if his spirit had returned after a short holiday.

Our own spirits also started to rise as we turned off the highway. Our hangovers receded in the brilliant morning sun and the bitumen stretched before us like an endless trail of promises.

We rode past green cow- or vegetable-filled fields along a gently winding road. The chance and thought of police pursuit faded with the miles and we looked forward to a great day. Ahead of us lay Bellingen, then the Great Dividing Range and the steep climb into Dorrigo.

We suddenly noticed Jabba was no longer with us. I slowed down to an idle and waited for Zorro to catch up.

'You were riding last,' I yelled. 'Where'd he get to?'

'He kept looking at his back wheel and then he stopped,' Zorro shrugged. 'I was going to stop, but he waved me on. It's probably nothing.'

Impossible, I thought. There was no way it could be 'nothing'.

Just then, a petrol tanker went roaring past, airhorns blasting and lights flashing wildly. The driver was scowling, shaking his head and pointing to his temple with a finger. We watched him disappear around a bend.

'Jabba!' we yelped in unison.

We tore back up the road and found Jabba sitting on his Triumph in the middle of a field of cabbages.

'What happened?' Mark yelled at him from the road.

Jabba just closed his eyes, pointed to his rear wheel and began to shake uncontrollably.

We didn't find out the details of what happened until much later. It seems that when Jabba had pulled over to find out why his Triumph was wobbling so badly, he had discovered that his rear sprocket had sheared off all its holding bolts except one, and that one was loose. Bellingen wasn't far, so he tightened the remaining bolt as best he could and decided to ride into town. Unfortunately, as he was making careful progress at

20 kms per hour lest the sprocket depart the rear wheel, he discovered a petrol tanker bearing down on him from behind. The driver beheld Jabba at the same time and started madly gearing down and braking to avoid running over the top of him. Jabba remained staunchly in the middle of the road undeterred by the screech of rubber or the hiss of air brakes. He said he wasn't initially concerned about the truck because he knew they had great brakes. He only started to worry when the hissing stopped and he heard the truck accelerate. He became frantic when he looked over his shoulder and almost banged his head on the truck's bull-bar. The driver had obviously had enough of his 'I'm riding slow' shit for that day.

Jabba somehow managed to wind the ailing Triumph up to about 60 kms per hour, but the truck continued to pursue him too closely to allow him to pull over. He told us he felt he had two choices. He could either continue riding in this fashion until the truckie tired of the game and ran him over, or he could wait for a corner and keep riding in a straight line. With a bit of luck, the truck would probably not pursue him into the fields.

He soon found a suitable bend and launched himself off the road. After thirty crazed metres of wild bouncing and cabbage excavation, he ground to a halt. And that's where we found him.

'Can you get to Bellingen?' Mick demanded.

Jabba looked back at him dumbly. It was an impossible question.

'Because if you fucken can't, then you should set fire to the fucken thing right fucken here and then go fuck yourself!' Then he fired up his bike and rode off.

Jabba appealed mutely to the rest of us for support.

'Mick might have a point, mate,' I finally said. 'The bloody thing has been nothing but trouble since you got it. Do yourself a favour and torch it. It's possessed. You can ride on the back with me.'

Jabba wouldn't hear of it. 'I can fix it,' he declared. 'If I can get it into town, I can fix it.'

'You do that then,' Mark said. 'I'm going.'

We rode into town, parked our bikes and were finishing our second joint when a familiar sound broke the quiet Christmas morning.

'I don't fucking believe it,' Mick shook his head. 'He made it.'

Jabba made it all right, but not by much. His very wobbly sprocket kept spitting his chain off every 500 or so metres. Undeterred, he'd stop and put it back on, repeating this all the way to Bellingen – a distance of some fifteen kilometres.

Once in town, he faced the unhappy prospect of how to fix the problem permanently, or at least until we got back to Sydney. It being Christmas, Jabba began accosting people in the street, much like a medieval beggar, to whom he bore a remarkable resemblance. But his luck was holding out. One of the blokes he stopped turned out to be the town's Nissan dealer. After much waving of arms, soulful looks and nodding of heads, the bloke agreed to look for suitable bolts in his workshop.

We sat under the tree across the road from the Nissan dealership, sipping from Ben's thoughtfully produced bottle of scotch, smoking joints and watching Jabba dog the Nissan bloke's footsteps all the way up the street to the dealership. Eventually he emerged with five extra-long bolts and thirty-five washers to make up the space on the over-long bolts. He then retightened the sprocket, checked his oil level, frowned and went to bludge some oil off the Nissan bloke.

'I don't believe it,' Mick said again. 'The cursed thing has finally run out of fucken oil.'

Jabba topped up his oil, ran a final critical eye over his machine and pronounced himself ready to continue. He then kick-started the Triumph, which promptly emptied the newly added oil all over itself and stalled.

Jabba examined this development with interest. 'I probably overfilled it,' he decided, scratching his head. He stomped on the kickstarter and we set off for Armidale.

Halfway between Armidale and the coast is Ebor, which is really only a petrol station, a pub and a length of Armco to prevent people from getting too close to the edge of Ebor's one tourist attraction – Ebor Falls.

We filled up with petrol, had a few beers at the pub and decided to view this natural wonder. We started our bikes and waited a few minutes while Jabba entertained a coach full of Japanese tourists who insisted on being photographed posing with his bike.

'Are you coming?' Zorro yelled over the excited babble of Japanese and the click-whirr of expensive camera gear. Jabba nodded grimly and kicked the Triumph into life. The Japanese applauded wildly, as if they'd just witnessed a miracle.

A few metres past the pub we turned onto the road leading to the falls lookout. Jabba misjudged the turn and bounced off the road and into the undergrowth. We skidded to a halt and watched in horror because it seemed that his merrily leaping

Triumph was hell-bent on throwing itself over the cliff. Three metres from the edge, it ran into a large rock and stopped. Jabba stared at the edge and then looked back at us. We cheered loudly as the dust settled around him. Then we dismounted and went to look at the falls.

Five minutes later we were back on the road. Two o'clock saw us in Armidale. The temperature was well into the thirties and our bodies craved beer and shade. We found a pub that was open and left Jabba examining his bike, which had only broken six spokes and the headlight lens since leaving Bellingen. We sat in the cool semi-darkness of the trendily refurbished public bar and waited for the multitudes of horny uni students to leap on us. Jabba eventually joined us.

The morning's ride had swollen Jabba's hands to epic proportions and rendered them useless for holding anything. They were large, blue and puffy, like dishwashing gloves full of air. He ordered a beer at the bar, then realised he couldn't pick it up to drink it. In fact, he couldn't even get his wallet out to pay for it. Ben paid for the beer and got him a straw.

Conversation was sparse. We had hoped to spend the night in Armidale, replenish our supply of dope and maybe find some female company. Two hours of waiting and drinking later, Mark made a grim deduction.

'We are not going to get laid tonight,' he stated morosely.

'Why not?' Mick demanded.

'There's no fucking women here,' Mark explained.

'They might get here later.'

'I mean there's none in town.'

'Where the fuck did they go?' Jabba wanted to know.

'Where everybody who lives in the country goes for their holidays. Sydney.'

We were geniuses. Absolute geniuses.

'Tamworth's nice,' Ben grinned. In minutes we were back in the heat and heading for Tamworth.

We stopped at a small servo somewhere between Armidale and Tamworth for a drink. It was very hot and seemed to be getting even hotter as the afternoon wore on.

Jabba had now added a furious case of sunburn to his list of problems. Anybody who's done any long-distance riding in summer knows the value of a good sunscreen. Accordingly, we'd all anointed ourselves with scads of florally scented goo. Except for Jabba, who'd denounced us all as 'poofters', claiming real men had no need for such effeminate nonsense. He now had third-degree burns and incipient melanoma to affirm his manhood.

It was still broad daylight, still very warm and Jabba's luck was still holding out when we arrived in Tamworth about 7 pm. We located a pub with several Triumphs parked out front. As we pulled up, the owners of the bikes walked out to have a look. I knew immediately that Jabba had found three kindred spirits. They all had the same hunted, persecuted look about them, were uniformly grimy and their pockets bulged with tools.

The heat had turned Jabba's Triumph's oil into something the consistency and appearance of watery coffee. Consequently, it ran out through the cracks and holes in his motor at an even faster rate than before. Amazingly, every time Jabba inspected the oil tank, he'd declare there was 'still heaps'. Since the bloody thing hadn't yet seized, we had no choice but to believe him.

The three Triumph owners gathered around Jabba, nodding their heads and commenting on this modification or that alteration. Jabba sat astride his bike (there was no immediate place to lean it against), holding court and displaying his and the bike's injuries with the pride of a war veteran.

We accomplished our intended purpose of getting nauseatingly drunk by sundown and somehow managed to wobble a few hundred metres down the street to a large park, where we collapsed into unconsciousness.

The next morning we realised Jabba had stayed at the home of one of the Triumph riders he'd met at the pub. We had snored on the grass of the park like the reeking drunks we were, while the two of them had spent most of the night going over Jabba's bike and had seemingly fixed many of the issues – like the Triumph riders they obviously were. The holes in the motor had been sealed with new caps, various gaskets had been replaced and the rear end's sprocket issues had been addressed. The bloke had even given Jabba a thermos full of fresh coffee for us. We took turns sipping from the thermos and marvelling at Jabba's indomitable luck. For every catastrophe that beset him and his bike, a bizarre solution of sorts would ultimately present itself and enable him to carry on.

We were only some five hours away from Sydney, and it certainly looked as if Jabba's suffering was at an end. He had done it. He had almost completed our annual Christmas run. So by mutually unspoken consent we let him ride in front, and contented ourselves to ride along at about 90 kms per hour as we rolled out of Tamworth.

It was extremely fortunate that we did let him go first. Otherwise the exact location of Jabba's bleached and fox-gnawed bones might still be perplexing the search teams.

We had managed to make it almost as far as the Halfway Roadhouse on the Putty Road. We were still some 100 kilometres from home, but on comfortably familiar roads when it all went finally and irrevocably to shit for Jabba and his Triumph. He was happily riding in front of us when we heard his exhaust note suddenly change from a drone to a scream, just as we also saw his arms jerk upwards, still holding onto the handlebars. Of course, this is an action which is only physically possible when the two big bolts holding the handlebars to the top triple clamp above the forks fall out. So Jabba went from being in control of his bike, to being in control of his handlebars, which were now only linked to the bike by the throttle cable. And because he had instinctively pulled the bars upwards when they came loose, he had jerked the throttle wide open, which allowed him to spear straight off the road and into the scrub at about 120 kms per hour.

The ensuing crash proved to be the straw that broke the Triumph's back. It also broke Jabba's arm. So there was no question of him making any attempt to rebuild anything that afternoon.

Mark and I made him as comfortable as we could, and used some sticks and four of the many ocky straps lying around amid the wreckage to immobilise his arm. Zorro, Mick and Ben rode for home to get the ute. There was an unspoken agreement about not involving ambulances and cops. None of us would have welcomed the scrutiny their attendance would have provided. There were bodies in Nambucca Heads we just didn't want dug up.

'Well, you almost made it, mate,' I said, sitting beside him as he reclined against the trunk of a large tree, his face an interesting combination of pain, satisfaction and determination.

'Yeah,' he sighed. 'Almost.'

'Come on,' Mark grinned. 'It was a great run. We're going to remember it forever.'

'That's right,' I added, putting a consoling hand on Jabba's shoulder. 'No one remembers runs where nothing happened. This one is legendary. Everything that could happen, happened.'

Jabba nodded silently, more in consideration than agreement.

'And don't worry about the bike,' Mark said, his arm indicating the dinged and grimy wreckage sitting between the road and our tree. 'You'll get some money for the wreck and get yourself something . . . um, else.'

I knew he had been going to say 'decent', but had thought better of it.

'No,' Jabba shook his head. 'I'm going to rebuild it.'

Mark and I could only stare at him in silent awe. He was beyond us. He had transcended his base mortality and had morphed into something entirely supra-human.

'And I'm going to paint it black,' he muttered through his pain-clenched teeth. 'Black as the devil's soul, black as the midnight sky, black as the ace of spades . . .'

And of course, he did do just that.

JAM TO JUPITER'S

*I first wrote about this event in 1996, the year it happened. It was
slated to appear in the launch issue of RALPH magazine, and the
editor was wet about the nethers with excitement about the yarn and
the publicity it would doubtlessly generate. I was more concerned
about how many years I would spend in prison for not only organ-
ising and participating in an insanely illegal road race, but then
also having the temerity to brag about it in a national magazine.
My concerns proved to be groundless. The story was pulled at the last
minute when various advertisers starting shrieking about the subject
matter. Bitches.*

```
'Conquering any difficulty always gives one
   a secret joy, for it means pushing back a
 boundary line and adding to one's liberty.'
```

HENRI FREDERIC AMIEL

It was a hell of an idea.

A number of motorcyclists would gather at a given place in the Sydney CBD on a Friday evening. If you were one of them, you would have paid 100 dollars for the privilege. Then, at exactly 6 pm, a man would shout 'Ready, setty, GO!' and you would run across the road to where your motorcycle was parked, jump on it and ride about 925 kilometres to Jupiter's Casino on the Gold Coast. Through the night.

If you were, by some bizarre twist of fate, the first to arrive at Jupiter's, you'd collect $2000 for your efforts – a not inconsiderable amount of money given the average Australian wage in 1996 was around $30,000 per annum. People have had sex with farm animals for less.

Then, if you were fortunate enough to win the cash, the richly hedonistic atmosphere of the Gold Coast would work its sorcery upon you. Perhaps you would find yourself drinking beer off the floor and chasing naked whores around dank nudey bars. Perhaps you would burn the whole wad on the flip of a card at one of Jupiter's many gaming tables. Or perhaps the cops would take turns anally raping you with a police-issue baton for getting drunk and chopping down the ornamental palm trees on Cavill Avenue. Anything could happen after an event such as this.

Just as anything could happen *during* an event like this. A Cannonball Run–type dash through the night from Sydney to the Gold Coast on high-powered motorcycles is an order of magnitude riskier in every way than, say, trying to kidnap one of Sea World's dolphins.

Especially since there were no rules. Rules would only have made the Jam to Jupiter's less appealing and more complex, so they were dispensed with. High appeal and wholesome simplicity. And massive testicular fortitude. That's what it was all about. And I made sure the advertising I booked in a few motorcycle magazines reflected this.

Predictably, the advertising made the New South Wales Police profoundly and deeply mental. In fact, the cops were very upset *and* deeply mental at the same time. Which is not how I like them.

That they were in this highly agitated state of profound discontent was obvious by the way they kept driving up and down in front of Harry's Café de Wheels half an hour before the Jam's start, all bitter and twisted with their guns gleaming and their surveillance cameras bristling.

I had chosen Harry's as the departure point for our Le Mans start because a) it was a Sydney icon; and b) it was packed with peak-hour traffic. So it would be easy for some of the interstate entrants to find, and the traffic would hinder the cops if they chose to mount any kind of pursuit or make an attempt to seal the road.

So there we all were at 5.30 pm. The cops and the fifty entrants, watching each other watch each other.

The cops were obviously gathering further 'intelligence' to go with the 'intelligence' they had already acquired, which had informed them that exactly 300 to 500 outlaw bikies aided and abetted by several promiscuous women were all manifestly up to no good. Furthermore, that these bikies, all maddened by industrial-strength methamphetamines and riding stolen motorcycles, were planning to conduct a Cannonball Run race–type thingy and distribute the aforementioned methamphetamines in the process. This was pretty major shit as far as the cops were concerned. There could well be the odd high-speed pursuit in the offing. And maybe even some overtime.

Exactly how fifty people, most of whom had never met before that day, were meant to distribute drugs while simultaneously engaged in racing their bikes through the night was never explained to me when I met with police after the event, but as far as they were concerned that was the deal. And it all looked downright nasty to them.

So as the starting time crept relentlessly closer, the cops watched us, and we watched them watching us and wondered what bubbling pit of noisome shit I had dropped us all into. Even I was starting to wonder what the fuck I had done. It had seemed like a great idea when me and my best mate, Brother Silverback, had come up with it a few months before. Sure, we were a little drunk and not a little crazy at the time, but how can a motorcycle Cannonball Run *not* appeal to any human male with a functioning man-gland? Of course, we weren't dumb enough to state it was a race in the advertisements we had bought in the motorcycle press, but no one was fooling anyone in the months leading up to the event. It was obvious what was going on here. The motorcycle media had rubbed itself into a bit of a rash, and there were moans from some conservative quarters about how events like this would only bring motorcycling into disrepute and that I was driving yet another nail into the coffin of motorcycling respectability.

Brother Silverback and I, however, had never equated 'motorcycling' with 'respectability' and I was vaguely insulted that anyone would. The only reaction of concern to me was that of the NSW Police Force. But it was very slow in coming. We did not hear a squeak from the police until three days before the start.

'You cannot give out 2000 dollars cash for the first rider to arrive,' came the advice from the Police Traffic Branch. 'And you can't give out any prizes for the most speeding tickets.'

'Oh? Really?' I replied. 'Why not?'

'Racing on public roads is illegal.'

'And rightly so,' I agreed. 'This isn't a race, but.'

'Well, what is it?' the spokes-drone from the Traffic Branch demanded to know.

'It's a rally . . . um, except we're all leaving together and at the same time.'

'No one is allowed to win!' the spokes-drone shrieked.

'I understand that. But according to certain immutable laws governing our universe, and with careful and due regard to sections of the *Traffic Act* which forbid motorcyclists to ride fifty abreast on public roads, even if we all leave at once, it follows that someone has to arrive at Jupiter's first.'

'So it's not a race?'

'Certainly not. That's illegal. We would never do anything illegal.'

'You must inform everyone of that.'

'Already done it. We've told everyone it's not a race.'

'Tell them again.'

'No problem.'

'We will be watching.'

But they did a little bit more than just watch, as I discovered not long after kick-off.

However, they were still only watching at 6 pm, when 168 centimetres of poisonous sex princess went hot and live. Blaze, a *Hustler* magazine model whom I knew and had co-opted to start the Jam, certainly gave us all something to look at. She stalked into the middle of Cowper Wharf Roadway in killer fuck-me heels, a skin-tight top and tiny leather shorts, and waved a little Aussie flag at the grinning riders assembled in front of Harry's. Immediately, in a classic Le Mans start, all fifty riders began waddling across four lanes of slowly moving traffic to their bikes, which were parked across the road.

And then it was on.

I still hold it to be a miracle most of us weren't made into roadkill in those first frantic seconds. Luckily, Blaze the sex princess was the focal point for both car drivers and cops that evening. Understandably, given she was standing in the middle of the road with the waxed edges of her reproductive organs peeking cheekily out from her shorts. And as the cars slowed to assess them and the cops focused their cameras on them, we fifty road warriors hit the road.

Drivers in the Sydney Harbour Tunnel were quite suddenly treated to an international array of freshly fuelled two-wheeled weaponry hammering madly past their car windows – closely pursued and eagerly awaited by what seemed like every single cop that had ever crawled out from under a mossy rock. But I am getting ahead of myself.

Right then, everything from long-haul custom Harleys delicately punted by scowling dealer mechanics, to shit-hot Honda Fireblades straddled by mysterious Greeks with cobras painted on their helmets, was getting out of Sydney in the most efficient way possible, and heading north. There were 250cc slingshots smelling of screams and two-stroke terror; nasty big Cosworth Triumphs made out of carbon fibre and ridden by long-haired priests malodorous with bourbon; great electronically enhanced Suzuki Cavalcades with 'Grow Old Disgracefully' stickers on their panniers and Pavarotti on their stereos; ultra-fast ZX750 Kwakas piloted by future World Superbike champions who'd arrived from Brisbane five minutes before the start and were now riding straight back the way they'd come (these two blokes frightened the shit out of me); late-model BMWs bristling with uber-designed Teutonic technology; old bikes, new bikes and bikes that were much faster than they looked. In short, the entire gamut of Australian motorcycling was engaged in this glorious folly and heading north with conviction.

And then there was my own personal riding rig. It had been created one manic night in Brother Silverback's garage, amid a welter of half-eaten pizzas, cold beer, sweet-smelling joints the size of brickies' thumbs, and four cans of matte black spray-paint. It was dubbed The Hezbollah Express that same evening, for reasons more to do with us all being catastrophically stoned and addled by paint fumes, and less to do with any sympathies with the Palestinian cause. And it was utterly matte black. Only the headlight, the blinkers and the instrument cluster remained not black. The rest of it was like a light-sink. Underneath all the blackness, it was a 1980 R100S BMW with a slightly warmed motor, twin 100-watt spotlights appended to the little bikini fairing, and a forty-litre Heinrich petrol tank that gave it a range of more than 550 kilometres. Most bikes have the fuel capacity to do between 200 and 300 kilometres, which means the rider is only in the saddle for about two hours. So there aren't many riders out there who can or even want to ride non-stop for six hours straight. But there was going to be one that night, and boy, was I ever pleased with myself when I set off! I'm so fucking clever, I thought, hurtling down the Gore Hill Freeway astride the motorcycling equivalent of a supertanker. I've got the rest of these blokes buggered. I got away in second place because I waddled across the road faster than most, and then I saw the bloke in front of me getting booked just the other side of the Sydney Harbour Tunnel. This meant that I was now in front and because I don't have to stop for petrol until I hit Coffs Harbour, I was a fucking genius.

But ten minutes after the start, the long night and whatever horrors it might hold was not even a consideration for me. This was because The Hezbollah Express had, in a bid to get a jump on the pack, turned left, and was now being ridden haphazardly through the back alleys of Artarmon by one dumb, wrong-turn-taking, no-attention-paying twat. Me. I still would have looked hell cool, but I was lost in Artarmon. And that was not fucken cool.

When I found the highway again, I realised I didn't know where the fuck I was in relation to anyone else. Cursing continuously in three languages, an ability that has served me very well over the years, I headed north, weaving steadily through the traffic. My eyes twitched madly from the road ahead to the road behind as it was reflected in the bike's mirrors. I could see no cops, and I could see no bikes. And this struck me as very strange. I kept my speed to a shade over the posted limit, and breathed a sigh of relief as I finally turned onto the freeway.

I was almost to Newcastle before something on two wheels passed me. It was the Greek guy, who I'd learned was from Melbourne. He had arrived at Harry's about an hour before the start in a rented truck. The truck held his bike, his girlfriend and two mates. His mates wheeled out the bike, a hot-as-hell Honda Fireblade, while he shook hands with me and said this was the greatest idea he had ever heard of. He showed me his totally illegal portable radar detector that lived in a pocket of his leathers and explained how it had an earpiece that made the cops think it was attached to a Sony Walkman whenever they stopped him. He struck me as a man who had every intention of getting on his motorcycle and riding flat-out until he either got to Jupiter's Casino, or the cops ran him down like a dog.

As he went past, he shook his head in disgust. Like me, he had been through two 'random' breath tests – one at Ourimbah and one at the northern end of the freeway. And while I had been breath-tested rather disinterestedly both times, I was photographed and recorded on a clipboard with much more enthusiasm.

Then, just as I was rejoicing a little as I saw the Greek bloke pull in to get petrol just north of the Hexham bridge, Werner went sailing past me at about 160 kms per hour.

Werner was immediately interesting to everyone at the rider's briefing just before the start when he asked what, if any, impact his 2500 dollars of outstanding traffic warrants might have on his journey, and what, if anything, he should do about them.

'Pay them now,' was the excellent legal advice proffered by a lawyer I'd brought along for the occasion.

'Fuck that,' said Werner, and went to confer with his pillion, Paul – a fellow he had brought along solely for his amazing ability to roll joints while on the move.

Werner was astride an ancient Kwaka 1100 shafty he'd bought specifically for the ride. He'd last ridden a bike some ten years before when he was a tank-driver in the Austrian army, which may have accounted for why Paul looked a little tense and peaky on the back. Of course, the fact that Werner also had a tendency to overtake everything on the left-hand side, whether there was bitumen there or not, was also probably not helping.

Happily, Werner stopped for fuel at Raymond Terrace and I wafted by, snickering and patting the monstrous Heinrich tank. Then I got stopped by the cops at Raymond Terrace for yet another 'random' breath test. And again at Karuah. And once more at Bulahdelah, but just then Werner howled past us at what I deemed a very thoughtful speed. So while he was explaining himself to Highway Patrol car No. 76, The Hezbollah Express and I motored on. But I still had no idea where I was in relation to the other forty-seven riders. The Greek was still behind me, as was Werner. No matter. Mathematics was on my side. I could and would ride for 500 kilometres without stopping. All of them would be passed at some stage. All of them would taste the bitter tang of defeat and know that mathematics and BMWs are not to be fucked with.

And then it started raining and it got very dark. I fishtailed my way through the Bulahdelah Mountains, twin spotties aflame, alone with the trucks and rain. It rained harder. I squinted as the rain needled my face, and sucked a little moisture from the bandanna shielding my mouth. Fuck it, I thought. I have wet-weather gear. I should probably put it on.

I pulled into the servo at Nabiac and was immediately surrounded by six Highway Patrol cars that came whooshing in as the rain continued to hammer down. I'd passed them setting up a breath-testing extravaganza a kilometre back, but they paid me no mind because it was raining. Now they came swooping into the servo like soggy schoolboys from a teeming playground.

I was pulling on my rubber overboots as they folded themselves out of their cars and started bitching loudly about the weather, and how it had prevented them from fucking up our drug-dealing bikie shit.

Then one of them noticed me, huffing and puffing and hopping around one of the bowsers wrestling with a recalcitrant overboot.

'Doing a bit of camping, mate?' he asked, mistaking the giant roll of Jam T-shirts wrapped in my swag for camping gear.

'Yep,' I nodded, grinning like a retard. 'I sure hope to, officer. Pity about the weather.'

He nodded, glancing at the downpour. Then a light came on in my head. *He doesn't realise I'm part of the Jam. None of them do. They're looking for outlaws distributing drugs, not soggy fools on black BMWs.* The arrival of yet another police car confirmed this.

'They're comin'!' leered the very senior officer at the wheel. His triple-striped sleeve was soaked, but he still had it hanging out his window so everyone could tell at a glance he was the Fleet Admiral.

'Geddout and get 'em!' he said, waving to his assembled minions. They all left just as the Greek pulled in for juice. I left as he was filling up, shaking his head and glaring at me like I was to blame for everything. I noticed he didn't have any wet-weather gear. Ha! I thought, rolling out into the downpour. Suffer, you fast-riding, radar-detector-toting cunt.

Things got deeply ugly after that. I was pulled over in Purfleet, ten kilometres out of Taree. Once again I was randomly breathalysed and photographed and had my details recorded. I was pulled over again just before the Taree bridge over the Manning River and randomly breathalysed once again. More photographs of me and the bike were taken and more of my details were entered on a sheet of paper.

Oh just fucken fuck this, I thought.

'Why are you photographing me, officer?'

'It's standard breath-test procedure,' he replied.

'Yeah?'

'Yeah.'

'Then you won't mind if I take your photo too?' I said, pulling a neat little camera out from under my jacket.

'What are you fucking doing?' he shouted and took a step backwards.

I clicked the shutter and he turned his head as the flash lit up the area around us.

'I'm taking a picture of a sworn officer of the Crown in the execution of his duties,' I parroted.

'You can't take my picture without my permission!' he thundered.

I grinned. 'But you can take mine?'

'If that picture appears in any magazine anywhere, I'll . . .'

'You'll what, officer?' I said, suddenly amazed at the size of my testicles, which were now bathing in a lake of icy rainwater inside my pants. Fuck him, I thought, but then figured he might take it into his fool head to shoot me for being a smartarse. His hat was on pretty tight.

'I'll take action!' he hissed and waved a threatening finger in my face.

He *is* gonna shoot me, I thought. Then I noticed Werner pulling up behind me, yelling something about 'More bullshit cop harassment!' Hooray, I grinned. There was no way he was going to shoot me now. But he might well drum a few into Werner.

The police officer gave me a lingering look of pure hatred and went off to do Werner over. I rode away, wondering for the first time if this whole Jam thing was such a good idea after all. Still, it wasn't like I could call it off now.

I was stopped again fifty kilometres later, just outside of Kew. Thankfully Werner got to them before I did, having passed me at about 180 kms per hour just outside the town, so they quickly breathalysed me and got on with the entertaining business of doing Werner for speeding, arguing and speaking with an accent.

I skulked into Fat Albert's Legends café and servo which was fifty metres up the road from where Werner and the cops were yelling at each other, parked The Hezbollah Express and dismounted into the waiting lens of my mate Donk, the event's official photographer.

'How many bikes have gone by?' I demanded, as Donk rattled off some shots.

'You're the first thing on two wheels I've seen in three hours,' he grinned.

Great shitting Jesus. I was winning. Mathematics ruled! But I was feeling a little frenzied and fey. The cops had frayed my already jittery nerves. I just needed to stop for a bit and assemble some of my mental shit. It dawned on me that I was not yet in jail, so I felt a celebration of sorts was in order.

I celebrated with Donk, who had a fat joint rolled and ready to share. Then I celebrated with Werner, who came in cursing the cops in gutter German and demanding that Paul roll more joints. When the pair of them left, Paul swaying visibly on the back, I celebrated with the Greek.

An hour-and-a-half later, I had welcomed and subsequently waved off about twenty-five fellow Jammers, all of whom were now on the road in front of me. Incredulity and horror at the massive police action we had all been subjected to was bright in their fevered eyes. But there was also a hard glint of determination to finish this run, no matter what.

I left Kew convinced it was going to be a big night. I was right. The ensuing eight hours (it took me just over twelve to reach Jupiter's) went rather quickly, as they do when you ride with a purpose. They were also redolent with some amazing personal tales.

Some of those involved appalled truckies, one of whom spoke to me as I stopped for a stretch in Coffs Harbour. My arse was burning and my eyes were stinging with tiredness.

'Mate,' he said to me as I stomped and wriggled in the truck-stop we were sharing. 'I've been driving this road for twenty-four years and I've never seen so many bloody cops in all me life! Just what the fuck are you blokes up to?'

I was the picture of smiling innocence. 'We're just going for a ride,' I told him.

Other Jammers later recounted awesome riding duels through the hills of Ballina in the cool half-light of dawn. I personally chased one bloke on a Ducati who needed to have The Hezbollah Express's Teutonic black supremacy asserted over his rattling Italian garbage. I rode like a fucking crusty-eyed god after that bastard and I pursued him relentlessly and with great skill. I would have caught him too, had I noticed that he'd turned off somewhere, and I'd actually been chasing nothing but my headlight for about fifteen kilometres.

There were tales of yellow motorcycles being chased by the Highway Patrol through sleepy hamlets at speeds in excess of 220 kms per hour. But the priest with the yellow Daytona felt that these were obvious lies, since police cars didn't go that fast.

Still others recounted the astounding police exploits. Things like the cops sneaking up behind riders with all their lights off, then pressing all the buttons at once and filling the universe with 12 billion megawatts of searing electricity and sirens as the freshly blinded rider tried not to crash into a gum tree. Another frequent occurrence was to pull over riders and invent offences they could not possibly have witnessed, but were obliged to write infringements for anyway. And sometimes their intellect was so overpoweringly sharp, my guts roiled with fear and despair under its edge. Like when I was pulled over near Macksville. The squat young buck wearing jodhpurs questioned me at length over a speeding offence he was convinced I had committed. Mind you, he hadn't seen it and was not prepared to show me the radar readout he was quoting.

He just 'knew' I had been speeding. Then he spent several minutes waving his Maglite around his head and shining the light in my eyes.

'What colour is that?' he demanded, running the beam from his torch over the totally matte black Hezbollah Express.

'What colour would you like it to be, officer?' I said wearily, wide-eyed with horror that someone so intellectually endowed had been issued with a loaded firearm. My jaw was hurting a lot, and I was in a foul mood. The last 200 kilometres had been done with me holding my licence in my mouth and spitting it out at the endless supply of cops that kept stopping me every fifteen minutes or so.

He glared at me as if to judge which part of my skull would crack best under the onslaught of his baton. Then his partner nudged him and he refused to discuss the matter any further, concentrating instead on correctly filling out my speeding fine. And he still managed to put the wrong date on it.

I later learned that one lone rider braved the New England Highway (on a 250cc two-stroke, no less) and he regaled us with equivalent tales of persecution, which was much worse than we could comprehend, given that the 200-odd cops on the New England only had him to play with.

Many were the stories from that night. Police with chafing erections roamed free, and shit was happening, at speed, along those highways after midnight. Two blokes didn't manage to finish. One shredded his tyre before Newcastle and retired gracefully. One filled his pants with the shit of fear after being hunted like a dog by the cops, and hid himself in a sleazy motel near Taree until the morning.

Werner was arrested in Murwillumbah for his unpaid traffic warrants, but had almost enough cash on him to pay them off. He somehow managed to talk the police into driving him to the nearest ATM where he withdrew enough money to cover the outstanding amount, so they let him go.

Personally, I don't think I was ever more relieved than to see Jupiter's colossal casino rearing up on my left that November morning. It even gave me a slight fat, I think, but that could have been just because I badly wanted to wee. You get like that after being subjected to more than twelve hours of the most odious police harassment in the history of history. Now I could finally have a wee and shed the unmarked red XR8 pursuit car that had dogged my back wheel since Brunswick Heads.

I pulled into the car park, fell to the ground as I got off my bike, and was greeted with a ragged though hearty cheer. I was the twelfth rider to arrive.

The fifty participants had been stopped a total of 297 times, with myself scoring ten stops, four speeding tickets and one overtake on double yellow lines. My licence was something I had when I left Sydney. It would be suspended as soon as the fines were resolved.

The winner of the run was the Greek guy on the Fireblade. His time, given the circumstances, was an astonishing eleven hours and forty-two minutes. I was forty minutes behind him. The truck carrying his girl and his mates arrived a few hours after he did. As his mates loaded his bike, he shook my hand and thanked me for the ride of a lifetime.

'How did your radar detector go?' I asked.

'It was working really well. I got warning beeps five times before Port Macquarie. Then the earpiece fell out and I got nailed the other side of town.'

That night, when the Jammers had assembled at a nudey bar called Santa Fe Gold for the prize-giving and babe-ogling, I drank heavily. Everyone drank heavily. I think we all felt a little battle-scarred and battered. But also rather chuffed with ourselves, especially Werner, who came third. This was no small thing we had just, successfully, done. No one had died and no one was in jail. Certainly the night was but a pup in that regard, but as far as the ride itself was concerned – happy fun-time success. Not many motorcyclists get to race almost a thousand kilometres through the night, then party with an assortment of writhing strippers.

Me? Well, I'd blown several thousand dollars of my money in prizes and traffic fines. Getting drunker than a pirate and sticking money into a girl's G-string was the only way forward. Over the next few months I would be involved in a series of court battles and letter-writing campaigns to the then Police Commissioner, Peter Ryan, which culminated in a bizarre meeting with the head of the Highway Patrol, me, my lawyer and the State Ombudsman.

Nothing ever came of that meeting, and the police would not explain why their intelligence was so far off the mark. They really *had* expected several hundred bikies to rampage up the coast selling drugs, using the Jam as a cover for an orgy of nefarious narcotics peddling. It never even dawned on them that the Jam could be real. It simply did not compute that a bunch of motorcyclists would race 1000 kilometres through the night for shits and giggles and on the off-chance they'd win a couple of grand. They clearly didn't understand motorcyclists. Which was not surprising.

What *was* surprising was the fact that I did another Jam to Jupiter's the next year. Only that time, the winning time was seven hours and twenty-three minutes.

Not a single police officer attended.

(

THE WRONG
WAY DOWN

*My body still shits cramps whenever I even think about this ride. I
was no longer young, strong and crazy. I was middle-aged, thickset
and angry. I had no business attempting a ride like this. I had no
dirt-riding skill, or even any particular inclination to acquire any.
But I still pulled on my boots and went. If you get why, no explanation is needed. If you don't, no explanation is possible.*

```
'Bite off more than you can chew
      and then chew like hell'.
```

PETER BROCK

The plan was, in essence, quite simple. Which is probably why
it went to bastard shit so spectacularly.

Dave, Ian, Mick, Miles and myself were going to ride to
Phillip Island from Sydney. But because it was important that

we all felt especially super-duper about the trip, it was decided that we would eschew bitumen, and make the trip using only the plethora of amazing dirt tracks that separated Australia's premier city from Australia's premier racetrack.

It was to be a journey of around 1200 kilometres over some of the most beautiful and brutal terrain the Great Dividing Range has to offer. The five of us had three days to make the attempt.

But at the end of three days, one rider was in hospital with a truly horrific injury, two bikes were unrideable, no bike was undamaged, and I felt like I'd been pack-raped by drugged-up grizzly bears.

However, as we sat around Mick's house planning this epic man-odyssey, drinking beer, yodelling our determination and beating our mighty chests like Vikings before a raid, we decided there were only two major problems impinging upon our collective awesomeness.

Our biggest problem was how to acquire the motorcycles to make the trip. We all had road bikes, but they were simply not up to this kind of nonsense.

It turned out to be not that big a problem after all. Basically, I just went and asked for them. And on the strength of my working relationship with the magazine *Australian Motorcycle News*, and my evidently brilliant bullshitting abilities, three separate motorcycle importers very generously lent Ian, Mick and me the bikes for the trip – a Suzuki DR650, a Honda Transalp and a BMW F650 Dakar.

There were two other crucially important members of the team, but they were somewhat higher up the adventure-riding food-chain than us, and so had no need to borrow motorcycles.

The alpha-predator on the trip was Miles, BMW Motorrad Australia's marketing manager, and a dirt-riding instructor of some renown. Miles had readily agreed to come along (probably to ensure the Dakar wasn't abandoned at the bottom of some ravine), and was to ride a fully loaded and appropriately dubbed BMW GS1200 Adventure.

The last, but certainly not least, of our party was Dave, the expedition's vastly experienced dirt-riding guide, who was riding his personal well-kitted-out KTM 640. It was Dave who planned the route and it was Dave who was to lead us south.

Ian, Mick and I quickly and easily agreed on who was to ride what, since it is not dignified for grown men to squabble like fishwives over borrowed motorcycles, no matter how much beer has been consumed.

Mick was allotted the BMW on the basis that he'd once owned a BMW dirt-bike, knew what to expect from such a beast, and had some dirt-riding experience. Ian scored the Transalp on the basis that he'd worked for Honda in a past life and had more dirt-riding credibility than Mick or me, and should therefore be given the most street-oriented bike (and thus the most difficult to manage in very rough terrain) to pilot. And I secured the Suzuki DR based on the fact that I had lots of tattoos, was dangerously crap at riding on dirt and should therefore be given the easiest-to-ride-in-rough-bits and most dirt-oriented bike of the three.

These proved to be amazingly prescient choices.

Our second-biggest problem was the lack of contiguous dirt between Sydney and Phillip Island. No matter how many maps we threw around Mick's cavernous planning room, or what order we arranged them in, the conclusion we reached was the same. It is simply not possible to get to Phillip Island from Sydney without having to traverse some bitumen – about 300 kilometres of it, in fact. That left us with about 900 kilometres of dirt to do – much of it apparently benign and easily manageable. But some of it looked so revoltingly difficult and heartbreaking it made my head spin with nausea.

Dave had ridden sections of the planned route, so we had to be guided by his vast experience on this venture. To be perfectly honest, I was completely indifferent to whatever route was ultimately chosen. When you're really crap at riding a motorcycle on the dirt, what possible difference could it make where you crashed?

Both Ian and Mick nodded in agreement when Dave explained that the route he was considering was 'challenging' but should not prove too daunting for a motorcycle rider of my experience.

I was going to ask, 'What experience? Did you not just hear me tell you that I ride dirt like fat people ride rodeo bulls?' but decided it was pointless and kept my mouth shut.

Dave took the maps home, and when we met the following week I was presented with Das Route. It was highlighted on a contour map, and came with several of Dave's notations. I had learned to read such maps in my youth, and as I examined this one, noting the thickly clustered contour lines along our route and Dave's considered observations, I felt a little ill. What the fuck had I agreed to do?

The answer was spread out before me.

We were to meet at Wisemans Ferry West Crossing at 6 am on the day of departure. This was the ferry one caught to cross the Hawkesbury River in order to ride to the old St Albans pub – a popular Sunday beer-and-lunch spot for lots of Sydney's motorcyclists. But we weren't going to St Albans. We were turning left immediately after the ferry crossing and heading up to the Putty Road, then down a dirt road to cross the Colo River on some old wooden bridge that had been built by convicts a thousand years before Sydney got electricity. From there, we'd head up into the Great Dividing Range, to Bilpin and Mount Wilson via the Bells Line of Road and onto the Bowens Creek track – which, according to the knot of contour lines, was nothing but a narrow path cut into the arse of a great sandstone cliff with a surface designed to murder the stupid novice dirt-rider with immense malice.

We would then proceed off the range to Hartley Vale, on a surface which was a mixture of slightly less murderous dirt and broken bitumen, for an early lunch at the roadhouse in Little Hartley on the Great Western Highway.

After filling our bellies with cheap carbohydrates and bad caffeine, we'd hit the Coxs River Road to Hampton – a section that had been marked as 'fast' – and which I understood to be a place where I would crash at a much higher speed than I was comfortable with. Then, if I had not been airlifted to hospital, it would be back onto life-affirming bitumen to Jenolan Caves.

And this was apparently where the really awful shit started. The vile Kanangra Walls Road, which winds down to the deeply nasty Kowmung River Crossing before proceeding back up the range along some more 'fast' dirt through vast hectares of

191

glorious sternum-crushing pine forest, and into the small town of Taralga, where we would stop for fuel.

This was to be followed by about two hours of some very technical navigation, along many kilometres of immensely dusty and loosely packed dirt track until we hit the Hume Highway. We would then cross the highway and ride very, very fast along 'beautiful dirt' for twenty kilometres, until we arrived at the historic town of Collector, which sits beside the Federal Highway as it winds into Canberra.

We were then to sleep the sleep of the righteous and not-dead at the Bushranger Hotel, and be up at 4 am the next morning for Day Two. A day which had already been dubbed 'big' – as in the chances it provided for me to die.

Day Two was to begin with fuelling up, then following the bitumen through Canberra and out onto the Cotter Road to the Cotter Dam. But before plunging into the waters of the dam, we intended to turn right onto the Brindabella Road – which I saw came with its own handwritten aside for me to absorb. The aside said: 'You will die on this road if you do not pay attention and take it easy. It is steep, twisty and if you make an error, you'll plummet off a cliff and into one of the most beautiful valleys in Australia.'

Should I somehow make it to the bottom on two wheels, I would notice that Brindabella Road met Crace Road on a bridge over the Goodradigbee River. Ten kilometres further up, we would turn onto Boundary Road, then Forest Drive, Broken Cart Track and the Long Plain – which had been marked on the map as twelve kilometres of 'super-fast open plains dirt' – and a place I could crash the bike at velocities I had never even dreamed of.

We would then emerge, in my mind's eye like Morlocks from a cave, onto the smoothly bitumened glory of the Snowy Mountains Highway and head to Adaminaby for fuel. Then it was all normal tarmac to Jindabyne, Thredbo, Dead Horse Gap and finally a little bit of dirt to the Tom Groggin river crossing. Once across the Murray River, we would be at Tom Groggin Station and the beginning of the Mount Pinnibar Track – which had a hand-drawn exclamation mark beside it. I didn't know precisely what that meant, but saw with some dismay there was a ludicrously steep seventeen kilometre climb which appeared beyond the abilities of even the raunchiest four-wheel-drive to attempt. Then I was either having an IV drip attached by a para-medic, or riding the Mount Hope Road, which leads to Mount Anderson.

Should I be fortunate enough to summit this peak, I would then get to crash my brains out on a very rocky and sharply twisting timber trail that led off the range and onto yet more 'fast' farm roads, before I finally arrived at Omeo for fuel, sleep and weeping with relief.

The route for Day Three was somewhat more enigmatic, since there was no map, just some written instructions at the bottom of the map I was looking at. Apparently, there was to be a measured dash up the Cassilis Road, then onto the Upper Livingstone Road and the Birregun Road to Dargo. We would fuel up at Dargo for thirty-five kilometres of some 'very tight and twisty' dirt to the base of some feature appallingly dubbed the 'Billy Goat Track' and the longest vertical road-climb in Australia – 1200 metres of elevation in a scant seven kilometres (Mount Pinnibar rises 1200 metres in a much more reasonable seventeen kilometres) and on to Licola for fuel. We would then head to Rawson down the side of the Thomson Reservoir, cross the dam and head for Erica and ultimately petrol at Moe. Then it was all bitumen to Phillip Island.

I folded up the map and went home, feeling exactly as a man condemned to death by his own stupid bravado would feel.

———

Two weeks later, I stood on the banks of the Hawkesbury River at Wisemans Ferry staring silently into the early morning gloom. I was filled with bright excitement and grim foreboding in totally unequal amounts. The gear I was wearing felt alien, as did the Suzuki DR650 that was to be my companion over the next three days.

I was early, because I am always early for bike runs. It's how I am. Usually, I'm pacing restlessly as I wait for everyone else. This time, I just leaned on the bike and stared at the slow-moving river, my mind ablaze with discursiveness.

I really had no business pretending I was a dirt-rider. I wasn't. I wasn't even the odour off the shit of a dirt-rider. And my mouth was made dry by this knowledge. I sucked savagely at the tube running from my Camelbak, swallowed greedily and listened with some abstraction when I finally heard my companions descending the steep switchbacks into the river valley. I hated them all. Pricks. Vastly experienced dirt-bike-riding pricks.

When we had assembled at the ferry landing, the vibe was completely different from our normal road-riding meet-ups. The trepidation was palpable. And it all seemed to be connected to me.

Miles and Dave were all smiles and business, checking their gear, and looking at the maps. Ian and Mick were likewise full of cheer. But I kept wandering off to squirt tiny amounts of fear-piss onto the weeds by the side of the road, and it's not like no one noticed me taking a leak every few minutes.

I didn't feel any better when our support vehicle turned up. The sight of Dino, Al and Steve ensconced inside Dino's trailer-towing Land Rover only reinforced the profound seriousness of this venture. I suddenly felt I needed to have a shit but clenched my buttocks until the feeling went away.

In practical terms, there was very little actual 'support' on offer from Dino and the blokes in the Land Rover. They carried no back-up gear and were only on hand to pick up any bike and/or rider unable to continue. One of the requirements we'd made of ourselves was that we would carry everything we needed with us. There would be no truck full of food, tools, spares, doctors, lawyers or whores dogging our trail. But since none of the bikes actually belonged to us, we had to have a way to get them back to civilisation if it all went pear-shaped. Neither BMW, Honda nor Suzuki would smile upon us if at the end of the trip we gave them the coordinates of where one of their bikes had been left, rather than the bike itself.

'We should go,' I rasped, my voice betraying how I felt rather more than I would have liked it to. We promptly geared up, crossed the river on the ferry, and turned left onto the dirt.

Miles was immediately up on his pegs, on the gas and gone into the distance. Dave was just in front of him and leading the way up the rocky, but relatively stress-free track. Mick was making a vain attempt at keeping up with the two pros, and Ian and I brought up the rear.

I knew Ian was watching me as much as he was watching the track, and I was making every effort to look like I knew what I was doing. I didn't and despite many attempts to imitate Miles's carefree stand-and-deliver riding style, kept lowering my fat arse onto the seat each time I was uncertain of the terrain – which was every fifty metres or so.

Still, it didn't stop me enjoying the scenery that unfolded around me as we climbed and descended and climbed again through the series of sandstone-hedged valleys that surround the Hawkesbury and Colo River basin northwest of Sydney. We eventually popped out onto the Putty Road, rode down it a kilometre or so, turned left and began our descent to the Colo River and the old wooden bridge I remembered from the map.

We stopped on the other side of the bridge to deal with our first equipment failure. Ian's pannier had come off a few clicks back and almost took Mick out, so while Ian buggered about reattaching it, Miles asked me how I was doing.

'Pretty good,' I lied. 'I struggled a bit coming down that last bit, but all up, I'm coping.'

In reality, I had been struggling the whole way. Dirt-bike riding had little in common with riding on the road. I like my bike to be glued to the bitumen, not skittering and sliding and lurching like a horse on an ice rink.

But at least I looked the part. The jacket that dirt-riding legend Geoff Ballard had so kindly donated to my cause was a marvel of dirt-riding technology. The overpants Geoff also supplied likewise worked a treat when worn over my enduro strides and gave me a funky homeboy look . . . until Miles told me to zip up the bottoms so I wouldn't look like an utter twat. He also advised me where the strap of my goggles should sit at the back of my helmet – not at the bottom of the lid where I was in the habit of putting it, but around the middle just like the pros.

Newly enriched with Miles's styling tips, I set off after the others via the climb to Mountain Lagoon and finally the Bells Line of Road before plunging back onto the dirt and the back way to the hidden hamlet of Mount Wilson.

It was warming up and the climb was not difficult, though it was no longer very friendly to anything but a road-trail motor-cycle. A road bike would have failed this stage. Lots of large loose rocks and some tight stuff that was corrugated enough to give your fillings a bit of a shake-up, but other than Ian's pannier coming off again, I was left to enjoy the scenery and wonder for the umpteenth time if my crap dirt-riding skills were up to the trip. If it was all like this, I thought, I should be okay provided I don't get cocky and start pretending I'm a Dakar racer.

We stopped at Bilpin, shimmed Ian's rattling panniers up with pieces of a plastic iced coffee bottle and hit the spectacularly scenic Bowens Creek track that would take us to Mount Wilson. I also picked up Miles's mobile phone from the forecourt of the servo, and briefly considered transferring all of his girlfriends' numbers into mine, but the technology defeated me. Instead I tucked in behind the pack as it turned left and just tried to keep up as we hugged the sandstone cliff, moving into the thicker scrub on the other side of the valley and began the gentle ascent to the Mount Wilson picnic area. We stopped there, all smiles, and ate lollies like little kids while Dave pissed a little on my happy parade when he advised me that the journey thus far had only been a gentle introduction to the challenges that lay ahead.

Our path now lay along the Bells Line again, as far as the little track that leads to the bucolic Hartley Vale, then briefly out onto the blacktop of the Great Western Highway and a hot pie at the Little Hartley roadhouse. All still well within my limited dirt-riding competencies.

At the roadhouse, my hunger was such that I virtually inhaled the pie. In fact, I was to get into the habit of inhaling all my food over the subsequent days, like some kind of organic sludge vacuum. I learned to eat for nourishment rather than taste and in any case our schedule and route didn't allow for leisurely lunches in comfortable restaurants.

The Land Rover crew caught up with us, but we left them eating, and under the admiring glances of two hefty German backpacking fräuleins who described us as 'Sehr schön' set off for Jenolan Caves via the Coxs River Road. This also proved to be easy and undemanding dirt, but I was still unable to spend much time standing up on the pegs and wondered if Miles was wearing some form of leg-bracing shit under his gear. The only time his arse touched the seat was when he rolled to a stop to gently tell me to fix my goggles or to giggle at Ian and his rattling panniers.

We hit the bitumen again about forty clicks before Jenolan Caves and wound our way down the vast and amazing limestone cave entrance that spits you out at Caves House. Evidence of eastern Australia's longstanding drought was everywhere: the stunning turquoise stream that usually flows beside the cavern's entrance was dry and there was only a little water visible upstream. Ian's petrol tank was also kinda dry and we adjourned to the car park above Caves House so he could siphon some out of the seemingly bottomless tank of my DR – a procedure he would undertake with some regularity as the trip progressed.

While Ian refuelled, the rest of us gazed at the thirty-odd Ferraris that had also arrived in the car park. I immediately noticed a distinct lack of hot, high-bottomed blonde babes among the passengers. It would seem that another one of my long-cherished beliefs was to be smashed upon the rocky foreshore of reality. Blokes who own Ferraris are clearly quite leathery old farts with correspondingly blowsy fat hags for wives – which is probably the Road Gods' way of making us all feel better about ourselves.

The next bit was the Kanangra Walls Road to the Kowmung River Crossing. We were now into relatively more serious dirt, complete with metre-high spoon drains encroaching on the tracks, but did that slow Miles and Dave down? Did it shit. I grew used to Miles appearing a metre above me with both wheels of the huge GS over my head. As he passed me in mid-air he'd tell me to turn my blinker off. The ease with which he rode that big bike astonishes me to this day. The ease with which I subsequently crashed doesn't astonish me at all. It was inevitable. 'Dirt' rhymes with 'hurt' for a reason. I was going relatively fast and had a bad moment on a bend which I managed to somehow save more through luck than skill. I got straight back on the gas lest I be deemed insurmountably gay by my riding companions, and trowelled it into the undergrowth three corners later.

There's a lot to be said for full body armour. Just ask me. I'll talk your fucking ear off about its protective beautness. I'd torn a hole in my pants at the knee, but was otherwise unscathed apart from a slight twinge in my back. Suitably chastened and sweating like a brute, I carried on and very soon rolled down a very steep spoon-drained bastard of a hill and up to the Kowmung River Crossing.

Dave had already scouted it and advised us that the best path was between two big rocks in the middle of the ten-metre-wide stream, which had to be exited at something near full noise because of the steep bank on the other side. Failure to do so would result in you stalling, possibly rolling backwards and drowning in the Kowmung River like a sack of puppies. I stood on the bank and surveyed my doom.

Mick, who was polluted with a goodly dose of giardia that gave him the runs, went to spray some rocks with his illness, as I kept gazing at the stream and telling myself that it really didn't look very deep at all. There was a drought on and the rocky bottom was clearly visible, so how bad could it be?

As I watched Miles power through the ford and stall short at the foot of the opposite bank, it hit me that the Kowmung was about four times as fucking deep as it appeared.

'I think it may have sucked some water in through the airbox,' Miles yelled, half at the GS and half at us. Having apprised us all and blazed the trail, he fired up the big Beemer and flung it up the bank to drip and tick on the opposite side. I went next and bounced and lurched my way across and up the other side – simultaneously marvelling at my apparent water-crossing skill and my waterproof socks. I parked and watched as Ian got halfway across and stalled with water up to his petrol tank. He instantly fired it up again and came heaving out of the water – a testament to both Honda's engineering skill in building water-proof bikes and his own determination not to drown like a rat in front of his mates.

Across the other side, I saw the Land Rover had caught up. Steve and Al took some pictures, as Mick demonstrated a violent and altogether more splashy way to cross a river, rode through a small bushy tree on the other side and emerged dripping water from everywhere like a breaching whale. Dave was last and crossed with the dignity and panache only a man of his dirt-riding skill could. As Ian wrung out his socks and we prepared to move on, Dino was across the river yelling stuff about how high he thought he could bounce the trailer before it landed on the Land Rover's roof, and some other stuff about us all being bike-riding bastards and how it was not right that he should drive while we rode. His words were drowned out by us riding off in the general direction of Taralga.

For reasons I'm not entirely sure of, I began to apply myself with a will and made conscious efforts to stand on the pegs for as long as possible. The winding, smooth dirt road to Taralga made this easier than it maybe should have been, and I found the bike tracked and steered a lot better. Miles might have something there, I thought, standing tall on the pegs like a medieval ship's figurehead, my feet locked straight, my arms loose and funky. I suddenly had much more control and wasn't having my spine pounded into powder by the ruts and bumps.

With his small tank, Ian had concerns about making the distance to Taralga, so as the others hared off ahead, I tucked in behind him with my Suzuki supertanker. Sure enough, less than two kilometres from the town, his Transalp gasped its last and no amount of shaking and shimmying provided any more go-juice. Ian coasted to a halt and fished the empty juice bottle from his pannier. I parked the DR beside him, lit up a durrie and basked in the glow of the afternoon that embraced the gentle rolling plains outside Taralga. The country was open farmland and the road thus far had proved to be very rideable and only mildly challenging to a klutz like myself. I was feeling good about me and the world, and the fact that all I could taste was dust and sweat. I was actually riding to Phillip Island on the dirt and I was quite inordinately pleased with everything.

With a half a litre in the Transalp's guts, Ian fired it up and we coasted into the town and a proper petrol supply. We now had some very fast dirt ahead of us, which provided lots of dust. Combined with a setting sun into which we were riding and a profound feeling of tiredness, I was surprised that the pace increased. But it did.

The final run into Collector was a navigational nightmare. All fast, loose dirt and roiling storms of dust for anyone behind the lead riders – which meant Ian, Mick and me. But there was also the added bastard of lots of crossroads and turn-offs, so we quickly adopted the second-rider-must-wait policy and thus leapfrogged our way to the highest point of the Southern railway, about fifteen kilometres from Collector. There was a farmer there and a few other locals who'd gathered at the railway crossing after hearing about our exploits on the local radio. How the local radio got wind of our trip I do not know to this day, but it would seem that riding a motorcycle to Phillip Island from Sydney on dirt roads was of passing interest to country people.

'How far to Collector, mate?' I asked one grizzled old son of the soil.

'About ten miles,' he smiled, pointing at the dirt track on the other side of the railway tracks. We blinked the dust from our eyes, licked it off our lips, belted across the railway line and made for Collector at a rate of speed that in hindsight was truly frightening.

I was actually horrified much later when I remembered myself riding so very much faster than I'd ever ridden before. The dirt was smooth and white with long straights and gentle bends . . . and, well, testosterone got the better of me. Ian said later that he thought I was riding well above myself and of course he was right. I was on the razor's edge of control as I chased Mick, who was rather pointlessly chasing Miles and Dave, but I was standing up on the pegs like a pro and my goggle strap was in the right place. I even believe my blinker was off for the most part. The sunset was bathing my world with misty gold, galahs were flying off the road and I was in a zone that was completely new to me. I felt great and right and powerful – audacious in a way I'd never felt before. My mouth, nose, eyes and soul were full of dust, but Mick and I were both hollering like kids as we hammered into Collector for what was, up until the following Sunday night, one of the best-tasting beers of my life.

The Bushranger Hotel was our digs for the night and the publican was brand new. It was his first night there after years running some pub in Sydney and he made us feel very welcome.

Later that evening, as the rest snored happily in the dorm upstairs, Al and I were sitting on the steps outside busily engaged in sipping dry a bottle of Wild Turkey we'd bought over the bar. To my great delight, my mate PJ arrived from Canberra on his red-and-white Honda and joined us on the pub's steps that frigid evening. PJ wouldn't drink with us because he had to ride back, but we swapped some tales and told some stories until the power of speech deserted Al altogether and I figured that three hours of sleep would just have to do me as well. I bid PJ a fond farewell, and lugged Al up the stairs to put him to bed.

I shat richly and happily in the toilet and showered quickly as tiredness started to set in with a vengeance. I then fell into a bed that was more akin to a hammock, only to find Mick bellowing at me the instant I'd closed my eyes.

'Come on!' he yelled. 'It's four am, we have to go!'

Damn good thing I'd tucked the almost empty bottle of Turkey in Al's snoring arms before I put myself to bed, or he'd be shaking me even harder, I thought. I struggled to my feet and started to dress myself. I knew no one had shat in my mouth because I'd been hungover before and I was on familiar ground, but my head was sore and murky as I squirmed into my boots.

'Good job,' Ian grinned as he watched me curse and mutter and search for my wallet and phone which had somehow found their way under my mattress. 'I always get pissed on good whiskey before riding 400 kays of really difficult dirt,' he observed.

'Yeah, me too,' I growled back and swallowed some gooey spit that tasted rather more like some liquefied internal organ than I would have liked. Then I went downstairs, got on my bike in the frosty darkness and headed for Canberra along the Federal Highway.

I love Canberra. But not for reasons you may share. I find it a most beaut place to take my wife for a weekend of chest-thumping moose-sex. Nice hotels, attentive staff, and a general atmosphere of benign indifference where a man can take his woman out dancing even if she's dressed in two hankies and fuck-me heels, and not have to knife-fight all night.

Other than that, the place is beautifully roaded for late-night racing and all of the tracks seem to lead back to Parliament House or the sex-fest that is Fyshwick, so getting lost is not an option.

As I idled through the early Saturday morning traffic I was reminiscing about the last time my lady was channelling Jessica Alba for me on a coffee table inside one of the Canberra Hyatt's suites. It was all I could really do, because I could certainly no longer ride a motorcycle properly. All my bastard shit hurt. My helmet ground into my thudding skull and the rest of my body throbbed with a strained ache I'd only ever experienced the morning after a big fight with angry bouncers. As I sourly burped my way past the Mount Stromlo turn-off and the bitumen got twistier, my riding skills deserted me altogether. I must have been about a kilometre behind as I saw the rest of the crew turn off onto the dirt and head up into the Brindabella Ranges. The DR, its knobby tyres and I just could not get it together.

'Fuckshit,' I chanted over and over as I lurched and yawed up the winding track that had the traction of greasy kitchen lino. The dirt was hard-packed, but heavily peppered with shiny buried rocks that caused the bike to skitter alarmingly from side to side. I couldn't stand up on the pegs because I was too busy hanging on for grim death and it was getting colder the higher I climbed. Yesterday afternoon, I had been planning on entering the Dakar. Today I was planning on throwing up in my helmet.

Eventually I arrived at the top, and found everyone waiting for me. I got off my bike and sat down in the dirt. I was cold, miserable and whiskey-ill.

'Did you see my pannier lid?' Ian asked.

'No,' I shook my head. 'Did you leave it somewhere for me to find?'

'Funny bastard,' he grunted, jumped on my DR and shot off down the hill only to return ten minutes later with the lid tied to the back. While he busied himself refitting it to his panniers, Dave adopted a serious look and beckoned us all closer.

'Blokes,' he intoned sombrely, 'we are now going to descend to the Goodradigbee River along this road. You must be very, very careful here. There is no room for error. Absolutely none. Screw up a corner here and you won't stop until you hit the valley floor a kilometre beneath you.'

I pushed my galling helmet back onto my head, scraping off another layer of skin on my cheeks and settling the helmet against the pain-filled lumps it had created around my skull the day before. Part of me hoped Dave was just being dramatic. Another part of me knew he wasn't. I mentally made the sign of the cross – even though my arrangement with God has nothing to do with my believing he actually exists.

We rode off: Dave and Miles in the lead, Ian behind them, then me and Mick. I think Mick was riding shotgun on me in case I chose to die, and while I appreciate his gesture, I can't help but wonder how he planned to prevent me sailing into oblivion. I did stop on the very steep and rock-strewn descent, but it was only to marvel at the scenery. A literal kilometre below me, immense wooded valleys undulated off to both my left and right. They were partly submerged in low cloud and looked like nothing of this Earth. The air was sharp and cleaner than air has any right to be, and weak sunlight lent the whole vista a distinct otherworldly appearance. I was captivated and paused to take it in several times on the descent. Dave was right. If you took this road for granted, it would kill you. But if you took your time and picked your lines, the descent was far more spectacular than frightening. Nevertheless, his warning was timely and well heeded. At the bottom, we paused for a few pictures at the little bridge over the Goodradigbee and I saw signs indicating we were entering the Kosciuszko National Park and wilderness areas.

'It's not too bad from here,' Dave informed us, obviously pleased we'd all survived the descent. 'Just mind the ruts; it's been raining and there may be a few soft spots.'

The scenery just got more spectacular as we wended our way deep into the national park. We weren't exactly banging along, but we weren't hanging around either. Some of my skills had returned and I was standing on the pegs most of the time and starting to look fifty metres ahead – rather than staring fixedly at the track a metre in front of my tyre – and pick my lines with some success. Then I went over a slight rise and into some deep muddy wheel ruts some bastard in a four-wheel-drive had left behind. The bike's front wheel went into one rut, the back wheel into another and I found myself travelling sideways at about 20 kms per hour. I was also screaming, but I don't think anyone heard me over the sound of the revving motor.

'Nofrontbrakenofrontbrakenofrontbrake!' my inner-Borrie yelled and I listened. Somehow I made it through and toddled off after Miles, a big shit-eating grin plastered over my face. Of course, had I been paying more attention, I would have seen that both Miles and Dave had ridden around the ruts and saved themselves a challenge. I then realised I was riding on my own and stopped. It does not do to be riding on your own in the scrub – ever. I waited and eventually Miles and Dave rode back.

'Where are the others?' Dave asked.

I pointed behind me and they rode back the way we had come. I turned and followed and soon found myself back at the wheel ruts I had conquered. Mick hadn't conquered them, and was busy picking up pieces of his BMW from the track and holding his hand. I stopped my bike, eased myself off, and went to look at his paw. It was swelling quickly and had a large bruise forming in the palm. It was either broken or dislocated, but there is so much of Mick and he is such a determined human being, I doubted anything short of full decapitation would've stopped his trip. We shared the broken bits of BMW around (a pannier and a front guard), strapped them to the bikes, and headed off once again – still further into some of Australia's most glorious wilderness.

I elected to ride last, concerned Ian was going to run out of petrol sooner rather than later, but as I rounded a big bend I was suddenly stunned to see all of the bikes stopped ahead on a slight incline, with a motionless rider in the middle of the track. It was Dave. The other blokes were either kneeling or standing around him, so I pulled up and clumped my way up the hill (one cannot run in dirt boots) to see if I could help.

Apparently, a wallaby had come out of the scrub and taken Dave's front wheel out. He was doing about 60 kms per hour when this happened and his fall was very hard. Dave wasn't moving, but he was conscious and in stupendous pain, if the noises he was making were anything to go by. The headlight, instruments and levers were smashed on his KTM, which otherwise looked rideable, but certainly not by him. We later discovered he had broken his humerus clean across the ball-shaped bit that fits into the shoulder socket. That ball of bone had floated off behind his shoulder and the jagged remainder was stabbing into the vacant socket.

This was all sorts of fucked. We were truly in the middle of nowhere and our back-up truck was in Canberra being repaired (which was the last message we had before losing all mobile phone coverage), so there was no salvation from that quarter.

It's only in such extreme moments that you realise what your mates are made of – and mine are made of very fine stuff indeed. No one panicked, no one plunged into despair, and no one did anything except what needed to be done with an absolute minimum of fuss and with total purpose. All of us had had extensive first-aid experience and we did it by the book. Dave was going into shock, so I quickly stripped off and covered him with my riding gear. Mick was kneeling by him, speaking gently and evenly, assuring him he'd be all right and ensuring Dave could feel physical contact. Miles had Dave's signal-free satellite phone out and was planning to ride until the phone found the damned satellite or the damned satellite found the phone, and Ian was busily unpacking all the first-aid gear we had. Then Miles rode off and the three of us set about working out what injuries Dave had and how we could alleviate the pain of any of them. Dave wasn't bleeding that we could see, and his pulse was fast, but regular. I'd also located his Emergency Position Indicating Radio Beacon (EPIRB) and activated it. It 'eeped' reassuringly.

Dave was also eeping, but far from reassuringly. He was in great pain and it seemed to be his arm that was the main cause, though he did manage to pant out that his neck was also hurting. We didn't want to move him but the way he was positioned – head pointing downhill and half on his side – was maybe exacerbating the pain. Still, at least he was fully conscious and relatively lucid. He was well into shock now and becoming irrational, so Ian began to gently talk him through the craziness, and to see if we could get him to move his feet downhill so we could make him more comfortable.

It was probably Ian's tone that had more effect on Dave than anything else, and bit by bit, inch by inch, the big fella moved his legs so they were facing downhill. We put a sling on his arm and combined it with a folded jacket to take the weight off the injured limb. We then asked Dave if he thought he could sit up. He didn't think he could immediately, but if we were to help him when he got his breath back, he might give it a go. As we waited for Dave to collect himself, Miles rode back.

'I got through to triple zero,' he said. 'But they'd already got the EPIRB signal and said there should be a chopper here within the hour.'

I could see a collective sigh of relief run through us all at that moment. Help was on its way. Dave must have been encouraged by the news and said that he'd like to try and sit up. We arranged the loose pannier from Mick's BMW behind Dave's back and propped it with a rock to keep it from sliding when he put his weight on it, then Ian, Miles, Mick and I gently levered him into a position where he could recline against its smooth surface. This process made Dave scream – but screaming men are still breathing men, so I drew a little comfort from this. We next cut his Hydrapak off his back and gently removed his helmet. We figured this was okay to do because he was moving his head freely and only complained of a little pain in that area. But we did immediately put a neck brace on him and secured it around his neck with, of all things, an Andy Strapz luggage strap. That he was still in profound pain was obvious, but he was certainly now more comfortable. We even gave him a lolly and a small sip of water to occupy him until the chopper arrived.

On the dot of fifty minutes from when I activated the EPIRB, we saw the chopper in the distance making a beeline for us. None of us waved like you see in the movies. The chopper arrived and began to hover above us, assessing the situation. It then started circling and looking to find a landing spot. I realised this was an utter impossibility. We were in the middle of a billion acres of tall timber and the biggest and nearest clearing wouldn't have been ten metres across.

We then witnessed what Paul, one of the paramedics, told us was the longest rope descent they'd ever done – a stunning eighty-five metre rappel to the ground. As Paul made his way up the hill towards us, I went down to meet him and grab the big gear bag that he'd descended with. The other paramedic, Mark, was then descending with the stretcher.

What immensely good-natured and competent blokes these two turned out to be. Mark cheerily offered to inject some backbone into Dave for the forthcoming trauma of finding a vein for a cannula so that litres of happy drugs could be administered more efficiently, but there was also some humour as Dave's top-of-the-line BMW Savanna jacket parted like paper under the blade of Paul's rescue knife.

'I told you I would have given you a hundred bucks for that 'cos they were gonna cut it off,' Ian declared sadly. 'It would only have hurt a bit if we took it off.'

'But it's Kevlar . . . and Gore-tex . . . and armour . . . and . . .' Dave puffed, then went suddenly quiet as Mark pumped him full of morphine.

'It's now a bunch of rags,' Paul grinned, folded the knife up and started to assemble the stretcher. In short order, the paramedics had Dave trussed up like a Christmas turkey and we were lugging him down to where the chopper would drop its lift-line. Mark gave him another shot of something that was to keep him placid and calm on the journey up to the chopper, locked himself to the stretcher and gave the thumbs-up to commence the extraction. Paul was next on the line and the four of us stood as one and applauded them as they flew off. I don't know if they saw us clapping, but we could do no less for these incredible people. If we had women with us, we would have given them over freely.

The silence that surrounded us after the chopper left was complete and profound. There was only the wind soughing unremittingly through the trees. One of our party was gone and a poignant reminder of his comforting and competent presence was a shredded jacket and a smashed motorcycle. We re-geared in that silence. I don't know about the others, but I was quite shaken up by this turn of events.

Miles had found a crossroad about three kilometres up the track and he and Ian relay-rode Dave's KTM up to it. When they returned, we all saddled up and rode there to stash Dave's bike and gear, plot the position on one of the GPS units so the Land Rover could collect it at some stage, and work out what to do next. We were now about four hours behind schedule and the whole trip suddenly had a dark and altogether shit-filled cloud hanging over it. There was no question but that we would continue. Surrender was not an option and Dave would have been very disappointed had we thrown in the towel. I was just working this through my head while Ian and Miles were stashing the damaged KTM behind a stand of trees, when I noticed several bees buzzing around me. I looked to my left and was horrified to discover about a thousand beehives not five metres away.

'Blokes,' I peeped, my voice reedy with primal fear. 'Blokes . . . um, I cannot fucken be here.'

'What's wrong?' Mick asked.

'I don't get on with bees. If I'm stung, then the men in the chopper will be making another trip out here.'

'Piss off outta here then!' Ian yelled, and I did just that.

Mick followed me and we made our way about five kilometres down the track and pulled up at another crossroads to wait for Ian and Miles to finish their business. As we sat there, I saw a sign on the track to my left. 'Long Plain 15 km' it read.

'Weren't we supposed to ride something called Long Plain today?' I asked Mick, who was prodding his busted hand with a finger.

'I think so,' he blinked. 'Why?'

I pointed. ''Cos it's in that direction.'

Mick rifled about in his jacket and produced a map. 'This says we should stay on Boundary Road and go straight ahead.'

We decided to wait for the others, who duly arrived and we began to compare notes, maps and GPSs. One GPS stated we should go straight ahead. One GPS stated we should turn left. The third GPS informed us we were floating in the sea fourteen kilometres off Bribie Island. We put that one in a bag and looked at our maps and notes. One map agreed with the first GPS that we should go straight ahead. The other, along with our notes, said we should make for Long Plain, but didn't mention anything about any turn-offs to Long Plain. The bloke who could have settled this was probably being levered out of the helicopter and transferred to a stretcher as we sat and pondered the charts he had prepared for us.

We took a vote, pretending democracy was meant to work in a situation like this, and agreed to go straight ahead in the hope this road also eventually spat us out at Long Plain. It didn't. And some fifteen kilometres later my inner compass told me we were heading north, when we should have been heading south. We were actually on our way back to Canberra.

The others didn't take much convincing. We quickly performed a U-turn and headed back towards the crossroads with the Long Plain sign. I later learned this U-turn would utterly confuse the champions in the Land Rover who were dogging our route. Unfortunately, Dino, Al and Steve had been reduced to following our tyre tracks by sight as they searched for us, because *their* GPS told them they were just north of Adelaide.

We rode back to where we'd rendezvoused earlier, turned left and were regaled with a technical twisty and rocky track for almost exactly fifteen kilometres. By now I was standing on the pegs and carving corners like I'd done it my whole life. I felt good and the bike felt right under me. I was still miles behind Miles in terms of ability, but was having no difficulty getting the bike to go where I wanted it to. Miles even gave me a hint about the accursed spoon drains. 'Roll off the throttle as you come up to them, feather the clutch and let the momentum carry you up and over, and then gun it a bit . . .' Before long I was actually looking for the humpy bastards and my progress was much smoother.

Suddenly the trees cleared and we found ourselves in an immense open area with massive power cables running overhead – this was Long Plain and we were no longer lost. We turned off our bikes, ate some muesli bars and lollies, and Ian rode around a bit on Miles's GS as we discussed our position. We were now around six hours behind schedule. It was 4 pm and we only had about an hour-and-a-half of day-light left. There was no chance of us climbing Mount Pinnibar or going anywhere near Omeo, which was to have been our overnight stop.

I wasn't quite sure what we were going to do right then, but I still had lots of petrol, water and lollies, some sardines and a big fuck-off knife in case a *Lord of the Flies* scenario began to manifest, so I wasn't too concerned. I was also radiant with self-confidence – hugely misplaced, given what later transpired. But at the time my balls were the size of moons.

Then, to my immense surprise two four-wheel-drives emerged out of the scrub to our left and disgorged their drivers.

'G'day, Miles,' one of them said. 'What brings you out here?'

'Just riding around with these blokes,' Miles grinned.

It turned out that the drivers had done one of Miles's dirt-riding courses and were out for a weekend with their families in what I was now thinking was a very small world indeed. They then asked us if we knew who the three blokes were in the silver Land Rover with the bike trailer. We admitted that we did indeed know them. But how well we knew them would depend entirely upon what crimes they stood accused of.

'Christ, that bloke was on fire up there,' said one of the drivers, inclining his head back the way he had come. 'He passed us doing about 90 fucken miles an hour. Then he pulled us over, asked if we'd seen any bikes, then took off again like a mad bastard when we said we hadn't.'

That would have been Dino. We later learned that Dino had heard via his CB radio that one of us had crashed in the wilderness, slammed the bonnet shut on the mechanic's head in Canberra and hightailed it for where he thought we might be. As he, Al and Steve roared around the alpine wilderness looking for us, they stopped at the beehive intersection and Al spotted the bike in the scrub. They quickly assessed it was Dave's, then Dino kicked bits of it straight and Steve got kitted up to ride it out, since they figured they could all go faster if there wasn't a bike on the trailer. They then followed our tyre tracks for a while, but that all went to shit when they missed the fact we had doubled back. The blokes in the two four-wheel-drives had come across Dino as he was howling through the bush looking for us in some kind of crazed search pattern.

We had a quick meeting and decided to head for Thredbo. We decided this on the basis that Miles said he 'knew' the receptionist at the Alpine Hotel and that she could probably get us somewhere to sleep at short notice. There was a big jazz festival on at Thredbo and it was booked solid, but Miles felt sure his friend would look after us. That settled, the four-wheel-drives drove off and we set to with a will.

I rode the ensuing and amazing bit of dirt faster and better than I'd ever ridden any dirt ever, and even managed to round Mick up eventually. The surface was smooth, clean and grippy and I was standing on the pegs like a veteran desert racer and 'bringing it' as they say on hip-hop records. I had one awkward moment when the front washed out and pushed me up a bank, but I recovered and hammered on until, almost without warning, we found ourselves on the Snowy Mountains Highway. We were grinning like murderers and backslapping each other like Grand Final winners. I was stupid with endorphins, light-headed with hunger and my helmet had worn divots in my face and skull, but all we needed to do now was tool into Thredbo for pizza, showers and beer. But we had to do it before the kangaroos came out at dusk.

We paused briefly in Adaminaby for a 5 pm breakfast, then made for Thredbo as the sun began to dip below the range, lining the immense black cloudbank that hovered over it with pale gold.

Miles's friend had found us a chalet that slept twelve, let us in and left us to sit around in our underpants until Dino, Steve and Al finally turned up at about ten that night. They'd eventually hit bitumen and mobile phone coverage at about 6 pm, but on the wrong side of the Great Dividing Range and spent four hours driving like madmen to Thredbo when they got our SMS messages. Like us, they had eaten nothing all day and were somewhat fey and loopy when they staggered into the heated chalet and commenced to snort the leftover pizza into their exhausted bodies.

For reasons I still cannot fathom, Miles and Ian went out to listen to jazz bands and drink psychotic cocktails with yet more people Miles knew. I just needed to put my head on a pillow and worry about tomorrow when tomorrow came around. After all, we were almost there, weren't we? One more day and we would be at Phillip Island. All we had to do was climb this Mount Pinnibar fucker and ride some more fucken dirt. How fucking hard could it be after what we'd been through?

———

The following morning it was cold and I was a little bit insane. Remember that song, 'Climb Every Mountain', sung by the Mother Abbess in *The Sound of Music*? That woman could sing up a storm, but she didn't know shit about riding dirt-bikes. Nor did I, and I have no idea why that particular song kept twirling around in my head as I strapped my gear onto the DR on Day Three. Clearly I was a bit mad by this stage of the game – but no crazier than Ian, who'd been introduced to the questionable joy of Red Bull with red wine the night before with Miles, and hadn't slept a wink. He was also out the front of our Thredbo lodge in the crisp dawn gloom and dealing with his luggage, mainly by muttering at it. Miles joined us and showed no sign of having been out the night before. He unlocked the top box on his GS, which made a very efficient and German sucking noise as the seal was broken, and tossed in some of his gear.

'Big day today,' he said to no one in particular.

I wondered how today could be any bigger than yesterday and a cold spike ran through me. Miles is not the kind of bloke to make overblown statements.

'Miles,' I rasped, fixing him with a gaze that must have looked like that of a spooked child. 'You've been up Mount Pinnibar haven't you?'

'I have,' he grinned.

'Tell me honestly. How fucking bad is it?'

Miles stopped grinning.

'It's epic.'

Ian looked at me and I looked back at him as Miles walked back inside to put his gear on. We didn't speak. There didn't seem much to say right then. We finished with our luggage and went inside to gear up. The clicking of the fasteners on my boots sounded like coffin nails being driven into a cheap plywood box, and I was the last to stomp out of the carpeted embrace of the chalet.

It was brisk and overcast as we made our way out of Thredbo and up to Dead Horse Gap. The last time I'd travelled this road it had been banked with snow and precipitated a hellish sliding ice ride that scared several kilograms of manhood out of me. There was no snow this time, but it was still altogether pointless chasing Miles on the big GS as I watched him disappear into the distance. Apparently with a few twists of the rear suspension's preload knob the wretchedly capable monster (the bike, not Miles) transforms into a sportsbike – and chasing sportsbikes through twisties is not something DRs, Transalps and Dakars excel at.

We got to the Tom Groggin campground and made a quick side trip to examine the river crossing we were meant to ride through the previous day, before Dave's mishap changed all our plans. There were lots of kangaroos in this well-cleared and pretty campground, and I watched them hopping casually off as we slowly made our way down to the ford. I used to shoot 'roos for money and I would have made a good night's drinking vouchers out of this lot, but short of running them down on the DR or throwing rocks at them, I could only hate them with a burning passion from afar.

We got to the crossing and Miles offered to essay it with my DR to see how deep and/or navigable it was.

'We're not crossing,' Mick suddenly declared. 'We cannot afford to drown one of the bikes.'

Miles shrugged and we rode back to the road, then along it until we turned in to Tom Groggin Station – the entry point for the Mount Pinnibar track and one of the most luscious and beautiful beef stations I've ever seen. The place was like a centrefold for *Cow Growers Monthly*. Green pastures, a meandering creek (apparently called the Murray River), chubby hooved steaks everywhere . . . and a bloody motocross track. It transpired that Trevor, the incredibly hospitable station manager and yet another of Miles's vast assortment of mates, had some kids who were quite good at riding dirt. His daughter was in fact the then Junior State Motocross champion, and one of his sons, Luke, raced competitively and later told me he and his mates frolic happily up and down the Mount Pinnibar track most weekends.

Trevor made us some coffee and watched with detached amusement as Mick fired a few puffs of Geoff Ballard's Monkey

Butt Powder into my bum crack. I was in no danger of arse-rash at this stage, but I had no way of knowing what the morning held and figured I may as well prepare for all contingencies. Considering a dirt-riding god like Ballard gave me the product, I would be a fool not to use it. At the completion of the process, my bum felt smooth and powdery. Much later, when I was sweating like a rapist and pinwheeling down the mountain, I would notice in passing that my arse crack wasn't a moisture-filled crevice of revulsion. Which was the only positive thing I could identify at that time. But right then we moved off behind Miles along a smooth farm track bordered by impossibly green grass untouched by any drought.

Two gates and about a kilometre later we commenced the climb – and it was immediately steep. Very steep. And wet. And clayey. And rocky. And rutty. And bedevilled with satanic fucken spoon drains. And unquestionably and despairingly epic. Knowing this, Miles had offered me some much-needed advice earlier that morning. 'Try and stay out of the ruts. Pick your lines and ride around them, but if you do get into one, just gas it on and ride along it. Do not try to climb the front wheel out of it.'

It was fabulous counsel. But less than a kilometre into the seventeen-kilometre climb I plunged the front wheel into a pit-deep rut, shat myself, and tried to ride out of it. Bear in mind that I was also riding up an incline you would have trouble standing upright on. So as I jerked the front wheel out of the rut and gassed it, the DR did what any great bike would do; that is, exactly what it was told. It was not the bike's fault the teller was an idiot. And that idiot watched with dismay as the front wheel came out of the rut and up the side of the bank edging the track. Two things then happened simultaneously – I parted company with the bike and began rolling backwards down the hill, and the bike rose straight up into the air and flipped onto its side, before sliding down the hill with me.

Mick and Miles were ahead of me and Ian was behind me, so I was only vaguely surprised to see Ian parked sideways several metres into the scrub to my left when I finally crashed to a halt.

'You okay?' he yelled.

'Great!' I yelled back. 'How'd you get there?'

'I don't know,' he laughed. 'One second I was belting up the hill, the next second I was going backwards and sideways. And here I am.'

He was making every effort not to tumble further down and was sitting astride the Transalp, trying to figure out how to proceed. I got up and immediately fell backwards once more. I got up again and saw Miles coming back down the hill on foot. Fucken swine was as agile as a mountain goat about it, too. His bike and Mick were about 150 metres further up the hill on a level spot.

'You good?' he asked, helping me wrench my bike upright.

I nodded. I was okay physically – again a breathing, sweaty testament to the sanctity and glory of body armour.

'I'll ride it up to the level bit for you,' Miles offered kindly.

'I'll have your fucken babies for you if you do,' I muttered, but I don't think he heard me. I then watched agog at the ease with which he did just that, with Ian right behind him. I took a deep breath and commenced to clump up the cliff face after them. In ten metres perspiration was cascading off me and I was puffing like a blown horse. In twenty metres black spots were exploding in my vision and there was not enough air on Earth to satisfy my needs. I stopped, hands on knees and retched emptily into my helmet. It smelled like old lollies. Miles, Ian and Mick watched my glacial progress from above.

'When were you giving up the smokes, Borrie?' I heard Miles ask from on high.

Since my remaining time on Earth was measured in minutes, I didn't waste it replying. I resumed clumping up the hill, got on my bike and went at it again.

But the scenario I just described was to repeat itself several more times. Sometimes Ian helped me, sometimes Miles helped me. Once, Mick almost ran over me, which would probably have helped by putting an end to my misery. I'd stopped sweating. There was none left in my spasming glands and I'd just about sucked my Hydrapak dry. So much of my body ached and pounded with pain, but I was too tired to cry. Of course, I did have moments of sublime genius. There were steep bits that I did ride up and didn't crash on, and longish sections of easy and relatively flat dirt. But each time I told myself I was doing great, another nightmare of a 300-metre-long climb would rise before me, and I would find a suitable gear, dry-swallow and hurtle up it. Or some of it. Then I would pick up my bike, and if no one was available to help (we managed to become separated by several hundred metres at times), I'd carry on. Sometimes for as much as a whole metre. Sometimes less.

The last crash I had was about a third of the way up. Some three hours had passed since we commenced the ascent, which was worrying, 'cos we figured it would only take us about

223

forty-five minutes to do the seventeen kilometres. We were once again way behind schedule, but I was ahead of Ian and just behind Mick. Miles had probably already ridden seventeen kilometres just going up and down to help Ian and me, and it just happened to be my turn this time.

'This time' I think I just fell off from sheer despair. As Miles lifted the DR off my legs, he grabbed hold of the clutch and made a face.

'Your clutch is gone,' he said.

I remember thinking where such a vital piece of equipment could have gotten to, and if perhaps it had somehow run off during one of the many cartwheels the DR and I had performed that morning.

'Where's Ian?' he asked.

I waved in a 'down there' direction and when I turned to look, I could see Ian about 200 metres below and not really upright. Miles then made several trips back and forth, searching for tools, then ultimately riding my crippled DR back down to Ian to see if it could be fixed.

I sat on my powdered arse for a while, then painstakingly made my way, sometimes on all fours, a few hundred metres up the hill to where Mick and Miles's GS had been sitting and watching.

'I'm fucked,' I wheezed.

'This is hard,' Mick blinked slowly and I remembered how banged up his hand was from yesterday.

'My bike is fucked, too,' I informed him. 'The clutch has gone.'

Then I saw my bike, revving its mighty guts out, coming

up the hill with Ian on it, followed by Miles on the Transalp. In seconds they were beside us.

'Your bike's fucked; the clutch is gone,' Ian advised me as he and Miles took off their helmets.

I was wide-eyed. 'How did I do that?'

Ian grinned. 'You didn't. It wasn't properly adjusted to begin with and all this work has just fried it. It was nothing you did.'

'What do we do now?' I asked, already knowing the answer.

After a brief discussion, we decided Mick and Miles would continue, and I would descend to Tom Groggin Station and make an attempt to repair the clutch.

'I'll go down with you,' Ian offered. 'I'm struggling with the Transalp anyway, and we can't send you down alone. If something happens, we won't know for hours.'

'I'm not wrecking your trip,' I moaned, sounding a bit like Eeyore in the Winnie-the-Pooh books. 'I'll go alone.'

'Mate, I'm fucked. I'm really struggling. The tyres on this are just not right. I doubt if either of us will make it and the choice is simple. There is no fucken choice. You cannot ride up on that bike, and you cannot ride down alone.'

And thus it was settled. I shall not go into the appalling details of our descent – the memory of which still causes my stomach to reel sickeningly. It's enough that you know it was the most technically harrowing motorcycle ride I have ever experienced. I never imagined I would succeed in making it down unscathed, given that I certainly didn't make it up that way. The clutch was certainly fried, my entire weight was on the back brake, two fingers of my right hand barely caressed the front brake. One gram too much pressure there and my wife would have been a widow.

And inch by torturous inch, Ian and I crept down that bastard mountain. I distinctly remember being perched atop a spoon drain and staring with dismay down the final 300-metre incline. I could see Ian at the bottom and the lovely green fields of Tom Groggin Station through the trees beyond him. And I just could not go on any further. I had hit the wall and there was no more left. My chest, arms and shoulders burned with dire cramps, and I knew I could not make this descent. I had not really been in control of the bike since I began coming down and that only looked like getting worse the more exhausted I became.

'What are you doing?' Ian yelled as I sat there in despair.

'Resting!'

'Dirt-bike riding is all about choices, mate,' he informed me from below. 'You have to make one now. And you know you can't stay up there.'

'I fucking well can!' I lied.

'Bullshit. Get down here!'

And I did. Somehow. Without crashing.

Both Ian and I were laughing like stoned hyenas as we idled back to Trevor's tender mercies. We had not made it up Mount Pinnibar, but we had made it down in one piece and that was an achievement all by itself.

Once again, I was humbled by Trevor's country hospitality. In short order, as Ian wrung out his jacket and re-dressed – he'd actually taken most of his clothes off halfway up, and was wearing his jacket on bare skin – Trevor got his son Luke to load my ailing DR onto the back of one of their utes. We lacked the bits needed to fix it, but provided I didn't ask it to climb hills and didn't load up the clutch, I could nurse it along for a while.

'I can't have you ride four hours to Omeo,' Trevor shook his head when he heard of our original plan. 'I'll get Luke to run you up to the logging trail at the top of the hill. Omeo's only forty minutes from there. All pretty easy downhill dirt.'

And so the DR and I enjoyed a twenty kilometres transport stage along a much less steep and evil track that wound its way gently up and around Mount Pinnibar. Ian followed and half an hour later we were unloading the DR and thanking Luke. For the second time in two days, I wished I had women to give away.

When Luke left to head back down the mountain, the silence of the bush cloaked us utterly. Ian and I stood around for a while, just taking it in.

'I feel like I've been riding for weeks,' I finally said, but I was smiling.

'We should get going. Omeo isn't far and I'm so hungry I could eat a cow.'

'Wanna snake?' I asked. I had come to rely on those lovely squidgey lollies. They had sustained me whenever the abyss of fatigue yawned wide. But Ian was already on his bike and riding off, so I poked a snake in my mouth and set off after him.

The road wound steadily downward, and I was standing comfortably on the pegs and cruising with confidence across the corrugations. Before I knew it, we were off the range and the sun was out. Ahead of us stretched a marvellous ribbon of white dirt – smooth, wide and bordered by green farms, which were in turn hedged by the foothills of the Great Dividing Range. We were the only vehicles on the road, so this gave us lots of time for sightseeing and navel-gazing.

I was coming to understand why people do this adventure riding stuff. In the space of 100 metres, you can go from a dizzying high to a vein-opening low. Extremes rush at you and you must deal with them on the instant. It is not at all like bitumen touring, where there are often long, boring sections – complete with cops, speed cameras and crazed car drivers. Out here on the dirt, there is nothing but you and the next challenge.

I found myself suddenly captivated by an enormous rock formation that reared ahead of me. I even stopped to take a photo of it. It was spectacular and majestic – much like I imagined my dirt-riding now was. I was thus mildly disappointed that the dirt ended on the other side of the formation, and Ian and I motored sedately into Omeo. The whole crew was there, fed and anxious about our whereabouts. As it turned out, Mick and Miles did make it to the top of Mount Pinnibar, to their eternal credit.

As I ate the best hamburger on Earth, we had a summit regarding our next move. It was about three in the afternoon and we still had a fair way to go to make Cowes on Phillip Island. The DR was struggling, but provided I was gentle with it and it wasn't asked to do hill-climbs, I figured it might make it all the way. Fixing it was perhaps an option, but at the expense of the time available to us. I had arranged to meet some friends at the Euphoria Café in Cowes, and I had every intention of keeping the appointment. This meant we were not to do any more dirt if we hoped to get to the island before midnight. I would like to say I was devastated, but I was actually relieved . . . with a small tinge of disappointment. I was willing, but circumstances had conspired against us. So be it. There would be other times.

Miles said his goodbyes and set off for Melbourne on the magical GS. I was prepared to carry him there on my shoulders had he asked me to, such was my gratitude for his help. I settled for hugging him.

Then we climbed on our bikes and made for the island on the bitumen. But because of my clutch issues, Ian and Mick soon left me far behind. I was about 100 kilometres away from Cowes and riding along in pitch blackness when the valiant Suzuki DR finally gave up. Its clutch ceased to clutch and my forward progress slowed to walking pace. I knew Dino and the Land Rover were not far behind me. I put my blinker on, left the headlight shining and waited. Within ten minutes, the Land Rover appeared and hurtled straight past me. I hauled out my mobile and prayed for network coverage. One bar. I dialled.

'Why the bastard fucking fuck didn't you fuckers stop!?' I shrieked, almost insensate with fatigue. All I had left was hate. 'I was the only fucken vehicle on the road! You cunts couldn't have fucken missed me.'

'I thought you'd stopped to have a piss,' Dino said, sounding hurt. 'I've pulled over. Can you ride it five kays up the road? I can't turn around here.'

I rode the five kays, the motor screaming, my feet paddling at the road and the clutch frying itself even more. Then it was duly loaded onto the trailer and I was ensconced in the back seat of the Land Rover. An hour later, we were rolling into Cowes.

'Stop the car,' I demanded.

Dino stopped. I climbed out, put on my jacket, wedged the shiteful helmet back on my head and perched myself atop the DR in the trailer.

'Onwards!' I yelled.

We idled past the Euphoria only to see it was closed.

'To the pub!' I hollered, betting that if my friends were still here, that's where I'd find them.

And I did, waddling into the pub to be greeted by Uncle, Yer Maun and Island Mick. I hugged them all. In that moment I loved them like a mother loves her children.

That night, after I had miraculously located the only open restaurant in Cowes, I would sleep the sleep of the righteous and utterly exhausted. But first I had to eat, and so did the others. I think the waiter imagined I was going to rob the joint when I limped through the door as he and the owner were closing up.

'Can I help you?' he asked.

'If you can serve us five steaks and ten beers at this late hour you certainly can help me.'

I think it may have been the pathetic glimmer of tears in my raw, wind-blasted eyes that convinced him to agree. The restaurant fed us royally and I spent several immensely satisfying minutes gnawing at the bone of the greatest King Island scotch fillet ever carved off the happiest steer that ever pranced through those wind-blown paddocks. When sleep claimed me not an hour later, I had a smile on my face that was undeniably self-satisfied. And I cannot be blamed for that.

RON'S RIDE

We don't venerate our elders like some cultures do. As thanks for their contributions to our society, we stick them in nursing homes to slurp on gruel, bathe in kerosene and shit their adult nappies. It's a bit of a shame, really. We could be putting them on motorcycles instead. I'm pretty sure they'd find that much more enjoyable.

'None are so old as those who
have outlived enthusiasm.'

HENRY DAVID THOREAU

Sitting in a deserted motorway truck-stop at 5 am while reeking of Ewan McGregor's new signature fragrance, Adventure, is not the stuff my dreams are made of. Nor was the candy-apple-red CBF1000 that Honda had kindly supplied me with – but my dreams were not what this particular journey was about. This trip was to be all about Ron Beck – a man I consider to

231

be one of Australian motorcycling's living treasures – and at seventy, the oldest person I've ever ridden with.

McGregor's toilet water, on the other hand, was not a motorcycle treasure at all. It had been sent to *Australian Motorcycle News* by some marketing company, so the editor, with tears of laughter rolling down his furry cheeks, passed it on to me to see if I was interested in 'testing' it.

'Sure,' I said to him. 'I'll test it up a storm for you.' Then I threw the bottle into my backpack and promptly forgot all about it for a few weeks. I found it again as I was packing to go to Phillip Island for the annual World Superbike races with Ron. What the hell, I figured. Rather than spraying it on my dog's mattress to sex up its stench, I'll spray myself up for the trip and see what comes of it. But in the pre-dawn gloom, surrounded by giant trucks and equally giant truckers, I was wondering if maybe I should have waited until later to give it an outing.

Thankfully, Ron was as ever on time, so I didn't get to find out if the cologne was having any effect on the truckies. After a brief greeting where Ron referred to me as 'young Boris' and told me that I 'smelled funny', we set off down the Doom Highway – prepared to put up with a mindless transport stage to Gundagai for a total overload of twisty goodness later on.

Ron was no stranger to the Doom. He was a retired truck driver (among other things) and knew the road with a level of intimacy not available to most people. We paused briefly for fuel and coffee at Pheasants Nest and continued south. As we rode, I remembered my first encounter with Ron, whom I had dubbed Master Yoda minutes after meeting him in my pit garage at Eastern Creek – because just like Master Yoda, Ron packed a shitload of kung fu into a rather small package. A former aircraft engineer for the Royal Australian Air Force, Ron had won the legendary Rolls-Royce Award for being the best apprentice in the known universe – and since I was the worst road-racer in the known universe, I was profoundly humbled to have him in my corner that day.

I had always wanted to repay Ron for his kindness, concern and expertise during my completely forgettable foray into motor-cycle racing. He'd come all the way from Queensland to Sydney to spanner for me for one afternoon of British, European and American Racing Supporters (BEARS) club racing, and worked like a madman on the race bike until I crashed my brains out on Lap One and we all went home early so I could cry about my broken ribs in the peace and quiet of my lounge room, rather than the pit garage. So as a way of thanking Ron for his efforts, my mate Ian and I hatched a plan to fulfil one of Ron's long-held dreams before his credits began to roll. We would procure a bike Ron had always aspired to ride (a BMW R1200RT), take him to an event he dearly loved but hadn't been to in millennia (the World Superbikes at Phillip Island) and use the opportunity to sit at Ron's feet and absorb the pearls of motorcycling wisdom that would doubtlessly issue forth from him when I got him sloshed.

A large part of me hoped the route I had in mind wouldn't overwhelm a seventy-year-old and that the weather would cooperate. Larking about the Snowy Mountains when they're pretending to be the Himalayas on a bad day is no one's idea of fun – and while I was pig-headed enough to push on through just about anything the Road Gods would send down, I was in

233

no position to insist that Ron do likewise. And if we got stuck and had to sit it out for a while, the old bugger looked way too stringy to eat.

As we fuelled up in Tumut, I spent a lot of time looking at the sky, searching for hints of forthcoming climatic evil. But it was clear and blue and the sun shone warmly upon our endeavours. Ron was grinning from ear to ear and proving to be a very likeable and easygoing travel companion. You learn a lot about people when you ride hefty distances with them – and five minutes after we left Tumut and the sweepers began, I learned that Ron could happily turn the Beemer's throttle to the stop and piss off into the distance. I knew the man could ride (he did punt a brutally powerful, hand-built Vincent until recently), but I didn't expect to be passed on the outside of a very fast sweeper at speeds that would make the Highway Patrol wee themselves with joy. Thankfully, the CBF1000, despite looking like a wardrobe on wheels, is no slouch on the open road – and after a brief prayer of gratitude that it was equipped with an immensely willing and tractable Fireblade donk, I set off in pursuit.

Ron was obviously in the zone and I watched his smooth, pin-accurate lines with admiration, and wondered if he'd remember to turn off at the Cabramurra sign. Because I would have to break all kinds of laws, both state and Newtonian, if I was to catch this ancient hooligan when he suddenly had a 'senior's moment' (as he called his rare lapses of memory) and carried on to Cooma at 200 kms per hour.

As it turned out, I eventually managed to pass him on a big straight just before the Cabramurra turn-off by pinning the

CBF's throttle, putting my head down and trusting the cross-winds wouldn't slam me into the side of Ron's BMW, courtesy of the spinnaker effect the Honda's massive top box offered at very high speed. Imagine a motorcycle with three large suitcases affixed to it: two either side of the rear wheel and one particularly broad and deep bastard behind the seat. And while such marvellous luggage is great for carting all sorts of crap around, at speeds over 140 kms per hour it tends to play utter havoc with the bike's handling.

'Moves around a bit,' Ron observed as I cleaned the bugs off my goggles at the turn-off.

I smiled ruefully. The BMW had no top box, and was thus not enslaved to the vagaries of high-country crosswinds like I was.

'I like to give it a bit of rear brake to settle it through some of the faster bends,' Ron continued, even though I'd not even seen a flicker of brakelight, and was left wondering just what Ron considered 'fast' bends.

We paused for an indifferent lunch at Cabramurra then made our way down the other side of the range and into some nasty squalls of rain and wind. Bark, branches and leaves flew horizontally across the road as we wended our way past Tallangatta, and rain lashed us mercilessly. But as we turned into the Kiewa Valley, the micro-storm stopped just as suddenly as it had started and I began to look for a pub. I found one in the small village of Dederang.

'I thought you'd never come to your senses,' Ron observed as we entered the pub. 'How long were you expecting me to ride without a beer?'

Feeling like I'd failed some vital test, I bought Ron a beer and listened to his tales of trucking hazardous liquids around the place in the days before Occupational Health and Safety legislation. I was especially intrigued when he told me about the time he needed to deal with thirty tonnes of LPG that was trying to ignite itself, by closing the offending valve with his bare hands – an experience he felt was akin to 'Having forty sparrows up your arse with the last one trying to get out first'. He added that afterwards, he was not game to bend his fingers in case they snapped off.

We finished our beers and made our way over the Tawonga Gap, where another brief rain squall escorted us into Bright. That evening, our company had expanded to include our mutual mate, Ian, another elderly war horse I knew called Mr Oddjob (but he was only sixty-five) and Tim, who had shadowed Ron and me from Sydney.

That evening will stay with me for the rest of my life. Ron told tales that dropped my jaw and convinced me that the love of motorcycling does indeed transfer from generation to generation.

Ron spoke of his father, Ron Senior, who was a motorcycle mechanic at Hazell & Moore in Newcastle, and who'd built a bike for Les Hoffnung – the bloke who invented motorcycle speedway racing at the Maitland Show in 1926 to keep the lunch-time crowds entertained. Ron Junior was later employed at two shillings a night to turn off the stadium lights when the flag dropped for the starts.

Ron Senior also worked with the celebrated Col Crothers, who held the Australian Motorcycle Land Speed Record of

152 m/h (later to be upped to 172 m/h on the salt), and which was set on a public road between Collingullie and Narrandera, New South Wales in the 1950s.

And then, as my jaw slackened even further, Ron spoke of an amazing and utterly unique 1947 Vincent Rapide he'd owned. Its original owner, an Englishman called Alex Phillip, bought it new then crashed it at the Ramsey hairpin during its first outing at the 1949 Isle of Man TT. He crashed right in front of the legendary Phil Irving, and bent the front end. The following year, Alex went on to win the 1000cc Clubman event at the Isle in record time. But on the way home from the race, Alex and his wife had a bad accident that left them both in hospital for five months.

The race-winning Vincent was subsequently sold to none other than Colonel 'Mad Jack' Churchill who, among many other astonishing feats, went into battle at Salerno in WWII wielding a Scottish claymore and captured forty German prisoners – perfectly normal for a bloke who also parachuted in a kilt. And in a Norway raid he was the first man ashore, just so he could play 'The March of the Cameron Men' on his bagpipes as his troops advanced. But after the war the race-winning Vincent 'disappeared', seemingly lost to the mists of time.

In 1982, Alex Phillip, the original owner of the Rapide, decided he would search for his bike (he had the engine number, YJ 9840) and sent feelers out around the world, hoping to track down Churchill, whom they eventually located in England. But he no longer had the bike. Amazingly, just as Alex was resigning himself to never locating his beloved Vincent Rapide, Ron Beck read of his search in his local paper and wrote to him, saying that YJ 9840 was sitting in his shed in Queensland. Ron had bought the bike in boxes in the '70s, totally unaware it was an Isle of Man winner. He just wanted a Vincent Rapide.

'I have had the engine for six years, complete, but in pieces,' Ron wrote to Alex. 'I bought it from a man who had it in a Cooper racing car.'

Alex Phillip was content. He had found his bike and it was in the hands of an enthusiast as passionate about the marque as he was. The bike stayed in Australia and was subsequently restored to its original grandeur by Ron and his mate, Terry Prince, and was back on the road and regularly blasting around racetracks from 1992 until Ron finally sold it in 2000.

I left Ron holding forth to Oddjob and Ian at the pub and went back to the motel. I was done for the evening. I'd been relatively stressed all day, worrying (needlessly, of course) about Ron, and once we got safely to Bright, I probably let off a little more steam than I should have by glugging several gallons of beer and a few joints. I only fell over once walking back to the motel. I think.

As I lay in bed that night, still reeking of Ewan's man-fume (I'd given myself a good wetting prior to dinner, hoping to odour the local babes into submission), I was actually quite sad. I knew that there were other men like Ron Beck, living repositories of motorcycle history, whose stories would never be told, and at whose feet I would never be honoured to sit.

———

The next morning I could have gladly killed the lot of the we-don't-need-to-sleep-late-after-a-night-on-the-turps-'cos-we're-leathery-old-bastards as I watched an altogether too sprightly Ron beaming at my stenchy hungover mien. After breakfast, Ron, Ian and I ascended Mount Hotham at a leisurely and dignified pace; Ron was taking it easy because he was old enough to know better, and Ian and I were freezing to death in the three-degree temperature, so we couldn't go any faster anyway. We stopped at the summit for pictures and so I could dampen myself with more of Ewan's signature pong. I figured it'd be much fairer to the ladies of Victoria if I could disperse the fragrance into the alpine winds so they would receive a suitable preview prior to the full up-close treatment. But I was pretty quick about it. It was unremittingly cold, and my hangover and I wanted to find a more congenial lower altitude as soon as possible.

Rain, wind and roadworks haunted us the length of the normally glorious Omeo Highway, and I was impressed to hear the theme from *Cats* coming from the stereo on Ron's BMW when we stopped in Bruthen to wring out our gloves. We still had a fair way to go before the end of our journey, so we left Bruthen in a wail of speed and purpose. Ron let himself go a bit with the throttle on some of the backroads I'd discovered on previous trips, and when we stopped for a warming bowl of soup in Welshpool, he impishly asked Ian if there was something wrong with the 1000cc Suzuki sportsbike he was on.

'It's great,' Ian declared. 'Why?'

''Cos I could have stuffed it right up the inside of you several times,' Ron grinned.

Having watched the performance in my mirrors I had no doubt that he could have done just that, and then nailed my sad arse as well. The little old bastard was certainly not afraid – either of speed or the cops.

'I'm too old to give much of a shit about my licence,' he laughed when I asked him how much jail time he reckoned he could do when he was booked for 220 in a 100 zone.

We made it to the island on sunset, and Ron's Superbike experience began with a vengeance. I'd managed to blag him a pit pass and got so much joy out of seeing how much he relished being within arm's reach of the big boys' pit garages, I still smile about it today.

As we walked around the pit-lane carnival that is any great international motorsport event, Ron gave me a running commentary outside one of the garages when Noriyuki Haga's pit crew went into crisis control during qualifying, when his Number One bike wouldn't start. A pit garage during any of the major motorcycle races is a sight to behold. Each one of them is a unique microcosm literally emanating purpose, pressure and tension on a level few people can comprehend. Lives hang in the balance. Forget to tighten a nut and shit can get real when it comes off at 300 kms per hour. But as the remaining qualifying time ticked down and Haga's bike still refused to fire, shit was getting real right there.

'That's the head mechanic,' Ron nodded at the man dancing lead in one of the most intricate ballets on Earth. 'And that's the bloke who's paying for it all. You can tell by his laptop and the expression of anguish on his dial.'

I learned much from Ron that weekend. I learned what it was like to have the companionship of a man who didn't talk any shit whatsoever; talking shit apparently ceases to be a prerequisite to socialising once a man attains a certain age. His observations about the bikes, the riders, the race lines and the technical aspects of the sport were more valid and honest than anything I've ever read or heard before. His *joie de vivre* was unmistakeable and unalloyed and not at all what I expected of a man of his years.

And I could see that he really liked the bike he was riding. His care and precision when dealing with his motorcycle were purposeful and revelatory. When you're Ron's size (he's not a big bloke – hell, he's not even a medium-sized bloke), you need to pay attention when parking your bike – especially when parking something as hefty as the BMW R1200RT.

At night, back in the house we'd rented for the weekend, Ron told tales of going AWOL to ride bikes and chase women when in the Air Force and I wept with laughter. He knew people I'd only ever read about in books. Hell, he had ridden with many of them and lived through events that for me were the 'stuff of legend'. All weekend I wallowed in his immense good humour, manners and wisdom like a supplicant. And he was an immensely caring bloke.

'You make sure the girls get home safe if that stinky stuff you're wearing actually works on any of them,' he told me in measured tones, when I decided I needed to go out some more after I'd brought him home. And in case you're wondering, Ewan's sex-water did work, in that none of the promo girls I asked were repulsed by its odour or called security, while the wife of my good mate, Island Mick, actually said it smelled lovely; it was just a fucken shame it was coming from me.

On any level I hold to be important, my time with Ron on the road and at Phillip Island was a singular privilege and honour. Our society offers little respect and even less time to our elders, and is a good deal more impoverished because of that. Sure, they can be cantankerous, opinionated and set in their ways. But they can also be like Ron – annealed by experience, filled with wisdom and profoundly uplifting to be with.

When they pass, we are a little poorer.

DEMON NIGHT

David 'Davo' Jones was the man who started the Far Rider concept in Australia in early April 2006, launching the organisation online on 17 June 2006. I was fortunate enough to meet him when he arrived at Nambucca Heads on what was the third Australian Far Ride. Prior to this meeting, Dave and I had only ever communicated via emails and on a website. He was a most jolly gent of middle years, with a ready smile and a well-used, incredibly equipped Kawasaki GTR. He rode immense distances in times that made my shit curdle and his fondest wish was to participate in the legendary US Iron Butt Rally, where riders must complete 1100 miles (1600 kilometres) each day for 11 consecutive days. This story concerns my participation in the Australian variation, Far Ride No. 3 – according to Dave, a gentle, introductory kind of thing for some of the new members. But I wasn't after membership in Far Riders (motto: 'It's just a road'). My curiousity was roused by the whole concept of riding purely for the sake of distance, and how that challenged you mentally and physically.

Dave was killed on Friday, 4 September 2009, living his dream and doing the Iron Butt Rally in the USA, when he struck a deer not far from the end of the challenging ride. The world of motorcycling has been lessened by this great man's untimely passing.

'Most glorious night!
Thou wert not sent for slumber!'

LORD BYRON, *CHILDE HAROLD'S PILGRIMAGE*

I have always known there are demons in the night. Fanged, red-skinned horrors, playing at the edges of your vision and capering through your mind as you ride.

Hemingway, in *A Farewell to Arms*, understood the night to be a time and place of great 'otherness' and wrote: *'I know the night is not the same as the day: that all things are different, that the things of the night cannot be explained in the day, because they do not then exist . . .'*

A mate sent me the above wisdom just before I set off at 11 pm one muggy Friday night on a run unlike any I'd ever done – and the words rang with a fierce truth. I am no stranger to night riding. I actually quite like it. I am also no stranger to banging out big miles, and I don't mind that, either. But doing 1000 kilometres in a twelve-hour period and riding 250 kilometres past my destination and then 250 kilometres back was something I'd never done before.

How this came to pass is not as important as the ride itself, though you probably need to know why I wedged myself upon a tiny, screaming 600cc Yamaha R6 and howled northward from Sydney through the murk.

A man called Dave had invited me along on what he called a 'Far Ride'. A Far Ride is a type of ride undertaken by a group of blokes known as Far Riders. They are a unique breed of motorcyclist, for whom the ride is purity incarnate – the be-all and end-all. Some of them have accomplished distance-riding feats that beggar belief and which prompt the question 'Why?'

Well, I know why because I did such a ride and they know why because they do these rides all the time – and I suppose whether you know why isn't really all that important. You can always find out by doing such a ride for yourself. What is important about this sub-genre of motorcycle-riding is precisely what Master Yoda meant when he said: 'Do; or do not. There is no "try".'

So at 11 pm sharp, I did. One thousand kilometres would be done in 12 hours or I would die in the attempt.

11 pm to 1 am

Damn, it feels good to be on the road. I'm warm and dry and between my legs is a shrieking motorcycle that's happier cutting killer laps on a racetrack than touring along a straight highway, but that only adds to the evening's delight. I can feel my night demons stirring and whispering to each other, wondering why I've suddenly let them out. I've been wondering that myself, but as I swing onto the northern freeway and give it a handful, the answer is self-evident.

The R6 is not even remotely uncomfortable at speed, which is surprising given I feel rather immense on it, like an ox upon an orange, and it's whip-crack sharp and purposeful. Provided I'm not shy about sawing through the gearbox to keep it in its happy place, it also goes like a crossbow bolt.

The two cups of coffee and cheese sanga that I had in my kitchen before leaving lie peacefully in my guts and I feel wide awake and as alert as a shaved Rottweiler.

'This 1000 kays is gonna be a piece of piss, sucker,' my demons hiss. Then giggle, stretch their limbs (something I can't really do on the Yamaha) and advise me that maybe I should turn it up a notch or three. There is a long way to go and not all that much time to get there. I hear them, sit the tacho on eight grand and 144 kms per hour and leer into the rushing darkness.

As a devoted insomniac, I spend lots of time leering into various darknesses, and as I chase my headlight up the almost deserted freeway, I wonder whether my sleep disorders will help or hinder this affair. The demons shrug and gibber. My sleep problems are their crèche. My insomnia nourishes them. We will see what we will see about this staying awake business, I guess.

Since time is a factor, sipping hot coffee at every stop is not the answer. The inventors of those 'energy' drinks are aware of this – and I vow to taste all their efforts this night. In fact, I plan to so load my system with Red Bull et al, sleep is going to be something other people do. How much guarana, ginseng and caffeine can the demons deal with? They shrug again and I nudge the R6 up another notch and wiggle my arse across the seat. One of my underpant seams starts to eat hotly into a buttock, but this passes.

I am making great time, I think, pulling into a servo at Hexham. Across the street is a closed McDonald's restaurant hosting some dope-smoking teenagers and I can smell the sweet tang of their hydroponically grown ganja on the air. I pay for my fuel, kick the Yammie's tyres, take a photo that makes me look like a goggle-eyed lunatic, neck a can of V and head back into the night.

A monstrous half-moon paces me on my right and thoughts of colliding with a thirsty kangaroo start to creep past the chanting demons in my head. I have chosen my 1000 kilometre route to Nambucca Heads with hydration-seeking kangaroos in mind. I figure the coastal bastards won't be as thirsty as their more parched inland brothers. The Pacific Highway, with all its trucks and rivers, is the best option during the million-year drought Australia is experiencing. Had I gone the Dubbo–Tamworth–Coast route, I may well have been dead already. As it turns out, the only 'roo I see is hopping leisurely through the town of Bulahdelah – which is also where I see the only police car of the evening. But he is going the other way and seems uninterested in me.

I top up again in Coolongolook, drink a Mother (for the very last time in my life), and decide I will never sleep again. The demons in my head are now so full of guarana goodness and night-speed fever, I can feel their claws scrabbling at the backs of my eyes. The only thing that makes them settle is revs – and the Yamaha has plenty of them.

1 am to 3 am

You understand there is not much to see at night, don't you? There's the road *waaay* in front of you, and the road *directly* in front of you, which always seems to move faster than the road *waaay* in front of you. Your world is the instruments, what your headlight picks up, and the odd blast of light that signals an oncoming truck. Then there is the howl of the engine and the roar of the wind. Of course, in my case, there are also the demons – now having a full-on joy jamboree in my head. My passing the odd truck in a shriek of revs is accompanied by a series of high-fives and backslaps. I am still profoundly awake and alert, though the taste of that last energy drink is like rancid cat-meat in my mouth. The turn-off to Port Macquarie flies by and the Yammie's clock puts me a little ahead of schedule.

You always ride faster when you ride alone, only because there's very little fucking about in petrol stations, waiting for your mates to clean visors or finish number twos in the toilet. My routine this evening is: pull up, fuel up, pay up, buy energy drink, drink energy drink, smoke cigarette, stretch, tell my demons to hush, and go. Well, it has been until I get to Kempsey. Parts of me are starting to hum with stiffness, so I suppose I am keen to stop. The only wiggle-room on an R6 is from side to side, but the ergonomics are so track-focused that when you slide your arse to the side, the seat actually pushes you down and to the front – towards the front axle. Perfect for racetrack cornering. Not so perfect for the Pacific Highway, whose rare and gentle sweepers are only interesting at 200 kms per hour.

3 am to 5 am

Why did I pull into the first servo I saw in Kempsey? I'm still asking myself that. It may have been the demons. Maybe I wasn't thinking clearly, or maybe I was thinking too clearly – which can happen when you're over-stimulated and yowling through the night on a crazy motorcycle.

And this is the Darkness before the Dawn, too. The time of night when people become werewolves and rip their neighbours' throats out. The time of night when nothing is possible but anything is likely. The time of night when you're most mortal, and yet feel immortal.

I'd consumed a Red Bull twenty kilometres back, and am now so wired I could do duty as a dingo fence. But I am comatose compared to the twenty young bucks having an ice-smoking party in the Kempsey servo I stop at. Three old cars, plastered with the Koori flag and various land rights logos are parked there. Around them, drinking and yelling and wrestling are some of Kempsey's more excitable residents. To have ridden straight out would have been an act of cowardly wisdom. To stop, turn off my bike and fuel up is the act of a crazed man – which I doubtlessly am by this stage of the game. The ice-smokers don't bother to stop smoking when I pull up, but since they only have one pipe between them, many of them are free to engage me in manly banter.

'Heeey, bro,' one of them says, his eyes glistening with insanity, 'Det your bike?'

'Yep,' I lie cheerily, willing the petrol faster into my tank and spilling some because my hands are trembling.

'Heeey, bro,' the lunatic smiles wickedly, 'you're shaking . . . hee hee hee . . . we'll hev to ride your bike for you . . . hee, hee, hee . . .' Then he stalks back to the group to report that he's scared the motorcyclist so badly he is shaking like a leaf, and that they would shortly be taking delivery of a new Yamaha R6.

I am actually vibrating like a drum-skin, but it isn't from fear. It is from the mega-litres of the guarana and ginseng and sugar and caffeine I seem to be made of right now. I quickly pay the terrified attendant, neck another V (what's the point of stopping now?) and amble back to my bike – which was now surrounded by several drug-crazed maniacs. I'll fit right in, I think.

'Heeeey, bro. Is det a police torch?' He is pointing at the top of my bag where I've strapped a half-metre-long Maglite torch, which can be unsheathed like a sword of vengeance in less than a second. (Do you foolishly ride at night without an instant source of bright light that doubles as a war club? Tsk, tsk, tsk . . .)

'Yep,' I say, unsheathing it and grimacing like a fiend. 'I just killed a cop in Taree and took it off him. Wanna see the cunt's skull chunks?'

This approach will either defuse the situation or not – and that is entirely dependent upon where they all are in the ice cycle. I don't much care, to be honest. I have so many jungle-boogie stimulants in my body right now, the Last Stand of the Maglite Warrior is going to be a beauty – right up there with the Spartans at Thermopylae.

'Hey, bro,' he stammers, his eyes bright with drugs and fear. 'It's cool. Be cool, ay?'

I sheath the Maglite, start the bike and hurtle back into the night, leaving the Kempsey boys to appreciate the Yamaha's exhaust note as I work my way up through the gearbox. I am panting like a runner, and leaking suppressed violence and adrenalin like an overfilled bathtub. I am also vaguely wondering how fast a man's heart can beat before it explodes. The fucking demons are dancing a polka in my head.

5 am to 7 am

Macksville, Nambucca Heads and Coffs Harbour roll past without my even noticing. I have a slight twitch of weirdness riding past my destination, but compared to the general strangeness in my head, it is barely noticeable. I briefly consider pulling in to Nambucca Heads and calling it a night, but to do so would mean that I had failed and was weak and soft, like the belly of a toad. I wriggle my arse, stretch my legs and bump the revs up another thou or so. This is a constant pattern throughout the night. Each time I feel like surrendering, or doubt enters my caffeine-enriched brain, I accelerate. And nothing centres and clears the mind as efficiently as acceleration.

Grafton arrives shortly before dawn. I need to shit so bad my spine feels like liquid. Given the gear I am wearing and what I have consumed during the night this is an eye-opening experience, which I proceed to have in the far right cubicle of the first servo on your left as you come into town. Because I don't want to take my pants completely off (or my boots, or my jacket), I am forced to shit with my knees pretty much together. This is distressing on so many levels. Try it one day after you've drunk two litres of sugared Ginkgo biloba and see what I mean.

7 am to 7.20 am

There is nothing of me but numbness interspersed with stabs of pain. Closing one eye at a time doesn't work. I'm so tired and wired, I want to throw up and die. I have hit the wall and I still have some 200 kilometres to go, back the fucken way I came, no less. I pull over and do some star jumps. They make my head spin, but wake me up. I push on. The demons in my head just won't stop laughing, and some of them have moved south into my neck. Apparently there isn't enough room in my head for them all.

7.20 am to 7.40 am

More star jumps. Probably not technically perfect, but good enough to stave off unconsciousness for a bit longer. I am now drinking water that I bought in a petrol station. My teeth ache from all the sugar I have consumed and I think my kidneys have failed. There is an iron band of pain across my lower abdomen.

7.40 am to 8.00 am

Star jumps and cigarettes and strange arse-pain are my entire world. I'm now doing twenty kilometre dashes before stopping to unglue my eyes with the saline solution I always carry in case something ends up in one of them. It is now doing sterling duty as a de-gumming agent. I cannot formulate a clear thought and I forget my PIN at the last petrol stop south of Ballina, so I have to pay by credit card. My signature is someone else's.

8 am to 8.10 am

I've crashed, haven't I? And I'm in some biker hell atoning for my evil thoughts about pushbikes. It's not hot, but I am sweating like a Mexican whore and squinting through eyes made of crushed glass. Thankfully, the R6 knows what it's doing and doesn't need my input at all. Lots of engine noise, but. Perhaps a gear other than third would help it along?

8.10 am to 8.30 am

I can now star jump and yawn at the same time. I have bitten my tongue, but there's no blood. Everything tastes like sugared vomit – even the water. I don't know why this is so, and the demons won't tell me. We haven't spoken in ages. They're talking to each other. I am just too fucken crazy to speak with at the moment.

8.30 am to 9.00 am

God bless Circadian rhythms. I'm starting to feel less awful than I was just feeling. And I only have . . . hell, I don't even know how far I have left to go. I'll be lucky to be able to read the turn-off sign. But at least I'm now prepared to ride in top gear and the screaming engine noise has abated somewhat.

9 am to 10.30 am

The final forty kilometres. I don't know what they were about, and I don't care. If you want to find out, do the miles and see.

All I know is I pull up outside Nambucca's V-Wall Tavern on a glorious sunny day. An immense feeling of achievement fills my sugar-crazed body. I have done it. I have challenged myself and been found worthy. I am unhurt, unbooked and so gloriously alive I almost kiss Thommo, the first Far Rider to arrive just after me, but that would have been very strange for both of us, 'cos we've not yet met.

11 am onwards

That afternoon, I manage to eat two T-bone steaks (one for lunch and one for dinner), drink a metric shitload of beer to flush away the evil energy-drink gravy that has been coursing through my body, and indulge myself in some very appropriate self-congratulations. My sense of achievement is vast. I even manage to sing some Johnny Cash songs with the jukebox. When my buzzing, demon-filled head finally hits the pillow in the small, air-conditioned cabin I have rented in the caravan park behind the pub, I am sure I hear familiar voices whispering: 'You done good, bitch. See you next time.'

THE LINE IN
WINTER

*Sometimes, I do shit for no other reason than I think it needs doing.
And sometimes, I do shit that I miss doing and haven't done in a
long time. And sometimes, like this time, it's a combination of both.
Of course, doing shit on a motorcycle is always more rewarding than
doing shit in a car because what might appear entirely mundane
when done in a car can be a life-affirming challenge on a bike.*

`'If you are going through hell, keep going.'`
WINSTON CHURCHILL

Once upon a time, if you tried a little, you could ride from
Sydney to Melbourne in under eight hours. But even if you
weren't in a rush, you could do it easily in nine.

You'd leave Sydney at lunchtime on Friday, and be sitting
in some St Kilda dive around nine o'clock sipping beer and

wondering what manner of dire mental illness had seized the people who chose to settle on the dank banks of the Yarra all those years ago.

When I first started riding it in 1979, the Hume enjoyed a reputation as Australia's most dangerous highway. It was the country's major road and, according to the papers, joined Sydney to Melbourne with bitumen soaked liberally in the blood and peppered heartily with the bones of innocent motorists.

Certainly, traversing the Hume back then could be a nightmarish voyage in a car. It was filled with amphetamine-jacked truckies hurtling along the narrow potholed road with scant regard for an HQ Holden full of family.

But as a motorcyclist, I never encountered anything but courtesy and consummate driving skill from the truckies I zoomed past. So my view of them and of the Hume was altogether different from that of the herd animals in cars. And that has not changed despite the passage of three decades.

But the Hume has changed. A lot. It is now an engineering marvel of divided, multi-lane highway for most of its length. Smooth, well-maintained and serviced with innumerable fast-food-and-petrol outlets, it bypasses all but two towns (Holbrook and Tarcutta) and is posted at 110 kms per hour for most of the way.

This being so, it is interesting to note that it now takes more than ten hours to get to Melbourne from Sydney – even if you don't screw around in servos getting food, stretching your legs or lying under a tree with tears of despair and boredom running down your face. My mate Nick likens riding the Hume to sitting in an old chair and staring at a blank wall for twelve hours. Most of the riders I know would rather date livestock than ride the wretched thing and will tell you it's actually cheaper (and more mentally stimulating) to fly.

So, given all the improvements in the road, truckie drug-management and overall vehicle safety, why does it now take longer to do the trip than it did thirty years ago?

I had an inkling it had everything to do with the cops and the sheer speedo-staring terror that we all ride and drive in today. And I was right. But to prove it beyond any doubt, I decided to do something I had not done in almost two decades. I decided I was going to chuck a sickie on Friday, ride to Melbourne for a Saturday night party, then return on Sunday and go to work on Monday.

It would be just like it was in my salad days, I told myself. But better, because on this trip I would be armed with uplifting music courtesy of my teenage son's iPod.

I packed lightly, as in days of yore. A sleeping bag, jeans, undies, socks, T-shirts, a cardigan, a tyre-repair kit, a bag of beef jerky and some fresh water against the rigours of the road, plus assorted odds and sods that always accompany me on any motorcycle journey. It all fitted rather nicely on the white Honda CB1100. Some in a bag on the back and some in a magnetic tank bag in front of me.

The Honda was no random choice either. Since I was getting in touch with a journey I'd made in my youth, I figured it'd be fitting to use a bike that was a stylistic throwback to those days. Honda's air-cooled, five-speed, retro-styled 1100 was ideal. The thinly padded seat was not so ideal (but there's not a bike seat made that cannot be improved with a sheepskin), and neither was the rather miserly fourteen-litre petrol tank. But at my age, I figured frequent stops would do me more good than ill.

I dressed myself as warmly as I could after being advised it was the coldest May in forty-one years (it was minus two-and-a-bit degrees in Goulburn the morning of my departure), consigned myself to the random mercies of the Road Gods and headed south.

The music being fed directly into my head was a novel experience for me. The noise that usually accompanied my trips was a combination of exhaust roar and wind whoosh. Having Warren Zevon hold forth quite melodiously about the importance of lawyers, guns and money was something else for me altogether.

John Fogerty's gravelly voice wondering if I'd ever seen the rain accompanied me along the freeway, and while I had, indeed, seen more than my fair share of rain, I was hoping I wouldn't see any on this trip. The sky was leaden, but I was thinking that was just because it was early morning, and it was cool (about eight degrees) as I sailed past Campbelltown, the Honda humming smoothly at just a shade over the 110 kms per hour limit.

Then as I started climbing into the Southern Highlands, the temperature began dropping. Inside my open-face helmet, Springsteen assured me these were 'Better Days', baby, but I had my doubts. It was cold and getting colder. With wind-chill factored in, I reckon it was about minus ten or twelve. That's right about the level where I start to question my sanity. My core seemed okay for the moment; there was no ice-wind seepage inside the jacket, but the gloves were at the limit of their design brief and my hands were starting to get their frost on.

Surprisingly, my face wasn't too bad. Two layers of Oxford neck-scarf did a pretty good job of trapping my warm breath, so my cheeks only vaguely resembled frozen chicken thighs.

But I could feel real cold-pain lancing through the gap between my goggles and my helmet. The tracks of Smokey Robinson's tears were not a patch on the ones leaking from my slowly freezing eyeballs as I pulled in for petrol at Marulan.

The ambient temperature was minus two. It was mid-bloody-morning and it was still minus fucken two. I decided Alice Cooper knew shit about nightmares. The petrol nozzle rattled as I guided it into the Honda's tank. I was shivering and panting, my joints stiff from the cold. Unlike Pink Floyd, I had not become comfortably numb. When I went inside to pay, the warm air almost made me whimper in gratitude. Thankfully, the nice lady who took my money spared me any inane 'You must be cold' observations. It was obvious from the way I dripped snot onto her counter that things were not all toasty in my world.

The next ninety-odd kays to Yass nigh on killed me. I actually almost turned back. I was living AC/DC's 'Highway to Hell', not just listening to it. Australia can be a cold, barren and blasted wasteland when it wants to be. Not three months ago, the country-side I was riding through was as green as Irish envy. Now, as I gazed at the vast Southern Tablelands rolling gently down to the Riverina, there was nothing but sere emptiness, cloaked in cold under a lowering and frost-bleached sky. My nose was a water feature. My extremities were seized up like an old two-stroke motor and the bone-deep ache of serious cold had me in its grip. Judging from the sky, there appeared to be nothing but more of the same ahead. As the clicks rolled past, I promised myself if it started to rain or snow, I was turning back. I'd tell my mates I'd suffered kidney failure to cover my shameful retreat.

But then it dawned on me. I was fifty. If I dogged it, it would be like admitting trips like these were now beyond me and it was time I sought an easier path. From there, it was only a short stroll to the land of liver tablets, Alzheimer's and incontinence pads. I resolved I would die before I turned back.

Then as John Hartford's magical 'Man of Constant Sorrow' came through my earphones, I started to dance. Well, it was either that or perish. One way or another, I had to get the blood moving through my body. By the time I had headbanged my way through AC/DC's 'Thunderstruck', I was ready to come on and feel all of Slade's glorious noise. I was singing and bouncing like a maniac in time to the music in my lid, and the distance to Melbourne kept shrinking. In retrospect, the Honda proved an ideal bike to dance astride. A totally neutral riding position, a silky-smooth engine, a hostile seat and an unshakeably non-judgemental demeanour provided me with an ideal dancing partner.

I was just as gone as Dwight Yoakam when I rolled into the big servo on the hill outside Yass. But the sky was a little less blank and the temperature was no longer in the negatives. I'd stopped aching some, but five degrees is still nothing to get nude over.

I gave the bike some petrol, fed my body some beef jerky and coffee, and smiled back at the well-racked hottie who gave me a grin as she walked her fine junk back to her car. Then I opened my heart to Russell Morris's brilliant 'On the Wings of an Eagle' and kept on south.

The sun came out a bit as I stopped for fuel in Gundagai, but the temperature stayed stubbornly in the single digits. My eyes burned like hoar frost. I wondered how I used to do this kind of thing with a leather jacket and a jumper. The Dainese gear I had on that day was simply exceptional.

More coffee and petrol at Holbrook and the temperature was now around thirteen. It was positively balmy after the Siberian bullshit I'd struggled through that morning.

It was now lunchtime and I had planned to meet my mate Jamie at Yea around sundown. Jamie would lead me to Uncle's house in the northeastern 'burbs of Melbourne, where a bunch of us would be celebrating Uncle's annual Goutfest & Monkeybike Stunting Extravaganza. Jamie would do this because he is a top bloke and racked with pity for my Melbournian navigational abilities after ten hours on the Hume.

I agreed with Porcelain Black's view of what rock'n'roll looked like, took Barnesy's word for the fact that there was nothing like the kisses of a jaded Chinese princess and resigned myself to the mindless runway the Hume turns into after Albury.

Victoria should be proud of itself. It has created the single most boring road in all of creation and stocked it with police cyborgs. I saw four different patrol cars taxing motorists for exceeding the 110 km/h limit on a road one could do 200 km/h on with absolute confidence. It's a road I *have* done 200 km/h on. It used to be the road you made up time on during your trip to Melbourne by putting your head down, your bum up, and aiming for the horizon with the throttle nailed to the stop. It was the done thing.

But not anymore. Now it's just a magically eternal cash register for the government.

But I grinned, I bore it, I agreed with Jon Bon Jovi that there should be no silent prayer for the faith-departed, and then I turned off the Hume at Euroa. The Merton Gap warmed the edges of my tyres, Marc Bolan informed me that Telegram Sam was my main man, and I pulled up outside the Country Club Hotel in Yea right on sundown. A light rain had just started greasing up the roads.

Jamie handed me a filthy scotch as I lurched through the pub doors, stiff from the road. We toasted my safe arrival, put on our gear and made for Uncle's house like vampires fleeing the dawn. One hour later, and ten hours and forty minutes after I left Sydney, I was in the warm embrace of good mates. There was a great fire, a functioning hot water system, several fridges full of beer, and a safe place to rest my head. Done right, this motorcycling caper rewards the soul on many levels.

The next day, Jamie indulged me and we visited some places I had not been to for decades. I specifically wanted to revisit the legendary Kew Boulevard, so we did that, and I heard a little of the song it used to sing.

Then we adjourned for some killer pasta on Lygon Street, and I heard another song I'd missed.

As much as I detest the fetid swamp village that is Melbournistan, I will admit some places there sing to me. Some pubs, souvlaki shops and dens of ill repute scattered about the joint I pine for now and again. Some wonderful people are likewise mired in that big southern bog town by the bay, lost like the Israelites in the wilderness.

Maybe that is why some of them know how to party so well. And that's why, while I dislike Melbournistan itself, I do so like visiting it.

The party went off like a bomb. I have some very good mates. Meaningful people I am honoured to know. I'd ride a hell of a lot further than I did to spend time with them.

Uncle, a deeply genial, intelligent and deranged Irishman, holds what he calls a 'Goutfest' once a year, when he opens his house to a bunch of selected friends and provides exotic foods on a scale and of a range that would shame Caligula.

So I consumed rare delicacies, drank fabulous beer, swilled outrageous wine, slammed medicinally smooth vodka and yelled my fool head off. I saw grown men put large boards on their bellies while other men jumped savage little motorcycles over them. I saw entire windows removed from Uncle's house (by Uncle) so the acoustic integrity of his industrial sound system could pass unhindered to the outside world. I laughed hard and long and slept the sleep of the righteous, stinking of sake, meat and two-stroke fuel.

As Sunday's dawn was breaking, the Honda and I were climbing out of the fog-shrouded northeastern suburbs and making our way back to Sydney. I was smiling like a fiend, and still stinking a bit of sake, for such is the nature of sake. And fiends. Jeff Buckley sang Cohen's 'Hallelujah' to me as I headed for Sydney. It was one of those moments. I was home in nine and a half hours.

Want to find some stuff out about yourself? Do the Hume in winter. Because you don't have every single brain cell devoted to staying alive (as you would if you were banging along a back road), you get to spend a lot of time inside your own head. I can understand that's not a happy place for some people. But those people should attend to Bruce Springsteen's views about how sad it is to see people who live inside their skin and can't abide the company. I reckon he's right.

Live a little. Learn a little. Listen to some songs. Do the Hume in winter.

THE FAST,
THE FIRST &
THE FEAR

This is an entirely fictional account of a completely fictitious journey to Phillip Island from Sydney, undertaken by four totally fictional characters, astride four totally fictitious bikes. It never happened and there is no evidence that it did. None of the events or actions described herein took place in the way described and it is only right and proper to soundly condemn individuals who would do the things referred to in this fictional narrative. If these individuals existed, jailing would be too good for them.

'I must not fear. Fear is the mind-
killer. Fear is the little-death that
brings total obliteration. I will face
my fear. I will permit it to pass over
me and through me. And when it has
gone past I will turn the inner eye to

see its path. Where the fear has gone there
will be nothing. Only I will remain.'

FRANK HERBERT, *DUNE*

Four of us left Sydney in the darkness before the dawn. That is
always the right time to leave anywhere. A man's soul is most
restless then. Unknown roads stretched before us, untold perils
awaited us, and the cool pre-dawn air was fragrant with unspoken promises.

I, the Bard, rode astride The Antelope.[1] The Door gripped the
Tyrannosaur[2] between his thighs. Crew clutched the bars of his
Bulldog,[3] and the Iron Hippy piloted his grumbling, death-grey
Conglomeration of Italian Disdain.[4] We rode in a tight, stag-
gered formation. The kind of formation men who have ridden
many thousands of kilometres together normally ride in.

The Door was drug-free as a nun; being a drinking man that
is how he rolls. But the rest of us were deeply and profoundly
and gloriously stoned, for that is the only way to deal with the
test-pattern madness of the road known as The Doom.[5] It was
once the most dangerous highway in all of Australia. It has now
become the most boring, hollow and bone-marrow munching
stretch of road in all of creation. The vampires who rule us have
seen to it that it is so. So we would only stay on it for as long as
we stayed stoned, and that would be for as long as it took us to
get to Gundagai. Then we would turn left and see if we could
ride ourselves into a proper Road-Pig Lather[6] without dying or
going to jail. There are no certainties in this life or the next, or
even the one after. But as long as there be crazy-fast motorcycles

and wild-eyed men who have to ride them like their lives depend on the outcome, it might be worth hanging around to see what happens next.

The Antelope thrummed easily beneath me. It is, arguably, the best motorcycle in the world, so I would expect nothing other than self-assured thrumming from it. In front and to my right The Door's Tyrannosaur hummed quietly as he stretched his not inconsiderable legs out on the highway pegs. No one on this earth manages a 600 kilogram motorcycle like The Door. He has wheelstood[7] the beast to almost-death in the time he has owned it; so hard and so often that all of the important electrical connections came loose and caused much angst and suffering at his bike shop. Which can only be a good thing. Not enough bike shops undergo angst and suffering in today's world.

Behind me and to my right, Crew, the man with the most aggressive riding posture ever seen, riding the angriest British motorcycle ever made, hurtled through the fading night. The back of his motorcycle sported a black hump of luggage the size of a small bison. Crew had informed me some days prior to departure that he was 'going off', and that this was to be viewed favourably by all.

Immediately behind him, the Iron Hippy and his Conglomeration of Italian Disdain brought up the rear. The Iron Hippy's comprehensive and overwhelming crash a year ago had assured him a near future filled with profound pain and suffering in one of his legs. That he even had that leg was a miracle. That he could walk and ride and now planned to bang out 3000 kilometres in four days was akin to the return of the living Christ.

Behind us the eastern sky began to lighten, so we paused briefly to lighten our bladders. I breathed deeply as my piss steamed into the grass by the road. It was now dawn and the landscape looked like one of those spooky Impressionist paintings the French were knocking out in the 1870s. I took a picture of it. I also took a picture of the Iron Hippy urinating. For some reason, this was a recurring theme over the next few days. My camera was full of images of him pissing. Tastefully, I took them all from behind him.

Then we rode to the big petrol station on the hill at Yass for fuel. And so that the Iron Hippy could repair his Conglomeration. Crew and I indulged swinishly in several recreational joints and laughed at him, braying like hyenas as he patiently disassembled his non-functioning tail-light. He put in a new bulb, reassembled it all, then discovered it didn't work anyway. This reduced Crew and me to hysterics and we were forced to recreationalise ourselves some more just to calm down enough to be able to ride on.

The ninety-seven kilometres from Yass to Gundagai wafted by in a breeze of mild paranoia and deep introspection. There were no armed revenue-raisers, but I had been reliably informed by an outraged Bloodbeard, who was already at the island, that there was some feckless Victorangian shitheel cop in an unmarked grey car conducting random drug-testings that were not very random at all.

The Iron Hippy felt it might be wiser to eat our drugs. I was of the view that chewing gum was the solution. Crew, the most greathearted and courageous of men, affected an air of sublime sangfroid. I quickly realised I would be less than a man were I not to follow his celestial example. Que sera sera, motherfuckers.

At Gundagai, more fuel was applied to the bikes, recreation-alisation took place again, and we aimed our motorcyclical weapons at the target of the Snowy Mountains Raceway. The transport stage was over. The sun was up. And I was full of Mars bars, energy drinks and the base urge to ride the Antelope until my inner hate liquefied and oozed out my pores like dark sweat. I got demons haunting me the like of which must never be allowed free rein. Flogging them into submission on deserted roads with high-powered motorcycles keeps me keepin' on. But one cannot explain that to the revenuers when one is in handcuffs and covered in one's own piss from their overzealous Tasering.

And I did not need to explain anything to Crew. He under-stood implicitly that this was a race. It had to be a race and it was always going to be a race. Our respective manhoods were at stake and we would have no peace unless we gave in to the call of the testicles. If he was behind me, it drove me mad. The drugs made me think I was holding him up because I was riding like a man who has sex with sailors and farm animals. If he was in front, it also drove me mad, because it confirmed I was riding like a man who has sex with sailors and farm animals. And then there was The Door, who would appear in my mirrors astride his monolithic behemoth and was impossible to lose, unless the going got really tight and brutal and bristling with destruction.

It is ninety-three kilometres to Kiandra from Tumut. We did it in half an hour. I believe I placed on the top step of the podium in that regard. The Antelope does not have a great big top end, but it's good for an honest 200–210. But since this is the road on which I saw an indicated 303 km/h on an MV Agusta[8] a few years back when I was young and strong and somewhat *demon-frei*, I did not panic when Crew lashed me on the inside of a big sweeper at what must have been 230. I had no top end with which to respond, so I had to wait until he slowed to about 190 before I tried to leg-check the swine into the shitty high-country shrubbery. And what is it with our alpine flora? It looks like crap. The European stuff is all pine-green and grassy and welcoming. Our mountain stuff looks like dung-covered fowls fuck on it, then roost in the dead grey trees. I decided it would be undignified to die amid such floral anguish. So I was grateful when the Cabramurra turn-off at Kiandra appeared and the race ended.

More recreationalisation had to happen because our nerves were totally shot. I was even hearing sirens in my head. This is not the shit you want to hear when you're pigging out on speed and dread, and not letting Crew past you despite the fact you're riding like a sweating pederast.

There was nothing left to do but race to Cabramurra. I believe I must have placed lower on the podium this time, because The Fear was vast in me. It's a narrow whore of a road, and when I came in too hot on one of those unmarked bends, my arse ate the seat, and I was forced by my immense terror to back the fuck off for the next twenty metres. But a race is a race and I was impelled to get back on the gas and get after Crew, when we were all suddenly pulled up.

Luckily, it wasn't by the Treasury Officials. It was a lovely council worker who was flagging people down to warn them. 'A bloke on a bike has hit a car up ahead and we're just clearing the road. You should be good to go in a sec,' he said. I took advantage of him talking by positioning myself higher up the grid, so that when the SLOW sign was shown, I could bitch Crew into the next bend. We hit it and the next corner was mine, but the one after was full of cops, and blood, and oil – and some bloke's red motorcycle being winched onto a truck.

The cops glared at me. I glared back at them. They knew it. I knew it. And we both knew we both knew it. What I knew was where all the cops in this area now were. At the accident. The cops knew I knew this. That is why they were glaring at me. They knew that as soon as I rode around the next corner I would be speeding like a twitchy new Hollywood movie zombie all the way down the mountain. And they also knew they would not be there to witness my progress.

Life is full of such disappointments.

The race down the mountain was interrupted by photo-stops. This made the race very interesting, and it is possible that The Door and the Iron Hippy may have placed highly or even won a stage or two. But since each photo-stop normally required some recreationalising, my memory is dim and by the time Crew and I reached the sea-levelly altitude of the Corryong-or-Khancoban T-intersection, we were baked like Bavarian hams.

And now we were in Danger Country. The Victorangian Treasury Officials roamed everywhere here – their hearts black with motorcycle hate and their minds full of ways to make you miserable.

It was clearly time for beer. The nearest boozer was in Corryong, which also happened to sell food, something we were all a little bit achy for. Now Corryong pub is famous for two things – intelligence on where the Treasury Officials are deployed, and the sheer hog-surliness of its barman. We got hefty doses of both while we enjoyed our repast. It seemed that Bloodbeard spoke the truth. There was drug-testing going on somewhere down the road.

Crew and I went outside and smoked a fat one and contemplated our options. The Iron Hippy still counselled eating it all. The Door drank beer and felt that if they were Tasering and Macing drug addicts they would hardly be interested in breathalysing drunks. The plan, for want of a better word, was to carry on down the Murray Valley Highway pretending we were a genial gentlemen's motorcycle touring club. Then just before Tallangatta (where intelligence advised the Treasury Official awaited), we'd hang a left and hit the Omeo Highway, fuel up at Mitta Mitta, chuck a right six clicks before Anglers Rest and climb the range to Falls Creek. Whereupon we would behold the majesty of the rolling hills Australia is pleased to imagine are mountains, look to sex up anything called Heidi, then race down to Mount Beauty to meet J'amie, Res and Dan.

Thus we arrayed ourselves upon the road, and cruised like moth-ball-reeking ancients to the turn-off, where we took some pictures of some water left over from the floods, recreationalised ourselves a little more against the rigours of the road and pissed out some of the beer we'd necked in Corryong.

Just as I was shaking off the last golden droplets, some ten raucous motorcycles took our turn-off and blasted off down the road with meaning and purpose.

'We have to catch those cunts,' Crew observed, passing me the recreationaliser.

'And so we shall,' I coughed.

We gave them a little more of a start because I couldn't find my gloves (they were in my helmet, but because I was stoned that didn't immediately occur to me), then set off after them with a will and the tinny taste of fear in our dry mouths. We should have waited longer. Crew and I caught this peloton of rectal-nuzzlers within ten kilometres and proceeded to crush their souls with a fly-by of pure venom. The Iron Hippy later told me one of them even had the temerity to shake his head in disapproval at being raped at twice the speed limit.

But one of them, and there is always one of them, figured he'd have a go and set off after us. I waved him past me and then boxed him between Crew and myself in the hope that he would shit his pants and crash when he realised that braking was for the effete and lisping.

To his credit, he did hang on for a bit. But then he made a wise decision to abort, raised his hands in surrender and got the fuck out of my way so I could chase Crew. Unfortunately, Mitta Mitta city limits appeared before I could close down the black Bulldog, and Crew took the top step of the podium that time.

We fuelled up here, because we are wise and seasoned travellers. Omeo is 105 somewhat difficult kilometres away and we had been using fuel at a great rate since we last topped the tanks at Corryong.

After fuel, we adjourned to observe the wickedly picturesque river that runs behind the pub, before going into the pub and being greeted by an even surlier barman than the one at Corryong. Oh well. Clearly having sex with native animals and one's relatives does not make for a cheerful mien.

As we sipped our drinks in the shade out front, the peloton of pusillanimity rode past glaring at us. The lady warding the petrol bowser outside the general store came out. 'They'll be back,' she said. 'Everyone who doesn't fill up here comes back when they realise how far Omeo is.'

Sadly, we couldn't wait for that to happen. We had a recreational, and banged on. Within twenty kilometres the peloton of penguins was returning, so I made the masturbating-my-head motion to advise that I viewed them as massive dickheads. I was crushed when they waved at us.

But very soon the bitumen disappeared and dirt became our world. The Antelope, as disgracefully capable as it is on the bitumen, was suddenly in its design brief. The next podium was mine. Victory was assured. I stood up on the pegs as I had been shown by dirt masters and just fucken brought it Dakar style.

I stopped after a while and waited for Crew to catch up. After all, if there's no one there to share your glory, you feel like a bit of a wanker congratulating yourself. Besides, it would give me a chance to pass him and spray him with roost.[9] And so it came to pass. I stood on the top step of the podium at the turn-off and watched the beautiful, fast-flowing river gurgle past. In quite short order Crew arrived, parked his bike up the hill from me and ran off into the bush.

'You okay?' I called, concerned that he had gone to get a club with which to beat me for having roosted him a few kays back. He is, of course, a ranga[10] and they are warlike in the extreme, so I am always aware of how quickly it can all go to crap when they are discomfited.

'You got any toilet paper?' he suddenly yelled from the scrub.

'Sure,' I yelled back. 'Come down and I'll give it to you.'

'I can't,' he moaned. 'Sorry.'

I climbed the hill and walked a few metres into the foliage where I beheld Crew performing a strange squat walk. He was nude from the waist down and clearly in extremis. I threw the toilet paper at him, made the sign of the cross, and retreated back to the road. A few four-wheel-drives cruised past as I waited for him. They had a clear view of Crew voiding his bowels. I can only pray there were no children on board.

The Iron Hippy and The Door arrived, Crew emerged from the bushes, returned the unused portion of my toilet roll, and we took some pictures, recreationalised ourselves against the effects of the altitude we were about to experience, and then climbed the newly sealed road to Falls Creek.

Christing buggery Jesus come to Earth in bastard glory. What a road. What a ride. I was panting like a bitch in heat halfway up and keening like a dying whore when we finally stopped at the summit of Falls Creek. The road is not a road. It is a racetrack designed by giggling, demonic geniuses. It winds and twists and turns and is this crazy salt-and-pepper colour which takes a bit of trusting, but is as grippy as anything.

Which was good, because it looked to be a kilometre down to the valley floor if your tyres suddenly felt you were being too demanding and said, 'Fuck off, stupid.'

But if it was at all possible, the ride *down* from Falls Creek to Mount Beauty was even more astounding and filled me with abject terror and vast elation all at once. This is the kind of riding that motorcycling is all about. This is its validation. Corner after corner after corner – relentless, unforgiving and without compromise. Death lurks on both sides while life burns with an insane incandescence between the twin Reapers. It is beyond explanation and understanding. It just needs to be done.

I cannot remember who won this leg. And it doesn't matter. When we rolled into Mount Beauty, we were done. Had we been hookers, there would have been sperm leaking out of every orifice and police in attendance. I had ridden myself out. There was nothing left. Everything was used. It was all I could do just to blink the crusty speed-tears from my eyes and leer like an imbecile at my companions, who all leered back at me.

'There are no chicken strips[11] left on these tyres,' Crew pronounced as we pulled over to have a calming recreational.

And then we left to find J'amie, Res and Dan – who were exactly where they were meant to be. The pub.

We had a few ales, checked into our motel, then went back to the pub. Across the road there was a fast-food outlet. We gave the man behind the counter money and in half an hour he walked six massive pizzas and two roast chickens across the road to us. We consumed them with exceeding savagery, much to the consternation of the locals in the beer garden, who were clearly concerned what would happen after we had stopped feeding.

They needn't have worried. The ride had sucked all the hate-juice out of me and all I wanted to do was sit quietly, drink some cold beer and smell the most astonishingly clean air in all of Australia. So we wandered back to the motel, sat under a few trees and watched the velvet-warm night engulf the Earth. I think I was in bed by ten.

But I was up at 5 am. And since I didn't wish to be alone, I woke everyone else up. Breakfast is for people brimming with gay pride. We were going to eat the Tawonga Gap for our morning wake-up.

Sadly, Dan, J'amie and Crew got the jump on me, but Res was somewhat handicapped by his bike – a borrowed Speedmaster[12] – which he rode above and well beyond anything its makers ever expected or designed for. The Antelope's dual-purpose tyres take a little longer to get some heat into them, but by the time I had crested Tawonga Gap and began the descent, I was banging. I caught J'amie, passed him and a few corners later came across some poor bloke on a fully optioned Antelope who was crabbing the poor thing around corners. I passed him so fast I don't think he even saw me. And then I could see Dan. Big, tall Dan – who is young and lofty and more than a dab hand with a camera – can actually ride very fast. The cunt. Certainly it was an effort to catch him, but I was reeling him in when the road ran out. Crew was simply uncatchable and took first, Dan was second and I was grateful for the bronze.

We proceeded with grace and dignity through Bright, got some petrol, and decided the first food in our mouths would be down the road some. Myrtleford went past and we turned left just shy of Gapsted, drinking in the stunning scenery and the stupidly sweet air, which was only briefly polluted when Res made a burnout[13] while I emptied my bladder on the side of the road. The big man was seething with unhappiness. I understand this unhappiness will not cease until he is back astride a beloved Busa.[14]

And it was doubtlessly this depression, coupled with an insect that flew into his eye, which nearly caused him to kill most of us as we stopped for breakfast in Oxley. That is because he didn't stop. And he didn't stop because he was blinded by the insect and didn't see The Door about to turn left. Thankfully, The Door heard the screeching of tortured rubber and aborted his left turn, allowing Res to skim past him inches away from motorcycle Ragnarok. The domino effect would have been fabulous. Many of us would be maimed and dead. But we weren't, so it was funny. Crew and I celebrated with a recreational, followed by some bacon and egg rolls made by a woman I feel was moist about the nethers for Crew. I have a sense about these things.

After breakfast we girded our sweetmeats for the hot bitusex that is the Whitfield to Mansfield road. Once again, I was a slow starter and J'amie and Crew kicked everything into gear and hared off up the mountain like hares with loud mufflers, sticky tyres and powerful engines. The first few kays of this road is blisteringly quick and consists of a series of magical bends you can see right through, and a steady climb. Then it gets tight and evil and nasty. There's no run-off and death calls to you from everywhere. But I was deaf to its fell cry. I passed J'amie and headed off after Crew, who, buoyed by his crushing morning victory, wanted to back it up with another one before lunch.

And then we came upon two fellows having their own race. One was astride a Monster, and one was in charge of what I think was an FZ1 – but I was too busy foaming at the mouth and screaming to see clearly.

Crew and I came up on them like Berlusconi on hot teenage bitches. They lasted maybe six corners. Crew slew the first and set off after the second bloke, leaving me to get around the FZ1 he just passed. Happily, the bloke realised it was easier to be my bitch than to end his days in a blaze of burning Yamaha cascading down a mountain. I did him like a teenage hooker, fast, hard and nasty, and then saw Crew eat the other guy, who suddenly saw nothing in his mirrors but angry Antelope, and gave up. Crew and I banged on alone for maybe another two kilometres, when we were forced, by my bladder, to pull into a lookout that was blocked by a wretched campervan full of dull peasants.

They all left when I unzipped myself. I don't blame them. They were only human.

Then everyone else arrived. We took more pictures. Res tore down a sign because it angered him in some way. Crew and I recreationalised ourselves in preparation for the descent and we made our way into Mansfield for petrol.

To my immense surprise My Mate Jeff[15] appeared in the servo as we were fuelling up. 'You blokes with a bloke on a Rocket and a bloke on a Monster?' he asked. We told him that was The Door and J'aime.

'Well, they're broken down about five kays out of town.'

Then Benelli Bob[16] showed up and told us that there was a Rocket Three towing a Monster three kays out of town. Seconds later, The Door appeared alone.

'J'amie's run out of petrol,' he explained. 'It's easier if I get some and bring it to him.' The Door's care and love for his fellow man is legendary. He is truly a great human being. He got the petrol, delivered it to J'amie, and in ten minutes, J'amie was in the servo being hostile and full of spite.

Which is probably why we all got hopelessly lost while he didn't and subsequently enjoyed a nice luncheon in Eildon. But I am getting ahead of myself.

'Where are we going next?' I asked him at the servo.

'We're going to ride around Lake Eildon,' he told me.

What he didn't tell me was that there was a turn-off to the town of Eildon, as opposed to Lake Eildon, which is a geographical feature and not a town.

The turn-off was just past the tiny hamlet of Howqua and before the town of Jamieson. So it was no surprise that Crew, My Mate Jeff and I went past that turn-off at about 210 km/h. If the wretched thing had been signposted with flashing lights and winking strobes we wouldn't have seen it anyway. There was a race going on. I was coming third. Then I was coming fifth when The Door and Dan went past me and set off after Crew and My Mate Jeff.

Clearly, yet again I was riding like a man who admires ballroom dancing, and I twisted the throttle a little harder to compensate. I slowly started to reel them in, but the arrival of the Kevington Hotel on our left called an early halt to proceedings. We regrouped, and headed out again and within a few kays, the tar turned to dirt and I was once again soaring in front like a stoned eagle among the pretty clouds. Except the only clouds were the dusty ones my dual-purpose tyres were kicking up.

Did J'amie mention dirt to me in the servo? I couldn't remember. He may have, but since I only listen to his every third sentence, it was possibly my fault. Then the dirt disappeared and some rather lovely undulating tarmac appeared. I waited a little and soon The Door, Dan and Crew appeared so the four of us made a fastish run along the smooth black ribbon until it stopped and was replaced by some rather more serious dirt. Well, serious for them.

The Antelope just took it in its stride. And I was on the pegs and up again. The road wound steadily higher and the dirt grew steadily worse. I remember passing some child-molester in a Hummer (as if anyone who wasn't a kiddie-fiddler would drive one of them – come on), then climbing higher and higher, until I stopped and wondered if this was indeed the road we should have been on. Crew emerged out of the dust behind me and I went to wave him down. He waved back at me and carried on. I went after him, passed him and once again tried to wave him down. He merely wheelspun his way around me and continued.

A race is a race, stupid, I thought, and set off in hot pursuit. I passed him again and saw a sign stating A1 Settlement. Strange name for a town, I thought. But no sooner had I thought that, than A1 Settlement disappeared and the road began to get seriously hard core. The corners were all signposted at 20 kms per hour, but they were savagely corrugated and brimming with large, tyre-tripping boulders and bone-crushing drops off the side. I started to pay lots of attention. Some twenty kilometres later, I stopped at a wide open area on top of a hill and saw the road stretching off into the distance. It was still all dirt.

A sign told me I was at Frenchmans Gap, elevation 1020 metres. Crew pulled up, followed by Dan. The Iron Hippy duly arrived, followed by The Door. No J'amie. And no Res. But as we were considering our options and having a calming one for our frayed and dusty nerves, we heard the cacophonous rattle of his Speedmaster labouring up the hill. Res later told me he and the bike made it up that mountain on pure hate. He was going to kill J'amie and eat his sodden flesh raw.

'Where is the cunt!' he bellowed as he skidded to a halt. 'I'm going to beat the fucken cunt out of him!' As if on cue, his phone rang. It was J'amie.

'WHERE THE BASTARD FUCK ARE YOU, YOU FUCKEN CUNT!?' Res shrieked into the phone. 'Eildon? What are you fucking doing in Eildon? Having lunch? FUCK YOU! Where are we? I have no fucken idea!'

Right about then some serious adventure riders[17] tootled past us, their jaws slack with amazement at the various jungle beasts, sportsbikes and rocketships docked on the side of the road. I waved one of them down.

'How far does this dirt go, mate?' I asked.

'Oh, another hour and a half, I reckon,' the bloke told me.

Apparently, we had missed the turn-off to Eildon in our rush to place on the podium. And despite J'amie not actually saying we were to go to Eildon, it was kinda hard to blame him for us not being there. We blamed him anyway, and that made us all feel better at having to turn around and ride sixty kilometres back the way we came.

I marvelled at the Iron Hippy's immense good nature and high pain threshold. His Conglomeration of Italian Disdain had held together amazingly well, and had only exploded a spare bottle of oil inside his remarkable Pelican cases.[18] Dan, astride a Gixxer, was completely unperturbed by the dirt and flat-tracked it back down the mountain in fine style. The Door was indefatigable. His mammoth motorcycle could carry him to the moon and he'd be totally blasé about it. Crew was equally cool about the whole bastard dirt thing, and Res's hatred burned like the sun. One could ask for no better riding companions.

So we descended, met My Mate Jeff halfway up, told him to turn around and made for the Eildon turn-off. We were hurting a bit emotionally at J'amie's abandonment, and aching with tiredness, but when we found the turn-off and a sign that indicated there were sixty-three kilometres of super bends between us and Eildon, it was on again.

Crew led from the front, followed by the Iron Hippy, Dan and myself, and we had to work hard for the next thirty-odd minutes. The corners were relentless and the surface was completely random. Sometimes there would be gravel all over the bends, and sometimes the surface would simply give way due to its newness and the bike would lose traction, recover, and I'd be setting up for the next twisty abomination. It seemed like the corners were only fifty metres apart the whole way, so we worked hard to stay alive. As did every electronic anti-idiot-crashing device the Antelope possessed – and I am grateful to the lovely Germans who designed these systems. I am living proof they work. And it would have been totally uncool to crash before Res had had a chance to beat J'amie like a dog.

We passed a few rally cars who narrowly avoided murdering us as we descended into Eildon (there was some stupid car thing going on that afternoon), and there was J'amie reclining under a tree. I waved at him and went to get petrol and to douse my head in water. I was dusted like a sponge cake with particles of dirt, and my throat was as raw as a wound.

If Res was going to stomp J'amie, I hoped he would wait until I was refreshed enough to watch.

But I think Res was too worn out to contemplate doing a *Romper Stomper* on J'amie's spine that afternoon. More's the pity.

The island was still a fair way away, and only the Black Spur[19] remained as a point of motorcycling interest. But since that was apparently carpeted with Treasury Officials (or so we kept getting told), the rest of the trip was not going to be a testicle-buzzing fright-fest.

So let me now move forward through time and alight you gently at the Mayor's island residence[20] and the joyous bon-homie that has become Turn 13, his bar/garage/sound studio and table-dancing arena. We may not get together all that often with the Southern Clan, but it is always grand to find a warm welcome after a hard and dangerous journey.

It was Saturday night and custom dictated that we present ourselves upon the main street of Cowes so that all could stand in our presence and suffer awe. We ate a mess of brilliant souvlakis at Kristo's souvlakiatorium, and adjourned to the Euphoria,[21] which had been extended out into the street, for cleansing ales.

There were police everywhere. Their presence was onerous and invasive and completely unnecessary. All I saw in Cowes was maybe 300 middle-aged bikers sitting around eating pizza and drinking a few quiet beers. Hardly the kind of get-together that required the deployment of legions of uniformed fascists. I would especially like to note the three bullet-proofed idiots who came to stand and watch us eat our souvlakis, as if our chewing fabulous lumps of succulent lamb somehow contrived to bring ruin to the public order.

That said, we did not encounter any police on the way down or on the way into the island. Others did and anecdotally, there were tales of fear and loathing that probably belong in a piece by Hunter S.

That night I was in bed by ten. Again. The next morning the Mayor, Crew and I went to sell pies at the track. This we do so that we don't have to buy tickets to the races, which are ruinously expensive. So we volunteer for three hours to man a few pie vans scattered around the track that sell pies to the punters with the proceeds going to the local school or penguin orphanage or somesuch. It is all very emotionally enriching.

After the race, the Greek eating theme continued, and after Res performed another burnout, a goodly amount of us were at a table in Rhyll at a restaurant called The Big Fat Greek. For me, this restaurant was the equivalent of the roads we rode down – simply astonishing. The food was marvellous and plentiful and we were all groaning like gunshot victims at the end. I was amazed that The Door and Crew were able to perform wheelstands on the way back home.

We left the island in the gloom of a cloudy morning. Groaning and gritty-eyed from too much of everything and too little of everything else. Situation normal – I always feel like this when I leave the island. Everything else was as it was when we had arrived; The Door, Crew and the Iron Hippy arrayed around me and upon the road in a tight, smooth-moving pack and the smell of recreation thick in the air.

All was as it should be.

Glossary of Terms

1 *Antelope* – a BMW R1200GS
2 *Tyrannosaur* – a Triumph Rocket III
3 *Bulldog* – a Triumph Speed Triple

4 *Conglomeration of Italian Disdain* – a Ducati Multistrada built in the Iron Hippy's kitchen while he was crazed on Endone and leg-pain

5 *The Doom* – Hume Highway

6 *Road-Pig Lather* – a state of excitement brought about by cheating death at high speed on a motorcycle

7 *Wheelstood* – past tense of wheelstand, the act of causing the motorcycle to rear up on its hind wheel like a mighty stallion

8 *MV Agusta* – F4 – the world's fastest production motorcycle

9 *Roost* – the stream of rocks and dirt and shit that flies backwards from the rear wheel of a motorcycle that is having its throttle twisted in such a fashion as to cause the rear wheel to break traction with the (normally dirt) surface

10 *Ranga* – a man with red hair, a descendant of the Neanderthal

11 *Chicken strips* – the portions of unused rubber found on the edges of the tyres' surface on bikes ridden by pooves

12 *Speedmaster* – a sadly misnamed model of motorcycle made by Triumph

13 *Burnout* – when the back tyre of the motorcycle breaks traction with the road, causing dangerous carcinogens to escape into the atmosphere

14 *Busa* – an abbreviation of Hayabusa, made by Suzuki, and arguably the fastest production motorcycle in the world

15 *My Mate Jeff* – Benelli Bob's mate.

16 *Benelli Bob* – My Mate Jeff's mate who rides a Benelli

17 *Adventure riders* – people who ride dual-purpose motorcycles on adventures

18 *Pelican cases* – large, practical hard luggage that looks like freight dropped from NATO cargo planes
19 *Black Spur* – a section of winding road in Victoria popular with motorcyclists who like to crash and get booked
20 *Mayor's island residence* – Island Mick's house
21 *Euphoria* – a café on the main street of Cowes that puts up with bikers

ACKNOWLEDGEMENTS

I must tip my hat to some quite remarkable people, who have helped me in so many ways to complete this book.

Firstly, my dear mate Mark 'Madart' Ambroz, who came up with the title and acts as my moral conscience whenever he feels I have misplaced my own.

My beloved friend and colleague of many years, Shayne Bugden, magazine editor extraordinaire and one of the angriest and most talented writers I have ever met. His editorial suggestions are without peer and without price.

The late and very easily great Ken Wootton, who was the editor of *Australian Motorcycle News* and brave enough to give me enough editorial rope to hang myself in issue after issue of that great magazine. His untimely passing has left a hole in the world of motorcycling that will not ever be filled.

If there is a photo of me somewhere in this book, then it was taken by award-winning cinematographer, photographer and KTM-rider, Andrew 'Son of Elvis' McClymont, with whom I have shared miles, beer and not a little mayhem from time to time.

Of course, I am quite pathetically grateful to the wonderful team at Hachette – my glorious publisher, Vanessa Radnidge, and my genius editors, Kate Stevens and Karen Ward, all of whom masterfully restrained themselves from calling the police when I came in to meet them for the first time.

And last, but by no means least, the amazing coterie of motorcycle hooligans, madmen and man-beasts who inhabit the endlessly effervescent cyberworld of www.bikeme.tv, offering advice like 'You should call your book *I Can Count To Potato!*' (Thanks, Boon) and who give me hope for the future of motorcycling. Do not ever go bloody gentle into that good night, blokes.

Some of the stories in *My Mother Warned Me About Blokes Like Me* **were published in different and abridged forms before they appeared here.**

'A Man Called Gronk' (page 5) – A very much abridged version of this story was first published as a three-part story in my column 'Twisty Bits' in *Australian Motorcycle News* (30 September, 28 October and 25 November 2009).

'The First Summit' (page 25) – A very short story vaguely similar to this was first published in *Australian Motorcycle News* in 2003.

'Tales from the Pillion' (page 39) – This tale was first published as a much watered-down two-parter in *Australian Motorcycle News* in 2009.

'Riding into Mordor' (page 47) – There was a much tamer and somewhat abridged version of this story published in *Australian Motorcycle News* in 2010.

'Rally Outstanding' (page 63) – A tamer and much shorter version of this story was published in *Australian Motorcycle News* in 2005.

'Outlaw Dawn' (page 87) – A similar tale appeared in *Australian Motorcycle News* in 2010.

'The Christmas Run' (page 117) – A different version of this yarn was first published in *Ozbike* magazine around 1990. In the original piece, I wrote a different ending, a happy ending, if you like. But that was not what really happened.

'The Wrong Way Down' (page 187) – A tiny part of this journey was recounted in *Australian Motorcycle News* in 2008.

'Ron's Ride' (page 231) – An abbreviated version of this story was first published in *Australian Motorcycle News* in 2009.

'Demon Night' (page 243) – A different version of this story appeared in *Australian Motorcycle News* in 2008.

'The Line in Winter' (page 255) – A version of this story appeared in *Australian Motorcycle News* in 2011.

If you would like to find out more about Hachette Australia,
our authors, upcoming events and new releases you can
visit our website or follow us on twitter.

www.hachette.com.au
twitter.com/HachetteAus

To find out more about Boris visit:
www.bikeme.tv

INTRODUCING

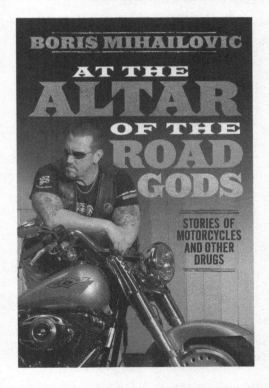

BORIS MIHAILOVIC

AT THE
ALTAR
OF THE
ROAD
GODS

STORIES OF
MOTORCYCLES
AND OTHER
DRUGS

ALSO BY BORIS MIHAILOVIC

LEARNING FAST

I am still at a loss to understand how I managed to survive my first five years of motorcycle riding. It can only be pure dumb luck as there was certainly no skill involved. Sheer craziness seemed to influence every aspect of my life back then. Like everyone I came to know who shared my two-wheeled fetish, I spent many years buying the fastest and most powerful bike I could afford at the time, then get into crippling debt making it faster and more powerful. The thing could never be fast enough, noisy enough, or angry enough. To my simple mind, there was a purity to the concept of a stupidly powerful engine bolted between two wheels, allegedly controlled by a set of handlebars and some squealing rubbish pretending to be brakes. Did that stop me and my friends pinning the throttles on deserted roads or empty (and not so empty) inner-city streets and measuring the girth of our cocks and the heft of our balls, in the hope that girls were watching? Did it fuck.

By the time I was nineteen I was a fully fledged, insane mutant pursuit machine. I would chase any motorcycle that passed me, or go after with a single-minded madness any bike I could see in front of me. Or, if no such challenge presented itself, I would chase my own shadow for the sheer heart-hammering thrill of cheating death and laughing at the law, which clearly did not apply to me. How could it? I was not dead, nor was I in jail. Sure, I'd come close a couple of times, but I've been told close only counts in horseshoes, hand grenades and thermonuclear weapons. It's got nothing to do with riding motorcycles, right?

> 'He who would learn to fly one
> day must first learn to stand and
> walk and run and climb and dance;
> one cannot fly into flying.'

FRIEDRICH NIETZSCHE

One of the consequences of riding motorcycles is that suddenly you lose all your friends. This is fine, because motorcycles quite effectively fill the hole those feckless, non-riding bastards leave in your life. So you don't really miss them at all. For a while, anyway. Eventually, the driving human need for socialisation with like-minded creatures kicks in and you begin to seek out people who laugh at the same things you do.

I lost my best childhood friend when I took to the handlebars. I didn't think I would, because Alex and I were tight. Hell, I had set him on fire when we were twelve and that kinda thing tends to make or break friendships. Immediately after I had put him out, it made ours. We were becoming increasingly attracted to the motorcycle thing, and as we approached our mid-teens we started making plans to ride around Australia. We even bought a map, seeing ourselves as the wog-kid version of Peter Fonda and

296

Dennis Hopper in the movie *Easy Rider*, except we were more like Corporal Serbia and Silly than Captain America and Billy. Anyway, upon finishing high school, the plan was to purchase motorcycles and hit the road.

It was a simple plan, but Alex still managed to screw it up by buying a car. He was a few months older than me, so he got his licence first, and two days later there he was at the door of my house with an orange VW Passat sitting on the street behind him.

'Whose is that?' I asked, peering over his shoulder.

'Mine!' he said proudly.

'I thought we were gonna buy bikes ...'

He looked a little uncomfortable, but he had clearly rehearsed an answer. 'Yeah ... umm, look, it's only until you get a bike,' he muttered. 'Then I'll sell it and get one too.' Except when that happened a few months later, he didn't. All of a sudden we didn't have much in common anymore.

By that time, I didn't really care. I had a motorcycle, which I had acquired via parental manipulation, extreme pleading and the telling of vast lies.

I had managed to save half the price of the bike doing part-time work, and then a bit more when I got some brief full-time work as the indentured servant of a crazy Holocaust survivor who ran an army disposal store in the city. In the three months I worked for Mr Aaronovich, and for which he paid me in small notes from the till every afternoon after I had finished sweeping the store entry and the footpath, cleaning the display windows and cases, and straightening the shelves that overflowed with musty-smelling ex-army gear, I vowed I would never again be taken in by classified ads seeking Trainee Assistant Store Managers, when all they really wanted were cleaners.

I was still short a grand, and after many high-level family summits, which began with my father vowing to put an axe through any motorcycle I brought home and eventually ended with my mother in tears on her knees before an icon of the Virgin Mary and my father's guarantor signature on a small bank loan, I was in a bike shop on Parramatta Road and buying the object of my eternal salvation – or damnation, if you believed the muttered prayers of my mum.

That object was a Yamaha XJ650. It had four cylinders, 650ccs and it was red. I was complete. I didn't need friends, I didn't need family. Hell, I even stopped paying attention to the pretty Greek girl who lived in the house behind ours and used to dance to the radio in her underpants most evenings. It was all I could do to keep a job for any longer than a month at a time because working ate into my riding time.

From the day at high school when my mate Gronk first appeared in the car park and let me have a go on his oil-splashed Honda XL250, I'd always had an idea that riding for real, as opposed to sneaking around in the alleyways behind his house, was going to be fun. But I had no idea just how much fun it was going to be.

The first fortnight after the purchase was spent in a haze of euphoric amazement. I even stopped masturbating for a while. My mother grew concerned I had suddenly become a little retarded because I would, in the middle of dinner, stop chewing my food and stare into space with a silly grin on my face. I was, of course, reliving a series of corners, or a particularly fast blast, but to her it looked as if part of my brain had turned into soap. The whole riding experience was so intense it was as if I had to relive it a few times in my head to absorb it and process it.

For the next eighteen months I funned myself stupid by riding everywhere all the time. I had no fear. There was no hesitancy in my riding, I just went at it with single-minded zealotry. I might as well have been retarded.

I didn't have any lessons and no one taught me anything. I lived in Marrickville, an inner-city suburb of Sydney, so there were no wide open spaces and dirt bikes filling my childhood. The only real-world motorcycle-riding experience I'd had followed hard on the heels of my mate Gronk's arrival, astride a disgraceful old Honda XL250, in my high school car park when I was in Year 10 – all of which is documented in my first book, *My Mother Warned Me About Blokes Like Me*.

Gronk's advent was the catalyst for my motorcycle addiction, and I spent many days jigging school and yammering around the lanes and back streets of nearby Camperdown on his bike – and learning whatever I could at the school of Trial, Error, Thrills and Terror. So whatever I had picked up astride Gronk's glorious shit-box, coupled with the fact that I had ridden a pushbike as a kid, seemed to have provided me with a skill-set sufficient to prevent a horrible red death. Which is pretty much how I explained it all to my terrified mother when she questioned me about how I knew how to ride a motorcycle.

'How you learnink raid dis?' she demanded to know one day.

'There's not all that much to learn, Mum,' I grinned. 'It's like riding a pushbike, but heaps easier 'cause you don't have to pedal.'

'Don't be goink too fast,' she pleaded.

My expression was immediately one of shock. 'Never!' I declared and followed that bullshit up with a lie of such epic grandeur it was a miracle the God to whom Mum prayed several times a day didn't strike me dead: 'They don't go that fast anyway.'

But they did. I loved what happened when I made the speedo needle go all the way to the right, but she didn't need to know any of that. In fact, the more ignorant she was of what I was doing, the more blissful I felt she would be. And to this day, I have not changed my mind about that.

So I rode and rode and rode. Day and night. If I couldn't sleep I would go for a ride. If I didn't know what to do on the weekend, I would ride to Brisbane and back. I rode dirt roads, I rode highways, I rode in peak hour, I rode in the rain, I rode with hailstones cracking off my helmet, I rode in state forests and I rode in national parks. I even rode along a beach on the NSW south coast until an incoming tide forced me to ride awkwardly up onto some rocks where I waited endless hours for the tide to recede so I could ride out again. In that year and a half, I clocked up almost 160,000 kilometres.

But I did it all alone. In many ways this was quite fitting, and a bit Zen. After all, we ride alone even when we are riding with a group of other people. If four blokes go for a ride, it's not at all the same as four blokes going for a drive. I got to know myself pretty well on those long rides.

Not every ride is a hell-for-leather death race of pitiless intensity and pulped organs if you screw it up. Once you've mastered the basics, many rides are just you churning out the kilometres, basking in the scenery and bathing in the wind. There's lots of space to think about things. So I did just that. I searched all the rooms of my soul and spent many hours poking about inside my own head-space. I discovered that I liked my own company. I discovered I did not like society all that much. I discovered I would never be a great singer, but I didn't mind the sound of my own bellowing too much and felt I did some of my best work with ancient Serbian battle songs, rather than murdering complex numbers like the Righteous Brothers' 'Unchained Melody'. I discovered I liked to sit by a campfire and stare into the flames and that the darkness held no fear for me. I discovered Australia was full of wonderful, generous, helpful and fascinating people, most of whom did not live in the cities. I discovered I liked speed and danger and risk, and being responsible for my actions. I came to like me and what I was doing with myself and where my life was going – which was nowhere in particular, but as long as it was going there on a motorcycle, I was ever so good with that.

So my life ticked along, until one day I discovered that I needed a new motorcycle. The one I had was simply not terrifying me in sufficient amounts anymore. So I took my XJ650 Yamaha back to the bike shop on Parramatta Road and traded it in for a bigger and vastly more powerful motorcycle. I still had no bike-riding mates, so I was on my own when I did this, and in a bit of a quandary as to what to buy next. I had read all the bike mags I could get my hands on, so I considered myself well informed about what was available. But I also considered myself to be a good rider, so what was one extra delusion in my arsenal of self-beautness?

The bike shop sold Kawasakis, Yamahas and Suzukis, which was fine by me. I had decided a few months back I would never buy or own a Honda because the company's advertising campaigns insisted that I would meet the nicest people on a Honda. Since I was not at all interested in meeting nice people, I was just not gonna buy a Honda. Had the ad campaign stated that I would meet sluts, werewolves, gunslingers, gamblers and drunks, I would have slammed my borrowed money down on the counter in a second, because despite its utterly anodyne ad campaign, Honda enjoyed a great reputation for reliability and performance.

I coveted a Harley, too, but I understood I needed a good deal more evil-ing up before I could carry off that whole hog thing. And besides, the wretched things cost more than twice what a Japanese bike cost.

I didn't have too many options. BMWs were, from what I could see, the province of bearded, Belstaff-wearing stamp collectors, train-spotters and balding middle-aged men who smelled vaguely of urine. Ducatis belonged exclusively to a subset of wild-eyed, long-haired fuckers who seemed to be hewn from obstinacy and delirium, walked with limps, smoked rollies and carried an array of spanners in their pockets. That only left Triumphs (which no one in their right mind wanted to buy in the early '80s as the only things keeping the company afloat were the crazed police departments of Ghana and Nigeria who kept buying them because the jungle drums had told them to do so), and Moto Guzzi, whose owners were several orders of strangeness and oiliness more deranged and oily than the mad swine who owned Ducatis.

My next bike was going to be another Yamaha, or a Suzuki, or a Kawasaki. So while Jerry, the twitchy, lizardy salesman who'd sold me my Yamaha and let me ride it home even though I could not produce a motorcycle licence when I bought it, was looking over the bike and deciding how worthless it was as a trade-in, I wandered up and down the showroom considering my options.

There was a dashing and rather lairy blue-and-white Suzuki GS1000S upon which I spent quite some time rubbing myself. It came stock with a bikini fairing, which caused me not a little anguish. About six months previously I had become overstimulated by press articles about bikini fairings. I immediately went and bought one for the Yamaha, for I very much wanted to be at the cutting edge of motorcycle style. Typically, I was unable to fit the small fairing to my XJ in any way that didn't make it vibrate against the headlight like a jackhammer. Nor could I make it sit squarely, no matter how many times I took it off and put it back on and swore at it. After nine hours of assembly, multiple test rides, fittings, de-fittings, re-fittings and temper tantrums, the cheap crap still buzzed like a Chinese sex toy each time I accelerated. The farce ended, as most of my mechanical farces end, in a sweary fit of Thor-like hammering and destruction of the non-compliant part. And though the Suzuki GS1000S's fairing had been fitted by the factory, I remained suspicious as to its integrity.

Beside it was a decidedly more respectable-looking GS1000G, in a muted two-tone orangey-red colour. But I was unable to take it seriously because it had a shaft-drive and the bike Jerry was de-valuing outside also had a shaft-drive. A shaft-drive, I had read in a motorcycle magazine, sapped much-desired horsepower from a motor. I wasn't having any of that. At my age, I needed all the horsepower I could get. It went with my manhood.

Next to that neutered blancmange was a monstrous dark-green and black behemoth that was one-third larger than any other motorcycle on the floor. Or in the world. It was the already legendary six-cylinder Z1300 Kawasaki and it was, to my youthful eyes, intimidation incarnate. I had no business attempting to ride this leviathan. It knew that and I knew that. And it cost two grand more than I had borrowed from the bank, so that settled my inner debate. But I felt like a bit of a girl when I turned my back on it. To this day I still do.

That left three serious contenders.

The Yamaha XS1100 was another shaft-driven monster, but one that allegedly produced enough horsepower to counter-act the shaft-drive's pussification. The bike beside the dirt-red Yamaha was another square-headlighted rocketship that had received a lot of praise in the motorcycle press, the new Suzuki GSX1100EX. It was tarted up in hateful, manly black, with three different blue accents on the tank and a motor that was the performance benchmark of the time.

Beside the EX was *ne plus ultra* of psychopathic Japanese motorcycles, the altogether jaw-dropping Suzuki Katana. It shared the same motor as the EX, but featured styling so far removed from the existing design paradigm of the time as to be almost alien.

I was standing on the threshold of a new age of superbikes, and I just couldn't decide. Should I go with the marque I knew, loved and trusted and buy the Yamaha? Should I sell my soul to the Lucifer-black GSX and its siren call of serious fuck-you power? Or should I take the plunge, bludge another grand off my mum and ride off into the sunset on the wildest, maddest and most outrageous motorcycle ever made and that had been named after the sword samurai warriors used to hack into their own entrails?

I had no idea.

'Okay, Morris,' Jerry declared happily as he wandered back into the showroom and forgot my name again. 'The best I can do on the XJ is a grand. It's got some big miles on it.'

That was about 500 less than I expected, but I was just not equipped to haggle with a man who was wearing a yellow body shirt, tight brown polyester flares and Partridge Family haircut. So I just nodded dumbly.

'So whaddaya reckon you might wanna trade up to?' he grinned.

'I don't know,' I said. And I didn't.

'You like the Katana?'

I nodded again.

'That one's sold, but I can get you another one next month.'

I did not want a bike next month. I wanted a bike now. Jerry, with the scent of my buyer's blood deep in his scaly nostrils, understood that perfectly well. It made him smile with disturbing intensity. I wanted to punch him in the face.

'I can do the black EX for you right now,' he said, showing me his crocodilian teeth. 'And I'll toss in a new helmet.'

I agreed instantly. I couldn't give a shit about the helmet; he was prepared to fuel this thing up and give it to me right now. And part of me wanted a change from the Yamaha and secretly feared its shaft-drive would cause me to sprout a clitoris. An hour later, I was riding my new bike home via Wollongong, a round trip of 250 kilometres.

Its power, after the relatively gentle exhalations of the Yamaha, dried my mouth and turned my eyes into saucers. It was noticeably heavier than my first bike, but it handled much the same, and when I opened the throttle that amazing engine spat me at the horizon with a venom that caused my arse to chew at the seat in delighted alarm.

And so began a love affair that was to last three years and some 260,000 kilometres. I spent money on that bike like a balding middle-aged fool pimping up his Filipina bride. But unlike the bride, the big Suzuki never let me down, always brought me home and ensured that I would now and forever serve as a high priest before the altar of the Road Gods.

But I still didn't have any mates. For a few months, that was still alright. My Suzuki and I were in our honeymoon period, and there was no room in my life for anything but it. Then one afternoon, as I was walking past the Hilton Hotel on George Street in Sydney, and admiring my splendid motorcycling self in the shop windows, I heard a bike gearing savagely down behind me. I turned and saw a nasty, noisy, matte-black Katana lurch to a halt almost beside me. Sartorially the rider was only some fur and a boot-knife removed from Toecutter in *Mad Max*.

'Mmonnis?!' said a muffled voice from inside a black-visored black-and-gold AGV helmet.

I narrowed my eyes and shifted my own helmet down from my wrist and into my hand, fully intending to defend whatever needed defending with my fibreglass bludgeon. The rider flicked up his helmet, and his eyes crinkled in amusement.

'Boris?!' he repeated, a little clearer this time.

'Who are you?' I asked, walking closer and peering at what little I could see of the rider's face.

'Hang on,' he said, put his bike on its stand, undid his helmet and slipped it off his head. 'It's me,' he said.

I still blinked in confusion.

'Frank. From school.'

And the penny dropped. It was indeed Frank from my high school. I vaguely remembered him, but we hadn't been mates – and what I did recall of him was that he was one of those nondescript kids. Neither a genius, nor a jock, nor a monstrous dickhead. And here he was now, looking very cool and very fast and riding what was obviously a horrid home-painted matte-black Katana with a buzzsaw-loud exhaust. And he had a walkie-talkie attached to his hip.

As we shook hands he told me he was a motorcycle courier and asked me what I rode. I proudly replied that I had a GSX1100EX, which you'll recall shared pretty much everything with Frank's Katana except the outlandish styling. So we instantly had something else in common apart from high school.

'I'm finishing work now,' Frank said. 'Wanna come back to my place for a beer? Remember Scott? I live with him. He rides a GPZ.'

I vaguely recalled Scott, Frank's mate at school, and I was inordinately pleased that he rode as well – and he rode a very mighty Kawasaki, which had recently been invented as competition to the GSX I was riding.

'Sure,' I said. It had been a long time since anyone had

307

invited me anywhere for a beer, and while I didn't want to appear pathetically keen, that's exactly what I was.

'Where's your bike?' Frank asked.

I told him it was parked around the corner.

'Cool. Follow me.' He waited for me opposite Sydney Town Hall, and in a few minutes we were barrelling down George Street to Frank's townhouse in the nearby inner-city suburb of Newtown. It was all I could do just to keep up with him. This had nothing to do with my bike, which was virtually as powerful as his. It was me – and this delusion I had about how fast I was. Or wasn't, as it turned out.

Clearly, Frank was possessed of riding skills, daring and ruthlessness when it came to traffic that had thus far eluded me. He lane-split at speeds that took my breath away, and hammered off the lights as if he was drag-racing for money. As we tore down Broadway, my speedo was nudging 130 kms per hour. His bike sounded glorious, crackling and popping on over-run through its aftermarket exhaust system. I vowed to buy one just like that the next day even if it meant I would once again cheat Mum out of the board I was supposed to pay each month.

And he looked far cooler than me. There was no doubt about that. I was dressed in my normal riding ensemble of blue jeans tucked into black Rossi-brand riding boots, a black leather jacket and some black gloves. My helmet was a silver-and-black AGV with a clear visor. Bar the helmet, which I got when I bought the bike, all of my gear had been bought from Omodeis – a wonderful shop that used to be on Pitt Street, just behind Central Station. I remember so clearly how it smelled of leather, waxed cotton and the ethereal promise of distant horizons astride a motorcycle.

Frank's gear looked a lot edgier and reminded me of the psychotic outlaw riders in what was then my favourite movie, *Mad Max*. Instead of blue jeans, he wore black jeans, and they weren't tucked into prissy black boy-boots. They were jammed into brutish Sidi dirt-bike boots, with cruel buckles on the side and steel reinforcement along the toes. His leather jacket was scuffed and collared with epaulettes (they call them Brando jackets these days), and much thicker than mine. Over the top of this he had a stained, faded sleeveless denim jacket.

I made mental notes as we howled through the busy shopping centre of Newtown, jaywalkers leaping back onto the footpath as Frank's exhaust popped explosions of hate at them.

Note 1. Buy an exhaust system. Do it tomorrow.

Note 2. Buy a Levi's jean jacket and saw the arms off it. Argue with mother about this. Do not lose argument.

Note 3. Buy dirt-bike boots or find someone who is prepared to fight you for his. And fight hard. You must not come second.

Note 4. Stop being a giant sack of trembling, hesitant, slow-riding bitch-poo. Turn the throttle. Do it now. If he can fit that Katana into that traffic gap, so can you. One hundred and forty kilometres per hour is a perfectly acceptable speed down the double yellow lines of a major inner-city thoroughfare. What the fuck did you buy this black monster for? To look at?

I was a somewhat altered Borrie when Frank and I finally pulled up in front of his two-storey townhouse just off the main road.

Scott was out the front washing his Kawasaki GPZ1100, and there was another identical-to-mine black GSX parked next to it, which belonged to a gentle-natured, careful-riding and somewhat skinny bloke called Barry. There was also a fabulous blonde with excellent tits and painted-on jeans sitting on the fence, swinging her legs, smoking and watching Scott wash his bike. She turned out to be Scott's girlfriend, Justine.

Like Frank, Scott was a motorcycle courier. I came to understand that their profession accounted greatly for just how fast these blokes were and how well they rode. As you might understand, a motorcycle courier's life span is mostly measured in weeks. They dance on the knife-edge of metropolitan traffic death for ten to twelve hours a day. They either learn to ride well, or they die. Both Frank and Scott had been couriers for about a year, and they were both very much alive. I was in the presence of minor riding deities.

They all greeted me with good humour, and quite suddenly, it looked like I might have friends again: friends who clearly shared my love of the motorcycle. In short order, I was drinking beer, laughing and passing around a joint as if I'd known these people my whole life. Another bloke called Craig joined us. He lived in the block of flats next to their row of townhouses and rode a big 1100cc Kawasaki shaft-drive. Despite this deficiency, he was as welcoming as the others.

I had to go home for dinner, so we all made some quick plans to go for a ride the coming weekend. We agreed that an excursion to Gosford, via the Old Pacific Highway, was in order. Since I was the new kid, a dash along that famously twisting stretch of bitumen would determine my place in the pecking order. I knew Frank was quicker than me, but I had no idea about the others. I did note that everyone was sporting the latest Pirelli tyres, which were the last word in adhesion back then. By today's standards it would be like riding on ceramic tiles but back then, as your giant, 130-horsepower Japanese bike oscillated and weaved its way around corners, always on the verge of tank-slapping you into the traction braces at the local hospital, you would congratulate yourself on having the stickiest tyres money could buy. And you would ride accordingly.

I will always remember that first ride with Frank and the others from Berowra to Gosford. It started fast and hard and didn't ease off – Frank and Scott engaged it with an intensity I had not seen this side of a racetrack. We must have been doing well over 200 across the Brooklyn Bridge, one of the only straight bits in what is a cornucopia of beautiful corners. They rode closely behind each other, obviously very familiar with themselves and the road, and while I also knew the road, I had never pushed as hard along it as I did that Sunday. We passed everything, and as we began the final, thrilling descent into Gosford, I was shaking my head in disbelief and trembling with adrenalin fizz.

Most Sydney riders are familiar with the Old Pacific Highway. It is a stunning section of bitumen that is rather close to the city. But what was a blessing to riders in the '70s (just after the Newcastle freeway opened for business), '80s and early '90s, has become their curse in the 21st century. The Old Road, as it is now known, was once a free-fire zone for motorcyclists. You went there to learn how to go fast around corners. And sometimes, in the process of learning, you would die or end up in a motorised wheelchair oozing faeces into a bag and swallowing laboriously through a tube. For such is the nature of learning how to go fast around corners on motorcycles.

The police now blanket the road every weekend, and the speed limit has been dropped from 100 to 60. But since many motorcyclists have pretty much become unskilled herd animals in today's world, legions of them still insist on riding up there, crashing their vestigial brains out and being booked for everything the Highway Patrol can come up with. I would rather gouge my own eyes out than go there today.

You will recall that the '70s and '80s were simpler and far more Manichaean times. Motorcycling had never been as magnificently Darwinian and more black and white than it was then. If you wanted to ride in those days, there was no room for any doubt or hesitancy. Your desire to ride had better burn with an incandescent fire, and you had to have an innate, almost instinct-driven ability to come to grips with your motorcycle in a short period of time. Failure to do this, and your time kissing the wind and surfing creamy waves of torque would be exactly as Thomas Hobbes observed – 'nasty, brutish and short'.

Do I have to tell you how face-scrunchingly appealing this was to a mildly crazy wog boy with a doting mother, or can you guess? It was the rite of passage into manhood I had always searched for. Sure, it wasn't exactly hunting cave-bears with a fire-hardened stick, but it was certainly a close second in terms of just how much pure screaming terror and manliness could be mainlined into your veins in a nanosecond ...